AMERICAN LAW AND THE AMERICAN LEGAL SYSTEM

IN A NUTSHELL®

SECOND EDITION

LLOYD BONFIELD
Thomas J. André, Jr. Professor of Law
Tulane University School of Law (Retired)
Visiting Professor of Law
Tulane University School of Law
Professor of Law and Director of the Center for
International Law Emeritus
New York Law School

WEST
ACADEMIC
PUBLISHING

Nutshell Series, In a Nutshell and the Nutshell Logo are trademarks registered in the U.S. Patent and Trademark Office.

© 2006 Thomson/West
© 2021 LEG, Inc. d/b/a West Academic
     444 Cedar Street, Suite 700
     St. Paul, MN 55101
     1-877-888-1330

West, West Academic Publishing, and West Academic are trademarks of West Publishing Corporation, used under license.

Printed in the United States of America

ISBN: 978-1-63460-645-5

For Lisa Bonfield, J. D.

PREFACE TO THE SECOND EDITION

It is pretension, bordering on arrogance, to write a book on American law and the American legal system that purports to be comprehensive. How can one justify such lack of humility?

This book was born of catastrophe, although the inspiration for it was not. The latter: in 2002, Marc Firestone, European Union General Counsel for Altria's Phillip Morris International subsidiary (later President of External Affairs and General Counsel of Phillip Morris International) decided that the lawyers under his tutelage should know more about American law and legal reasoning. He asked me to put together a program in Evian, France, which I was happy to do, and about a dozen of my Tulane colleagues participated. It was an experience never to be forgotten. The former: all thought of a book on the subject dissolved until Hurricane Katrina ravaged New Orleans in 2005. I evacuated to New York, without a single document pertaining to a book I was writing on probate litigation in the Prerogative Court of Canterbury in seventeenth-century England. What else was I to do? American law. Although I was asked many times to update it, it took another catastrophe, the COVID plague (during which I was also left without documents) to find time to do so.

For this second edition, I would like to warmly acknowledge Kirsten Kovats and Michael Kazamais, students at New York Law School for their dedication, good humor and hard work in helping me update the volume. Although not generally predisposed to the University of Chicago's Law and Economic mantra, I always believed that the transaction costs in employing student research assistants outweighed the benefits. Once again I was proved wrong.

PREFACE TO THE FIRST EDITION

I wrote this book because I thought I had something interesting to say about American law to both foreign lawyers and aspiring American law students. But as I worked through the various chapters, I realized that I also had a lot to learn about the subject in which I claimed expertise. Like our kin who work with the law in the so-called 'real world,' academic lawyers also practice law, we never really know it; all we do is to continue to learn about it and marvel at its complexity. So even though I have been at the podium for better than a quarter of a century, writing this book has been a learning experience for me.

I have been blessed with wonderful teachers. I have learned both from my elders (some sadly departed), and from those who constitute the future of the law teaching profession: my young colleagues at Tulane. While directing summer schools in Siena and Cambridge, this English legal historian learned American constitutional law, civil procedure, and evidence from two masters of the federal bench in New Orleans, the Honorable Morey L. Sear, late Chief Judge of the Eastern District of Louisiana, and his colleague and friend, the Honorable Martin L.C. Feldman. In the same unlikely venues, I learned American legal history from the 'Chief,' the Honorable William H. Rehnquist, camped beside students, listening to him talk about the

institution that he loved, the Supreme Court of the
United States.

At the other end of the demographic spectrum, I
must have bewildered the 'new' generation of
colleagues at Tulane, those hired in the twenty-
first century, Felice Batlan, Chris Cotropia, Onnig
Dombalagian, Jonathan Nash and Rafael Pardo,
with barrages of specific questions about the law in
their areas of expertise. While they no doubt viewed
the interrogation as a rite of passage for tenure, it
was merely to make sure that I got much of what
follows right.

Colleagues also read individual chapters and
made useful additions and corrections. Michael
Collins and Jancy Hoeffel took a double dose, as did
my cousin Arthur Bonfield of the University of Iowa,
who certainly must hold the record for the amount
of red ink that graced a single page of typescript.
Harvey Couch, Steve Griffin, Dan Posin, Brooke
Overby, Mark Wessman, and Anne Woolhandler
could only bear single draft chapters. Danielle
Babashaw provided excellent research assistance,
and would no doubt have done more had not a
potent young lady called Katrina played havoc
with her senior year at Tulane.

My wife Adriana and my daughter Lisa deserve
more than thanks for tolerating a person who thinks
of little else but the law, past and present, and who
runs the household like a classroom. I dedicate the
book to Lisa, with the following reverie. As a young
lad growing up in suburban New York, I once visited
the Ford plant in Mahwah, New Jersey. Bits of cars

would pass down the various conveyors, and every so often a yellow one would be assembled, destined for what I regarded as the worst of fates for an automobile, a New York City taxicab. The human equivalent, I reckon, is for a baby to roll down the line and be allocated to a law professor. She has more than met the challenge, and I love her dearly.

OUTLINE

PREFACE TO THE SECOND EDITION V

PREFACE TO THE FIRST EDITION VII

TABLE OF CASES XIX

Chapter 1. Introduction to American Law 1
Introduction to an Introduction 1
American Law: Rife with Contradiction 5
American Law: Complexity 7
American Law: The Moral Dimension 10
And Finally, American Law: Diversity 11
A Page of History 12
Conclusion 20

**Chapter 2. The Sources of Law and Common
    Law Reasoning 21**
Introduction 21
The Legal Saga: Framing the Issue 21
The Search for Law 23
Enter the Common Law 25
Policy Concerns 30
Old Wine in New Bottles—of Baseballs and
    Foxes 32
Conclusion 35

**Chapter 3. The American Constitutional
    System: Allocation of Governmental
    Powers 37**
Introduction 37
Our Federalism: Congressional Powers 39

The Commerce Clause 41
The Necessary and Proper Clause 48
Our Federalism: The Supremacy Clause................ 50
Our Federalism: The Powers of the President 51
The Third Branch... 58
Conclusion 63

Chapter 4. The American Judiciary:
Guardians of the Constitution....................... 65
Introduction.. 65
The Federal Bench in the Constitutional
    Scheme 65
The Federal Court System................................ 67
A Primer on Federal Jurisdiction........................ 69
Conclusion 72

Chapter 5. The American Civil Trial:
Ritualized Combat...................................... 75
Introduction.. 75
An Overview of the Federal Rules 76
Stages of the Trial: Pleading 78
Pre-Trial Discovery 83
Pre-Trial Motions.. 90
Pre-Trial Conference..................................... 91
The Right to a Trial by Jury............................. 91
The Trial 95
A Mock Jury Trial 97
A Primer on Rules of Evidence............................ 98
Appeals Process.. 100
Conclusion 103

**Chapter 6. Contract and Commercial Law:
A Promise Is a Promise (Maybe)** **105**
Introduction 105
Jurisprudential Aspirations of Contract Law 107
Contract Formation 109
Consideration 112
Promissory Estoppel and Unjust Enrichment 115
Contract Interpretation 115
Contract Performance 118
Excuses for Nonperformance 121
Remedies 124
An Introduction to Commercial Law 128
Payment 129
Transactions on Credit 131
Negotiable Instruments 132
Secured Transactions 133
Consumer Protection Law 136
Conclusion 138

**Chapter 7. American Tort Law: Venerable
Common Law on the Eve of Reform?** **141**
Introduction 141
Tort Law Reform 142
Links Between Criminal Law and Tort 145
The Link Between Contract and Tort 146
The Moral Dimensions of Tort 147
Intentional Torts 147
Battery 150
Assault 151
False Imprisonment 152
Trespass to Real Property 153
Trespass to Personal Property 154
Transferred Intent 155

Defenses to Intentional Torts.................................. 156
Negligent Torts... 158
Duty of Care 160
Breach 162
Causation.. 163
Contributory Negligence.. 165
Multiple Parties 166
Strict Liability 167
Damages in Tort... 170
Conclusion 172

**Chapter 8. American Property Law:
Plenty of Old Wine in Both New and Old
Bottles.. 175**
Introduction.. 175
Possession and Ownership in American Law 177
Adverse Possession 180
Real Estate Transactions.. 183
Eminent Domain 184
Land Regulation... 187
Zoning 193
Environmental Regulation 195
Nuisance 198
Estates in Land 201
Inheritance: Wills and Trusts 207
Landlord-Tenant Law 210
Intellectual Property... 212
Copyright.. 213
Patent Law 216
Trademark 218
Conclusion 222

Chapter 9. America's Business Is Business: And Business Lawyers Govern the Show **225**

Introduction 225

Forms of Business Entities: "Non-Corporate Forms" 227

Forms of Business Entities: Sole Proprietorship 228

Forms of Business Entities: Partnership.............. 229

Forms of Business Entities: Limited Liability Company 233

Forms of Business Entities: The Corporation 234

Corporate Equity and Debt 242

Corporate Mergers and Other Acquisitions 243

Securities Regulation.. 248

Antitrust Law 256

Conclusion 269

Chapter 10. American Labor Law: Laissez-Faire—Freedom to Contract; Limitations Regarding Discrimination............................. 271

Introduction 271

Employment Law 273

Employment Discrimination Law 276

American Unions.. 279

Conclusion 283

Chapter 11. Criminal Law: (Much) Crime and (Severe) Punishment in Modern America 285

Introduction 285

Basic Principles of the Substantive Criminal Law 288

Particular Offences: Murder.................................. 291
Manslaughter 293
Rape 293
Crimes Against Property 294
Racketeer Influenced and Corrupt Organizations
    Act: Innovating Crime...................................... 295
Defenses to Criminal Liability 296
Self-Defense 297
Insanity.. 298
Other Affirmative Defenses.................................. 299
Crime and Punishment... 302
Conclusion 306

**Chapter 12. Criminal Procedure: The "Long
    and Winding Road" from Apprehension
    of Criminals to Their Release...................... 309**
Introduction.. 309
The Criminal Justice Process: From Arrest to
    Appearance 312
The Criminal Justice Process: Pre-Trial Phase ... 315
The Criminal Justice Process: Trial...................... 317
The Criminal Justice Process: Post-Conviction ... 321
Parole 324
Constitutional Criminal Procedure: "The
    Criminal Goes Free Because the Constable
    Has Blundered" 326
Unconstitutional Searches.................................... 329
Unreasonable Searches... 330
Confessions 333
Exclusionary Rule Exceptions.............................. 336
Conclusion 337

Chapter 13. A Bill of Rights for All Seasons... 339

Introduction... 339

First Amendment: Religious Expression and Tolerance.. 342

First Amendment: Free Expression..................... 346

First Amendment: Assembly and the Right to Petition... 352

The Second Bill of Rights: Equal Treatment Before the Law 353

The Due Process Clause.. 354

The Equal Protection Clause................................ 357

Privacy Rights 363

The Second Amendment 367

Conclusion 368

Chapter 14. Administrative Agencies and Their Law: The Fourth Branch of American Law... 371

Introduction... 371

Functions of Agencies 374

Judicial Review of Administrative Acts................ 379

Legislative and Executive Control of Agencies 380

Conclusion 382

Chapter 15. International Law in the American Legal System: Is It Really There?... 385

Introduction... 385

American Process for Entering into International Agreements 388

Status of International Agreements in American Law... 390

Extra-Territoriality of American Law:
Substantive Law.. 392
Extra-Territoriality of American Law:
Jurisdiction... 394
The Interface Between European Union and
American Law: An Example of New Frontiers
of International Law 399
Conclusion 403

**Chapter 16. Conclusion: The American
Bar** **405**
Introduction.. 405
Regulation of the Guild... 407
The Practice of Law.. 409
Conclusion 410

INDEX... 413

TABLE OF CASES

References are to Pages

Alcoa, United States v., 393
Alice Corp. Pty. v. CLS Bank Int'l, 217
American Soc. of Composers, Authors, Publishers, United
    States v., 262
Arizona v. Johnson, 333
Arlington Heights, Village of v. MHDC, 195
Armory v. Delamire, 178
Ashcroft v. Iqbal, 79
Atkins v. Virginia, 306
Batson v. Kentucky, 320
Bell Atl. Corp. v. Twombly, 79
Belle Terre, Village of v. Boraas, 51
Berman v. Parker, 185
Booker, United States v., 304
Bostock v. Clayton Cty., Georgia, 276, 367
Boumediene v. Bush, 324, 394
Brown v. Board of Education, 63, 358
Burton v. Wilmington Parking Auth., 360
C&A Carbone v. Town of Clarkstown, 48
Cardoza v. City of N.Y., 95
Celotex Corp. v. Catrett, 90
Charter Township of Delta v. Dinolfo, 51
Chevron, U.S.A., Inc. v. NRDC, Inc., 380
Chiarella v. United States, 253
Citizens United v. Federal Election Commission, 353
Civil Rights Cases, 357
Cleveland Board of Education v. LaFleur, 363
Comstock, United States v., 49
Cooley v. Bd. of Wardens of the Port of Philadelphia, 47
Dames & Moore v. Regan, 389
Davis v. United States, 336
Defore, People v., 326
District of Columbia v. Heller, 368
Dolan v. City of Tigard, 192
Dred Scott v. Sandford, 17
Dudley and Stevens, Regina v., 300

Eldred v. Ashcroft, 1, 214
Elk Grove Unified School District v. Newdow, 345
Erie, City of v. Pap's A.M., 194
Facebook Ireland, Ltd. v. Schrems, 403
Fisher v. University of Texas, 361
Florida v. Powell, 334
Gibbons v. Ogden, 39
Gonzales v. Raich, 44
Gratz v. Bollinger, 361
Griswold v. Connecticut, 365
Gundy v. United States, 40, 375
Hadley v. Baxendale, 126
Hawaii Hous. Auth. v. Midkiff, 185
Henningsen v. Bloomfield Motors, 168
Jones, United States v., 330
June Medical Services, LLC v. Russo, 12, 62, 365
Kelo v. City of New London, 176
Lawrence v. Texas, 356
Leegin Creative Leather Prod., Inc. v. PSKS, Inc., 261
Little Sisters of the Poor Saints Peter & Paul Home v.
    Pennsylvania, 343
Lochner v. New York, 356
Lopez, United States v., 44
Loretto v. Tel. Manhattan Catv Corp., 189
Los Angeles, City of v. Alameda Books, 194
Louisville & Nashville R.R. v. Mottley, 80
M'Naghten, Queen v., 298
Malone, Commonwealth v., 292
Marbury v. Madison, 59, 66, 340
Mayo Collaborative Ser. v. Prometheus Lab'y, Inc., 217
McCulloch v. Maryland, 50
Mead Corp., United States v., 376
Medellin v. Dretke, 386
Medina v. Gonzalez, 89
Missouri v. Holland, 390
Montejo v. Louisiana, 335
Morrison, United States v., 44
NAACP v. Mt. Laurel, 194
National Collegiate Athletic Ass'n v. Bd. of Regents of
    Univ. of Oklahoma, 263
National Fed'n of Indep. Bus. v. Sebelius (Obamacare), 39
National Prescription Opiate Litigation, In re, 87

New York Trust Co. v. Eisner, 13
Nollan v. Cal. Coastal Com., 191
Obergefell v. Hodges, 366
Our Lady of Guadalupe Sch. v. Morrissey-Berru, 344
Penn Central Transport Co. v. City of New York., 188
Pennsylvania Coal v. Mahon, 187
Philadelphia, City of v. New Jersey, 47
Pierson v. Post, 21, 176
Plessy v. Ferguson, 63, 357
Popov v. Hayashi, 33
Price v. Leflore Cnty. Det. Ctr., 89
Ramos v. Louisiana, 320
Raniere, United States v., 296
Revlon, Inc. v. MacAndrews & Forbes Holdings, Inc., 247
Roe v. Wade, 62, 73, 365
Roper v. Simmons, 306
Schad v. Borough of Mt. Ephraim, 194
Schenck v. United States, 350
Security Nat'l Bank of Sioux City, Iowa v. Abbott, Lab'y, 89
Shelby County v. Holder, 354
Shelley v. Kraemer, 360
Skidmore v. Swift & Co., 380
Spector et al. v. Norwegian Cruise Line Ltd., 393
Spur Indus. v. Del E. Webb Dev. Co., 199
Trump v. Vance, 52
United Haulers Ass'n v. Oneida-Herkimer Solid Waste Mgmt., 48
Unocal Corp. v. Mesa Petroleum Co., 246
Van Gend en Loos v. Nederlandse Administratie der Belastingen, 401
Virginia, United States v., 363
Watkins, Ex parte, 323
Whole Women's Health v. Hellerstedt, 62
Wickard v. Filburn, 42
Wyeth v. Levine, 46
Youngstown Sheet & Tube Co. v. Sawyer, 57
Zubulake v. UBS Warburg, LLC, 85

AMERICAN LAW AND THE AMERICAN LEGAL SYSTEM

IN A NUTSHELL®

SECOND EDITION

CHAPTER 1
INTRODUCTION TO AMERICAN LAW

Introduction to an Introduction

Some contemporary historians have described the twentieth century as the "American" century. An intellectual property case argued in the United States Supreme Court at the turn of the next century, *Eldred v. Ashcroft*, involved copyright. *Eldred v. Ashcroft*, 537 U.S. 186 (2003). Jack Valenti, the president of the Motion Picture Association, was quoted in the press as touting the contribution that the celluloid industry has made both to the American Gross Domestic Product and to the otherwise dreadful balance of payments situation of the United States at the time. Yet, another American export has been even more important. It is neither McDonald's nor Coca-Cola. Rather, it is the American legal system or to be more precise, and variously stated: American legal ideas, American jurisprudence, or the American approach to the law.

Like it or not, intended or otherwise, American law casts a giant shadow over international commercial affairs. That is not to say that it has no competitors, or that other legal orders have capitulated to this jurisprudential imperialism. After all, other countries make movies, fast food, and soft drinks: nevertheless, they do not seem to have the same fascination and attraction as does America's. Likewise, I would argue that with American law, excuse my arrogance, the foreign competition is not that robust.

Perhaps my case for the predominance of American law is overstated. Regardless, given the number of overseas lawyers who take LL. M. degrees in the United States, it seems apparent, at the very least, that many non-American lawyers do indeed deem American law and its legal system worth learning. And rest assured that the reverse is the case as well; interest in the law of other jurisdictions is not a one-way street. Just as American law is relevant to aspiring overseas lawyers, foreign law is studied by American law students who study abroad in droves, particularly in the summer.

Moreover, non-American law (international and comparative law) is integral to the curriculum of American law schools. European Union law, for example, is widely-taught and has become a critical area of law for American lawyers. International Business Transactions is also a mainstay of the curriculum. In addition, there are courses in Public International Law and International Human Rights Law.

Besides international and transnational law courses, comparative law has also been a prominent part of the American law school curriculum since the 1930s. While legal orders should and probably do reflect their national culture and spirit, as the German legal philosopher and historian Friedrich Carl von Savigny argued in the nineteenth century, "national" legal systems also have borrowed extensively, both actively and passively, from one another for about as long as they have been in contact. It is for this reason that the connection between legal orders, "Comparative Law" has long been the object of historical and jurisprudential study.

Finally, there is interest in the private law of "foreign" jurisdictions. For example, there is considerable interest in America in the commercial law of Japan. With the economic power of China looming, can courses and programs in Chinese law be far behind? Indeed they are already in the curriculum at some elite schools. As trite as the term now seems, legally speaking, we inhabit a global village.

This book's agenda is to introduce readers to the settlement in this global village that is American law. Because American law is as much a process as it is a bundle of institutions and rules, our mandate is not merely to provide a sketch of jurisdictions and legal principles. To be sure, the reader will encounter legal rules. He or she will learn "diversity of citizenship" coupled with $75,000 in controversy triggers federal jurisdiction. Likewise, we will discuss whether a contract is binding without consideration. These snippets of procedural and substantive law are of use to a lawyer, albeit limited. What lawyers, American or foreign, must learn is the reasoning that underpins a rule of law: to determine what diversity of citizenship means in a specific context; or how courts have defined consideration so that one may measure doctrine against the facts of a case at hand.

Thus, this volume does not aim to be a compendium of laws. Rather, it proposes to introduce its reader to the foundations of American jurisprudence; how the American system of law approaches the making of legal rules, and how it engages in both dispute prevention and resolution. It strives to reveal American law's subtext, the shared understanding about the law that American lawyers have digested. Upon assimilating this background, lawyers in America can find, understand, use, and argue law. The latter lesson is well-learned, because, above all, the law in American society is rarely fixed, and it is usually in the process of dialogue and disputation. Once the code that is American legal discourse is cracked, assimilated, and the rudiments of American law understood, the determination of individual principles can be discerned quite easily, and a foreign lawyer can be invited into the seemingly endless dialogue.

Alas, though rewarding, ours is an arduous journey. All this learning generally requires the average American college graduate three years of serious study. After four years of immersion in art, music, history, political science, or another of the liberal arts (and now more commonly even business or engineering), the graduate is deemed prepared to be thrust into law school: three years to learn the law, a required obstacle for them to vault in order to go on to take the bar exam of a particular state, and then begin to practice as an attorney in that lone jurisdiction. Why not allow our newly-minted lawyer to practice all over the country? The answer is simple; though non-Americans generally view the United States as an undifferentiated political mass, or mess as the case may be, most of its law is enacted in state legislatures and decided and enforced in state courts.

National law, though relevant and important, is limited to defined areas. One's birth, marriage, and death are registered according to state law—how one's property, and even how one's remains are dealt with, are dictated according to the tenets of state law. More about this in later chapters.

How does one commence this journey? How can an American law professor introduce an overview of American law to non-American lawyers? By simplifying it beyond recognition? Why not? Suppose one were required to reduce the American legal order to a single word. The one I might select is "contradiction." If permitted a second, "complex." Allow me a third, "moral." And finally, a fourth, "diverse."

American Law: Rife with Contradiction

American law, like America itself, is riddled with contradictions and paradoxes. How can one explain them, and how did they develop? The hit Broadway show "Hamilton" proclaims:

[Burr] The constitution's a mess

[Hamilton] So it needs amendments

[Burr] It's full of contradictions

[Hamilton] So is independence

Pop culture notwithstanding, it is always best to start with the past. Professor John Reid has argued that American society was, prior to the twentieth century, *law minded.* John Phillip Reid, *Policing the Elephant: Crime, Punishment, and Social*

Behavior on the Overland Trail (1997). In his study of law on the Oregon Trail and also research on the mining camps (in the middle years of the nineteenth century), where in some sense Americans were beyond the law (and formal law enforcement), there was very little evidence of violent crime against persons and property, Jack Valenti and Hollywood to the contrary. Americans beyond the law were largely self-regulating. Law was a part of their psyche; today one might say it was in their DNA. It was followed intuitively—Americans beyond the reach of the law were nevertheless "law-minded"—an interesting and provocative idea.

Much time can be devoted to discussing the nature and reliability of his evidence, but assume that Prof. Reid is correct: what does law-minded mean? Social and economic relations can and should operate without law enforcers. It should operate upon those within the reach of law, as well as beyond the law. The law should be understood, and must be observed, intuitively. Just as complex ideas of government were reduced to a few words in the Constitution, private and public law should be redacted into a simple set of uncomplicated principles.

Of course, neither American private law (nor its public law) turned out that way: hence the contradiction. Why not? The response is a relatively easy one: the lawyers. No society disdains lawyers as much as does American. Finding out that your child is to marry a lawyer was, at one time, a source of great satisfaction. Now, it has become one of disgrace. And herein the contradiction: though despised as they may be, should tomorrow an American slip and fall, she will probably call an attorney before an ambulance, or at least very soon thereafter, unless, of course, a lawyer passing by has already slipped a business card into the victim's pocket.

Though disdained, the law, and the lawyers that create and distort it, those who have fashioned the contradiction, have become a national obsession. This ambivalence is another example of the paradox regarding law that is part of our national character. Switch on the hundreds of channels of cable television in an American hotel room (or log-on to Netflix or another streaming service), and you will probably land on a dramatic depiction of lawyers and the law. "Lawyer shows" abound. Trials, civil and criminal, plague the airwaves; on the ubiquitous talk show, little else is chattered about. Americans are obsessed with the law and the legal system that they purport to hate.

American Law: Complexity

Presumably, this law, which Americans may desire to be intuitively discerned, should be simple. Regrettably, the contrary is the case; modern American law is hopelessly complex. Again, the contradiction emerges; and again, the lawyers can be blamed. From a law that could and should be followed intuitively, American lawyers have imposed a legal order that is hopelessly complicated. Yet, this complaint is age-old. Recall Shakespeare. Of what was he thinking of but of America's jurisprudential ancestor, the English common law, when he depicted in *Hamlet*, the prince contemplating a human skull in the graveyard scene and musing: "Why be this not the head of a lawyer; where be his quiddities and quillets, his tenure and his tricks."

A better example of American law's complexity can be illustrated by moving from private law to public law. Modern American constitutional law inhabits a world of its own. No discipline of the law is more contradictory than constitutional law; no analytical framework is more arcane. Indeed, analysis requires the assimilation of a large body of vocabulary specific to constitutional analysis, and one that is absurdly nuanced. For example, in determining whether a statute violates a provision of the United States Constitution, courts use the following varying standards of review depending upon the constitutional provision in question: strict scrutiny, heightened scrutiny, intermediate scrutiny, loose scrutiny, rational-basis scrutiny, and so on. The differences among them are frighteningly arcane. Likewise, only specialist constitutional lawyers can aspire to understand with precision the structure of the debate over federalism, separation of powers, and individual rights, let alone the nuances of constitutional interpretation.

Thus, only the chosen few who have devoted their lives to the cause are able to speak the language of constitutional law. A layperson (and many a law professor who like myself plough other fields) is bewildered by obvious contradiction. For example, the First Amendment is frequently said to create a barrier between church and state. Yet, you cannot spend a penny or a dollar in the United States without being reminded that, in this country, it is "In God we Trust." Nor can an address by the President close without the words "God bless America." A wall between church and state? Like English monarchs, the President often appears to be the "Defender of the Faith." But there are contradictions in constitutional analysis, or so lay folk might discern. Sessions of Congress can begin with a prayer, yet a football game between two public schools cannot. Likewise, as to the Eighth Amendment's prohibition of cruel and unusual punishment: do late eighteenth century standards apply or "evolving" ones? The macabre debate over what which combination of poisons does or does not constitute "cruel and unusual punishment" (whatever that might mean) is bewildering. Regardless of which position on capital punishment the reader supports, one would have thought that after a couple of hundred years of discussion, the issue would have been resolved. It has not, and perhaps never will be, until the last capital offence is committed. That is unlikely to occur anytime soon.

Of course, constitutional lawyers refuse to see complexity or the contradiction of principles that govern their domain; all of these problems can be systematized or explained away. The language employed is sufficiently dense so as to be incomprehensible to the average American, let alone her colleagues who teach in other areas.

Likewise, much the same can be said about a variety of areas of private law. Oliver Cromwell, the revolutionary who led the British Isles as Lord Protector from 1653 to 1659, referred to the common law of England in the seventeenth century as an "ungodly jumble." It still is; and American law, though no longer strictly governed by the common law, remains at the very least complicated. I defy one to try to explain (as I must do to my Property law class) the difference between the following two future interests in land developed by the "common law": a vested remainder subject to open and to divestment, and a contingent remainder. Similarly, American statute law is complex, and for law student and citizen alike, unreadable. And there is a lot of it: state and federal. When you have a moment, browse the United States Tax Code. If American law began with the notion that it should be a law "of the people," it is now a law for lawyers, and specialty lawyers at that.

American Law: The Moral Dimension

Like the thirteen colonies, American law began its journey, above all, following a moral or cultural design. Our settlement was to be (largely) "a city built on a hill." American law strives to fulfill the moral imperative that governs the legal relation of those who dwell on this now quite large, and far more densely-populated, mountain range. But the idea that there is good law, just law, and bad law, unjust law out there remains. America's goal must be for its legal order to strive to find the righteous path. Just like America believes that its foreign policy is, and has always been, driven by moral rectitude, so too it is believed that its legal order should be so governed. That others might not perceive it precisely that way may be interesting, but beside the point. The goal of American law, then, must be "to dream the impossible dream," an ever-striving process of discovering what is the right law, the moral imperative of law, what the law in a given circumstance should be. Of course, once again, enter the lawyers who fashion the law. Just as lawyers led us down this path from law-minded to law-hating, they may have diverted us from a morally-just law. Their interest in law is as a businessperson, and not as a moral theologian.

And Finally, American Law: Diversity

My final stab at oversimplification is the much-worn term: diversity. But in this context, I mean the plethora of 'law-givers." In America, one is never at a loss for law, and lawgivers. Countless levels of government are constantly churning out the law. My own American law students are subject to a myriad of law: the "law" of Tulane Law School; the "law" of Tulane University; that of the city of New Orleans; of Orleans Parish; of the state of Louisiana; and, of course, of the law of the United States. There is enough law in America for the conscientious foreign lawyer to spend many years in active, painstaking, and detailed study. And from time-to-time each law-making sovereign seems to have a different idea about what the law should be. Recently, the legislature of the state of Louisiana believed that it was within its power to limit doctors who provide abortion services within its borders to have admitting rights in hospitals within a 30-mile radius of their clinic. The United States Supreme Court thought otherwise. *June Med. Servs. L.L.C. v. Russo*, 140 S. Ct. 2103 (2020). So, America, like all federal states, has a hierarchy of law, and one not easy to delineate, which we shall try to come to understand.

American society, then, is marked by ambivalence towards law; the belief in law as a moral exercise; and a disdain, or at the very least, a suspicion of and for formal law. The latter has led Americans over the course of the half-century (if not longer) to find "alternatives" to law, and in particular, to the courts. Alternative dispute resolution is frequently on the minds of commercial actors, and their lawyers, though it also was current in the reign of William III, when colonial "Americans" were British subjects. *An Act for determining Differences by Arbitration*, 9 & 10 Will. 3, c. 15 (1698). The contemporary preference has seemingly turned from litigation in the courts to arbitration, mediation, negotiation, neighborhood courts that are not courts, and the like. Though procedures are streamed-lined and law a bit less arcane, lawyers are as omnipresent in the process of alternative dispute resolution as they are in the courtroom.

A Page of History

An introduction to an introduction, like this one, cannot conclude without addressing American law's glorious past. If American law reflects the spirit of the American people, some understanding of our history must be required. Once again there is a need to be concise. That's what "Nutshells" are about! America's history, and its legal history can, and do, fill the pages of learned monographs. Our incursion will be brief.

Of legal history, Oliver Wendell Holmes, perhaps America's most erudite jurist, once remarked that "a page of history is worth a volume of logic." *New York Trust Co. v. Eisner*, 256 U.S. 345, 348 (1921). Though he dabbled in the discipline, he also wrote that "there must be better reasons for adopting a rule other than that it was law in the reign of Henry IV." Oliver Wendell Holmes Jr., *The Path of the Law*, 10 HARV. L. REV. 457, 469 (1897). A contradiction? American lawyers ascribe to both. History can and does shed light on the meaning of law; but history ought neither to direct, nor should it mandate its present guise. Before moving on, then, with apologies to Mr. Justice Holmes, *a page or so of history*.

Once upon a time there were many laws. European settlers came to a continent that had some notion of law; Native American tribes were not lawless. Foremost amongst the foreign law transplanted was English law: royal law, the statutes and the common law. Royal law was both a legal system and an amorphous body of principles of substantive law, and to the extent it was applicable, it governed a very different economic and social order. It crossed the Atlantic with the colonists, though likely in its most rudimentary form. But there were in England other forums and other laws, church courts, borough courts, and local courts. America continued to function "in English ways" for lack of viable alternatives. English law in the colonial period, both the common law and statute, was perhaps less complex than in the mother country, and it became deeply imbued with both religious and secular morality to varying extents in different colonies. Likewise, diversity with respect to forum and substantive law applied has always been a part of the English legal system.

Recall also, however, that other European settlers pillaged the North American continent. They brought with them Dutch and Spanish, and of course, French law. Successive colonization, therefore, added further layers: more diversity to a diverse law. And colonial law reflected this mix. As British rule was ensconced in the North American colonies, the law therein became diverse: the law of Anglican Georgia was the Anglican gloss on English law, Maryland, the Catholic, Massachusetts, the Puritan.

But, how long could these European legal principles and procedures continue unaltered in this virgin territory? The colonies had their own economic orders, and therefore, forged their own wrinkles and glosses on this polyglot that is called the English common law. Each settlement, then each colony, had its own courts and its own law. Supervision from across the pond, from England, was minimal. The colonists had little use for lawyers, and what little English law they knew, was derived haphazardly from the few texts that crossed the Atlantic. In the latter years of colonization, the most popular was Sir William Blackstone's *Commentary on the Laws of England*, an admirable volume, but one written for a different audience than colonial lawyers, and with a different agenda: to acquaint the ruling elite of the mother country of the basic tenets of English law, and its innate superiority to the law of other European nations. The work was originally published by the Clarendon Press at Oxford, 1765–1770. It is divided into four volumes, on the rights of persons, the rights of things, of private wrongs and of public wrongs. An American edition published in Philadelphia between 1771–72 sold out its first printing of 1,400 and a second edition immediately appeared. Nevertheless, Blackstone was neither compiled to educate lawyers, nor was it intended to serve as a codification of the English legal system. But it served as the colonists' guide thereto.

Diversity and naiveté were, therefore, terms that might aptly characterize the American legal order during the colonial period. The Revolution, of course, had a great impact on American law. In one area of the law, constitutional law, new ground was surely broken. In the area of private law, change was incremental. At first, the English common law was received into the decisional law of the newly-forged states *en masse* to the extent that it was not contrary to the federal and state constitutions. Because the economic and social environment of the republic differed so fundamentally from that of the mother country, the common law had to be Americanized. That speedily occurred in the early nineteenth century.

What does "Americanization" mean? For much of the nineteenth century America was a frontier society. A new continent had to be settled; huge amounts of land were given away to encourage that process; enterprise had to be fostered to tame the wilderness. Land law had to conform; it had to protect the rights of occupiers of land who put the soil to productive use, rather than to others who might claim title. Likewise, industrial development had to be promoted, and the law could assist, or at the very least not impede, it. Like American economy and the society, American law could not be static; rather it had to be dynamic. Thus, the law of nuisance first encouraged industrial enterprise by continuing to allow the first use to which land was put (and therefore, ultimately protecting existing use) even if it was noxious and conflicted with a more benign use to which neighboring newcomers wished to put their land. As industrial and commercial land exploitation burgeoned, a different balance had to be struck between protecting enterprise and promoting competition, and one that would bring about more investment in growth. Likewise, with respect to the railroads, the key to both the geographical and economic expansion of the new nation, tort law was initially hostile towards finding the railroads liable for negligence to encourage investment in the "iron horses." Later, as the population grew, and the need for expansion was less critical, tort standards became more favorable to passengers and to bystanders injured in railroad accidents.

In addition to economic expansion, much of the nineteenth century in America was devoted to the debate over slavery, the American Civil War, and the ensuing Reconstruction. Because it supported the slave system, law, both federal and state, was very much involved. The debate over slavery, and the extent to which it should be contained to existing states as the country expanded, was also an economic, political and moral discourse. Perhaps the most interesting single case to read is the much-debated *Dred Scott v. Sandford*, 60 U.S. 393 (1856). Although the viability of slave state economies is a continuing controversy amongst historians, southern states in the antebellum period had little doubt that their "peculiar institution" was at risk if further expansion occasioned admission of a greater number of free states (one in which slavery was not permitted). The Civil War devastated a generation, and after two decades of federal involvement in "Reconstruction" of the former Confederacy, interest was lost in improving the economic and political conditions of the former slaves, leading to more than a century of second-class citizenship for the descendants of slaves.

The experience of the Civil War and Reconstruction seems to have left America with little taste for national, as opposed to state, government. The half-century after Reconstruction witnessed cycles of economic boom followed by bust. It would take the Great Depression and the two World Wars to create the enormous social and economic problems that cried out for national solutions. President Franklin Delano Roosevelt's New Deal, a plan to combat the most serious economic downturn that the nation has ever suffered, brought the federal government into the forefront of American economic life, and witnessed the beginning of the federal regulatory state, the institution of what has been termed the "alphabet soup" of federal agencies, the SEC (Securities and Exchange Commission), the SSA (Social Security Administration), the FCC (Federal Communications Commission), the FTC (Federal Trade Commission), and the like. Thereafter, the role of the federal government was further strengthened; the Second World War and the Cold War required an active well-armed military which placed enormous demands on the public purse. Likewise, the civil rights movement brought the federal government into the forefront of the struggle for racial equality, a work-in-progress, and to fashion an American version of the social and economic safety net that modern governments provide.

Thereafter, for many Americans, history blends with current events. A country united at war, hot or cold, became divided by the variety of social and economic issues that separate so-called "conservatives" and "liberals." The liberal Democratic decade of Kennedy-Johnson administrations gave way to a conservative Republican reign of Presidents Nixon-Reagan-Bush (with a brief Carter interregnum), which passed on to Democratic President Clinton, and then back again to another President Bush. He was followed by the Democratic, President Obama, the first African-American president. President Trump followed in his wake. Americans seem undecided as the proper ideological bent it desires for occupants of the White House.

Exactly what ideological forces actually drive the political divisions in the United States is a matter for debate. Although conservatives claim to be driven by a nation of lean government, freedom from governmental interference, and fiscal restraint, there is little evidence that the nearly two dozen years of conservative rule has actually furthered that aspect of their articulated political agenda. The conservative President Trump is said to preside over the largest number of federal employees in history if government contractors are included. Much the same can be said for the liberals, who though they espoused greater economic intervention by government, and in particular a kinder, gentler approach to social programs for the poor, delivered a reform of the welfare system in the 1990s which eviscerated the partial successes of President Johnson's War on Poverty of the mid-sixties and that seems to have eliminated almost everyone from the welfare rolls. Likewise, the division is said to be directed by a different view of the role of law, and particularly the function of the federal courts in interpreting individual liberties in the United States Constitution's Bill of Rights. Though conservatives decry judicial activism, and liberals espouse the evolution of protection consistent with contemporary values, the position of judges, conservative or liberal, seems often to be driven by outcome rather than a conception of the proper role of an unelected judiciary in a democracy.

Conclusion

Reducing the first principles of American law to a very few, as we have done here, and its development over time, even over the relatively short history of the United States, is fraught with risk. One navigates between the Scylla of confusion and the Charybdis of oversimplification. The relationship between law and society and the economy is critical in trying to make sense of where we are, and where we have come from in the American journey. This conundrum does not make it any more straightforward to explain American law to the non-American lawyer. Suffice it to say that a complex society, one rife with inner contradictions, has produced a multi-faceted law that we are about to describe.

CHAPTER 2

THE SOURCES OF LAW AND COMMON LAW REASONING

Introduction

A wild fox is running across a public beach, chased by a hunter. As the huntsman is about to catch him, another, an interloper, grabs the fox and carries it away. Believing himself wronged, the huntsman seeks your legal counsel. How would you advise him? To what sources of law in your own legal system would you have recourse?

Nearly two centuries ago, another huntsman called Post entered his lawyer's office to complain that a fellow called Pierson behaved exactly as did the above interloper. That the case went to the highest court in the state of New York may seem remarkable given the value in controversy, that of a fox pelt, but then and now, Americans are by disposition litigious. That the case is still studied is perhaps even more extraordinary. No American law student gets his or her J. D. degree without coming to terms with (or not, as the case may be) the case of *Pierson v. Post. Pierson v. Post*, 3 Cai. R. 175 (N.Y. Sup. Ct. 1805).

The Legal Saga: Framing the Issue

Neither the progress of the action, nor indeed its outcome, is in itself remarkable. The huntsman Post sued the interloper Pierson for the fox (or more specifically its value since it had probably long since been made into a hat or stole) on the grounds that

Pierson had appropriated his property. Stated simply, Post's counsel alleged that the fox was his client's property, and that Pierson had wrongfully carried it away. The response from Pierson's counsel was equally straightforward: "No, it wasn't your property." The trial court awarded the value of the fox to the huntsman Post, but the Supreme Court of New York reversed, and oddly enough in a split decision, the majority held for the interloper Pierson, though Justice Tompkins, who wrote for the majority, duly noted that Pierson's conduct was discourteous.

Lawyers, of course, are required to phrase disputes at law in abstract legal terms. They are paid to translate transactions and disputes into legal parlance. So, the huntsman's lawyer did not merely march into court, tell the judge the sad tale, and demand justice for his client. Rather, he sued out a writ of trespass on the case, a common law writ in use in New York in the nineteenth century, though its origins hark back to medieval England, one that joined a single legal issue between the two parties, huntsman and interloper. Writs at common law were essentially entry tickets into court; today, they are called "complaints," at least in federal court. One began a cause of action at law by issuing a writ that summoned the defendant to court to answer to the formulaic allegations in the writ. Writs were specific to a particular cause of action. They outlined the elements of a particular claim. To prevail on an action in trespass on the case, the plaintiff, huntsman Post, had to allege and prove that another, here the defendant, the interloper Pierson, had interfered with his property. Because the huntsman Post never had the poor reynard in hand, he must have claimed that he acquired his property right by merely chasing it to the point at which interloper Pierson intervened in order to claim property in the fox. Counsel for Pierson, on the other hand, argued that Post could have acquired no such right by merely chasing the fox, and that the clever beast remained "unowned" until Pierson reduced it to his physical possession and carried it away.

So, the judges were rightly presented with what one of the learned judges, Justice Livingston, called a "knotty problem:" when does a person acquire property in a wild animal? Or to phrase the issue in more abstract and cosmic terms: how and when does society allocate property rights over things to individuals? A knotty problem, indeed, and not one confined to eighteenth-century jurisprudence. Are not similar questions of acquisition really the essence of intellectual property law? When does an idea floating out there (or running) in the minds of authors and inventors become copyrightable or patentable?

The Search for Law

Contrary to the views of American law students, judges, past and present, just do not make the law up as they go along. Post is a good chap; Pierson a scoundrel; verdict for Post. While that analysis might explain the verdict in the trial court, the justices of the Supreme Court of New York in the case did what judges in modern America do: they looked for controlling law that would dictate the outcome. The American legal system has sources of law, and judges must ferret them out and apply them. The highest source of law in the United States, proclaimed in Article VI, is the Constitution of the United States itself, as well as laws and treaties of the United States adopted pursuant to the processes set out in the Constitution for enactment and ratification; they are proclaimed to be the supreme law of the land. Unhappily for the justices in *Pierson v. Post*, the founders and early American legislators were occupied with other more trying issues. Federal law, though admittedly supreme, was decidedly silent on the issue before the court: the acquisition of rights in property in wild animals. And indeed, since the ambit of federal law is limited by the Constitution to particular subject matters, and property in wild animals was not one of them, Congress probably would have had no business allocating rights in property in foxes on public beaches in the state of New York anyway. The American system of law, which we shall refer to as "our federalism," allows the states to make law in most areas of property rights. So, the focus of the justices shifted down a jurisdictional notch. New York law should resolve the knotty problem. But, unhappily, neither the Constitution nor the legislature of the state of New York had turned its attention to the issue. And municipal law was likewise silent; ownership of the fox was a lacuna in the relevant law. So, was the search for law at its end?

Enter the Common Law

Not yet. New York is, and indeed all states, save Louisiana, are (and even judicial reasoning in Louisiana follows the American model), of course, common law jurisdictions. We must now confront this awkward term, mentioned in the first chapter, but where definition was studiously avoided, and at least try to explain its meaning. The common law is both a set of legal rules and system of analysis. It was forged in the English royal courts in what is often referred to as the Middle Ages, where it began as a dialogue between judges and lawyers, the judges themselves generally drawn from the elite of the legal profession. The substantive common law was seen as a basket of principles that could be applied to resolve actual disputes between the kingdom's subjects. Just what these principles were, and how they were found is difficult to divine. Reason, natural law, logic, customs, and previous decisions, as well as the interpretation of statutes, were all used by litigants to argue their cases in the royal courts, and therefore could be said to be components of the common law. Cases correctly decided added to the body of common law; they were precedent, and though possibly not binding, they would be used to resolve similar disputes, newly-decided cases grafted on to this existing, yet amorphous, body of common law.

Although largely principles of private law (contract, tort, and property), the common law also came to embody certain constitutional principles, and in particular, the notion that monarchical power in England was not absolute. Just as certain principles of common law govern private rights, there were certain principles that limited the sovereign hand in dealing with its subjects. The clash between royal power and notions of its limits arose most frequently in the area of taxation, where consent of Parliament came to be required to levy charges on the people, and in disciplining rebellious subjects, where imprisonment without trial was precluded in the Great Charter of 1215, the much-revered *Magna Carta*. These two limitations on sovereign power very much informed discussion between the American colonists and their sovereign, George III, and led finally to the American Revolution. Ultimately, the United States Constitution addressed many of the issues of sovereign power that had so vexed and troubled the colonists until they rebelled.

Having operated largely under the common law before the Revolution, the newly created states received it into their private law to the extent that it was not inconsistent with newly-created state constitutions and statutes adopted pursuant thereto. In the course of the following century, the common law was "Americanized," that is to say, the same dynamic processes of legal reasoning that were employed to create and then to elaborate upon the common law in England, continued to refine law in America. The arguments of lawyers and judges, in cases between parties, transformed the received common law into a body of principles more consistent with economic and social conditions and aspirations of the young nation. Because private law was state law, the several states might adopt rules of decision that varied, again due to the very different economic and social realities of the several states. Likewise, the nineteenth century witnessed the rise of a nascent regulatory state; legislatures began to enact statutes, which could and did vary from state to state. It was not until the close of the nineteenth and the beginning of the twentieth century that a movement began to rationalize and make uniform the private law of the American states, a goal which has yet to be achieved fully.

But the common law system also embodies a process. Return to our fox. After constitutions and statutes were consulted, recourse would then shift to decisional law. Had the courts of the state of New York addressed the issue of wild foxes on public beaches? Apparently not. And those of the sister states, likewise. And on the other side of the pond: what saith the English common law? The law of once and future enemy combatants, the common law of England, was received into the law of New York by its 1777 Constitution. But there was no English precedent either. Suppose there was? Would the case have been resolved by reference to precedent? Perhaps, even probably, but not necessarily. The use of the term raises questions about whether previously-decided cases, precedent, would necessarily control the outcome of our tangle between the huntsman and the interloper. Now, if a case that had exactly the same facts had been decided one way or the other, say in favor of interloper, Post's counsel would have had a tough rough to hoe. Yet, if the case that touched upon the same issue was factually similar, but not precisely the same, all might not be lost for Post; his cause might not be lost. Common law reasoning allows a lawyer to attempt to distinguish the case at bar from a previously decided case. One side might argue that precedent controlled, and the other might try to distinguish the facts and circumstances from the case in litigation and argue that it did not.

Happily, the court did not have to consider whether the outcome was directed by another case, and if so, whether the court was bound to follow it, or since the court was the highest in New York, repudiate the existing rule and articulate another: to revise the common law. The court could not ignore the constitution or statute law, but it could (and this is done rarely) have decided not to apply its own judge-made law. It could have found certain critical facts and circumstances sufficiently different to warrant a different outcome. For example, suppose the other case cited as precedent involved hunting elephants on private land. Is the hunted creature (non-indigenous rather than indigenous) or the venue (on private rather than public land) significantly different from the case at bar to warrant a different outcome?

Or the court could have decided that it was time to change the law because times have changed. The underlying logic of the previously decided case sometimes no longer fits contemporary conditions. After all, precedent binds, as Sir Edward Coke, the great champion of the common law in late sixteenth and early seventeenth century England, noted, not because it is simply there, but because the judges in the past had confronted the same issue and proclaimed a reasoned opinion. It is the logic within the past case that binds, not merely the fact that it was decided one way or the other. A wrongly reasoned case was not precedent, any more than a statute that had not been adopted in accordance with legislative process was law. A case decided in the past may no longer serve societal interests, and should be overturned. Because the common law should guide individual actions to the same extent as the Constitution and statute law, modifications or reversals of the common law are not undertaken freely and without due regard to the rights of the individual parties to the suit. Yet, the common law is not static. Indeed, sometimes the judges will enforce the "old" law in the case at bar, but announce that the court is inclined to follow different law for the future.

But there were no cases anywhere! *Pierson v. Post* was a case of first impression. Rights in wild animals as they were being pursued had not been allocated at common law. It was up to the court to find the law elsewhere. And in *Pierson v. Post*, the court ranged far and wide. One will note in the opinion, the names of Bracton and Fleta, learned (though perhaps long-forgotten) commentators on the laws of England of the 13th and 14th centuries. But the court searched more extensively, perusing the learned works of Justinian, Pufendorf, Bynkershoeck, and Barbeyrac, lawmakers and commentators on the civil law. The majority pondered these learned souls, and adopted the view of Barbeyrac: ownership in wild animals occurs when they are "wounded, circumvented or ensnared ... so as to deprive them of their natural liberty." A reasonable rule; but why did they select that one? Was it because they revered Barbeyrac? Did they feel bound by his wisdom, or was something else controlling the agenda?

Policy Concerns

The genius of judge-made law is directly related to the wisdom of the judges. Both the majority and the dissent in *Pierson v. Post* probably looked to logic in order to decide the case. The judges applied predispositions, perhaps differing ones since one judge dissented, about what goals the law should accomplish. In his dissent, Justice Livingston was persuaded that economic efficiency mandated a judgment for Pierson. While law and economics is a formal area of study in the legal academy, the common law has probably considered the effects, economic and otherwise, of a judgment and a rule before instructed to so by modern law professors. Justice Livingston's logic went like this: foxes are noxious beasts; they disturb farming, a noble and necessary occupation in our state; who would hunt, expend labor (not to mention keep numerous hounds to assist in the chase) to rid the country of these noxious animals if the fruits of such effort could be whisked away by another? Allowing the huntsman a property right in the fox after having chased him for a good long time, until upon the verge of reducing the beast to possession, would provide the required incentive. More broadly phrased, the law should encourage investment and enterprise. Justice Livingston's position was calculated to reward the person whose labor has brought the property into the stream of commerce.

Justice Livingston raised a further issue. Why, he queried, did the case come to the courts; would it not have been better to have referred the controversy to a cabal of sportsmen, who, he mused, would know precisely to whom the pelt should be awarded? There is a certain prescience to his comment; it surely has a modern ring. Avoid litigation; submit the dispute to ADR (alternative dispute resolution): arbitrate, mediate, or negotiate! And note that his preferred decision-makers are gendered: sports*men*. The evaluations of huntswomen are not welcomed here; modern feminist jurisprudence scholars would remind us that the prevailing legal order sought (consciously or otherwise) to create a law made by men to protect the interests of men.

The majority valued something else. Justice Tompkins wrote that rules ought to be made in such a way that they are easily enforced. Modern legal academics call such rules "administratively efficient." If the rule of the dissent had been adopted, that pursuit with a reasonable chance of physical appropriation would accord property rights in the animal to the huntsman, how would a person know when his or her chase was sufficiently far enough along to be certain that property rights would be allocated to him or her? And how could an interloper like Pierson know when the chase was too far along for him to intercede? The standard of "depriving the wild animal of its natural liberty" is a bright-line rule. It is easy to apply, it is "administratively efficient."

Of course, there was a moral dimension to the case. Did not Pierson's conduct run counter to prevailing ideas of morality? Wasn't he really a thief? American law is also comprised of a philosophy that incorporates societal as well as economic values. So both legal theory and jurisprudence are a staple of American legal reasoning, and the American legal education.

Old Wine in New Bottles—of Baseballs and Foxes

Why bother to read old cases? Because modern decisions are woven from them. The logic of past cases may direct controversies that subsequently come before the court. Old wine in new bottles. The discourse which follows is an interesting and amusing example of how a modern court "plays" with precedent.

On October 7, 2001, Barry Bonds hit his record-setting 73rd home run of the 2001 Major League Baseball season. You may be asking yourself: "How could a baseball possibly be related to a fox?" Allow me to explain. During the lead up to the game, it was widely anticipated that if Barry Bonds did indeed hit a new record-setting home run, the ball could be worth over $1 million. As you can imagine, the prospect of catching this baseball brought many fans into the stadium that day. Alex Popov being one of them; Patrick Hayashi being another. Well, Barry Bonds did hit that record-setting home run, and the ball soared through the sky and landed directly into Popov's glove. However, as the ball entered his glove, he was immediately attacked by a large group of fans also trying to obtain the flying fortune. This caused Popov to drop the ball, allowing it to roll into the hands of Hayashi, who had also been knocked down by the group. Popov, believing himself to be the rightful owner of baseball, decided to sue Hayashi for conversion, essentially demanding the return of the baseball or its value.[1] Sound familiar?

The court was once again tasked with deciding at what point possession and ownership are obtained. To that end, the court began by identifying some fundamental principles of possession. The court looked to the perspectives of various legal professors (sorry Justinian, Pufendorf, Bynkershoeck, and Barbeyrac—modern American judges are not so erudite) with an expertise in the area. Hayashi, following the argument of Professor Gray, suggested that in order to establish possession "the actor must retain control of the ball after incidental contact with people and things." Popov retorted, citing the logic of Professors Finkelman and Bernhardt, that possession occurs "by stopping the forward momentum of the ball whether or not complete control is achieved." In other words, possession occurs when the ball is "wounded, circumvented or ensnared ... so as to deprive [it] of [its] natural liberty." In fact, Popov specifically pointed the

---

[1] *Popov v. Hayashi*, WL 31833731, Ca Sup. Ct., 2002.

attention of the court towards *Pierson v. Post* in order to support his contention.

However, the court disagreed with Popov and adopted the conception of possession proffered by Professor Gray (Gray's Rule). They reasoned that the principles argued by Popov, that possession is obtained even before absolute dominion and control, were in response to the unique circumstances of the conduct they attempt to regulate. That the reason they are relevant in those contexts (capturing a harpooned whale, fleeing fox, or sunken ship) is because absolute dominion and control is impossible. Such is not the case of a baseball hit into the stadium stands. So, Popov loses, right? Not quite.

The inquiry did not stop there. Now that the court had decided on their definition of possession, it was time to apply it. Gray's Rule, as stated earlier, was that "the actor must retain control of the ball after incidental contact with people and things." Popov lost control of the ball. It was once again "wild" and subject to capture by another. However, his loss of control of the ball was not due to incidental contact, it was the result of a collective assault. The court then reasoned that Popov should have had the opportunity to complete his catch unimpeded, "to hold otherwise would be to allow the result in this case to be dictated by violence. That will not happen." The court, as a matter of equity and fundamental fairness, adopted a new rule which bestowed upon Popov a pre-possessory interest in the ball which constituted a qualified right to possession. So, Popov wins? Not necessarily.

While Popov had a pre-possessory interest in the ball, Hayashi had actually initially attained unequivocal dominion and control. Hayashi was not a wrongdoer and was also a victim of the violent group. Both Popov and Hayashi had a legitimate possessory interest in the ball unencumbered by the other. So, the court, relying on the concept of equitable division, did the only thing that seemed "fair." They declared that both parties had an equal and undivided interest in the ball and that the ball must be sold, with the proceeds divided equally between them.

While Pierson v. Post took place almost 200 years before Popov v. Hayashi, the process that transpired in the court and the principles relied upon are fundamentally the same. In both cases, the court looked for guiding legal principles from learned experts, considered the righteousness of each party's actions, and inquired into the policy effects their respective decisions would have. Although the Popov court did not follow the principles relied on by the Post court, they only did so after distinguishing their unique set of facts and context. The Popov court had the advantage of knowing the reasoning used by the Post court, leading them to a decision which uniquely addressed the issue at hand. Every relevant court decision will help guide the next court in reasoning their way to resolving the case before them.

Conclusion

All these issues, legal, economic, and societal, clash in many cases that have come before American courts and continue to grace the halls of justice. But of course, not all cases are decided by recourse to Barbeyrac, or even the various strands of logic that support the common law. Today most cases allocating rights in property probably would be decided by statute. Much common law has been reduced to legislation, and they are drafted with reasonable specificity, though perhaps not quite like a code. But statutory interpretation also can be influenced by the sort of policy concerns that were in play in *Pierson v. Post*. Legislatures ponder some of the same issues in drafting laws. These multifarious concerns render the study of American law a very complicated, but a very interesting intellectual exercise.

CHAPTER 3

THE AMERICAN CONSTITUTIONAL SYSTEM: ALLOCATION OF GOVERNMENTAL POWERS

Introduction

No two nations organize their governmental structure and allocate law-making authority in precisely the same manner. Even amongst modern western democracies, each country has its own constitutional peculiarities. Thus, the governmental structure and law-making authority of the United States has some elements in common with other nations, and others which are unique to our shores. Like other constitutions, the form that American government assumed was initially driven largely by its history. In particular, the American pattern of government embodied in the United States Constitution, which came into force in 1789 (and has been sparsely amended thereafter), reflected dissatisfaction with both the structure and substance of the British colonial government.[1] The Constitution was therefore directed towards limiting the powers of government, particularly the federal government, rather than enhancing them; powers not delegated to the federal government would either reside with the states or the people. Structurally, then, the

---

[1] The colonists, followed by the revolutionaries, and thereafter the Framers, were, after all, largely British subjects who had migrated (or were descended from migrants) and held a particular view of the rights of Englishmen and the proper function and power of government.

Constitution established two important principles: federalism and separation of powers. Federalism, it was believed, would limit governmental power by fragmenting it, insuring that law-making authority would be distributed vertically between the national and state governments. Separation of powers, grafted onto the federal political structure, would effectuate a system of checks and balances among each branch of the federal government; this horizontal division limited the authority of each co-equal branch to act (in certain circumstances) without the concurrence of the others.

Federalism is not unique to the United States. Most modern democracies are federal in structure in that law-making authority is not held exclusively by central government, but shared with regional or local governments which also maintain some residual power to make and enforce law. But "our federalism" may well differ. Generally, it is central government rather than local government that maintains greater control in modern democracies. Under the American Constitution, at least in theory, it is state governments that have plenary power (authority that is broadly construed); the federal government has only the powers expressed or implied in the Constitution. This conception of limited lawmaking authority in the federal government was arguably reaffirmed in the Tenth Amendment to the Constitution, which proclaims that, "The powers not delegated to the United States by the Constitution, nor prohibited by it to the States, are reserved to the

States respectively, or to the people."[2] Thus, if one were to conceptualize sovereign power in the United States as a large circular pie, the pie itself is controlled by the states and the people, and the federal government has been given merely a slice by the framers of the Constitution. This segment of the pie, the federal government's allocation of sovereign power, is fixed; its powers are enumerated, and the federal government can only exercise power specifically granted or "necessary and proper" to those delegated.

Our Federalism: Congressional Powers

Of course, the extent to which *enumerated* power is effectively *limited* power depends upon what powers are specifically delegated by the Constitution. But before considering Congressional power, first a word about the institution. Congress, like its ancestor (the British Parliament), is comprised of two houses: the House of Representatives and the Senate.

---

[2] Whether the Tenth Amendment serves only to reaffirm Congress's limited lawmaking authority is hotly debated. A narrow reading of the Tenth Amendment would assert that it is merely a reminder that Congress cannot act absent express or implied constitutional authority to do so. *See Gibbons v. Ogden*, 22 U.S. 1, 198 (1824). The counterpoint, favoring a broad reading of the Tenth Amendment, is supported by a canon of constitutional interpretation, namely, that language in the Constitution should never be read as being surplusage. A broad reading would construe the Tenth Amendment as an additional constraint on Congress's power, beyond those already delineated in Article I, so to protect the states from abuses of power by the federal legislative branch. *See Nat'l Fed'n of Indep. Bus. v. Sebelius (Obamacare)*, 56 U.S. 519, 647 (2012) (Scalia, J., dissenting) (arguing that the Tenth Amendment limits Congress from "compel[ling] the States to function as administrators of federal programs.").

However, the similarity between the two ends there. Seats in the House, though divided into districts wholly within an individual state, were, and continue to be, allocated to the states by population, each Congressional district having roughly the same number of citizens. The upper house, the Senate, was created to represent the states. Although now elected by the voters, two Senators for each state, the Senate was originally selected by the state legislatures in each of the several states, and reflected the will of state government rather than that of the people.

Because of the complexity of federal regulation, Congress frequently legislates in general terms, but leaves detailed rule-making pursuant to enactment to administrative agencies. For example, though complex, the statutes passed by the Congress setting out the federal tax system pales in comparison (both in number and detail) with the regulations established by the Commissioner of the Internal Revenue Service. Many sections of the tax code empower the Commissioner to adopt regulations to carry out the legislative intent. This delegation of lawmaking authority has attracted considerable controversy. Recently, the Supreme Court has flirted with the idea of breathing new life into the "nondelegation doctrine," which restricts Congress's ability to abdicate lawmaking powers to federal agencies. See Gundy v. United States, 139 S. Ct. 2116, 2145 (2019) (Gorsuch, J., dissenting) (arguing that revival of the nondelegation doctrine is necessary to protect individual liberty). In the end, the courts permit delegation, provided the statute delineates criteria to guide the agency's exercise of discretion (the Court's "intelligible principle" requirement), because Congress may countermand any ensuing regulation by merely passing a law with contrary terms.

Let us return to Congressional power. Article I, Section 8 sets out the law-making authority of Congress, the legislator in the American system, and lists its competency in a scant 18 clauses. Some of the enumerated powers seem today quite mundane; for example, in clause 7 Congress is granted the power "To establish Post Offices and post Roads." Others seem more formidable. Six clauses deal with the establishment and maintenance of the armed forces (clauses 11–16), and another group address financial matters such as collecting taxes, borrowing, and coining money (clauses 1, 2, and 5, respectively). Congress also has powers in specific areas of international concern, most notably the power to declare war (clause 11).

Two other clauses enumerating congressional lawmaking authority, however, have emerged as the most significant in extending federal power, probably beyond the scope originally imagined by the Framers. The first is the so-called "commerce clause" (clause 3); the second, the "necessary and proper clause" (clause 18). Each will be discussed in detail.

The Commerce Clause

In clause 3, Congress is given power "To regulate Commerce with Foreign Nations, and among the several States, and with the Indian Tribes." Neither the first nor the third area of regulatory authority in the area of commerce has proved significant. The regulation of commerce "among the several States," however, has been the cause of much controversy concerning the scope of Congressional power.

As a general rule, present-day commerce clause jurisprudence regards "among the several States" as encompassing three categories of activity in which Congress may regulate: (1) channels, such as interstate highways and railroads; (2) instrumentalities, such as goods moving through the interstate channels; and (3) purely intrastate activities which have a substantial connection to interstate commerce. This third category is the most tested and often serves as the vehicle for narrowing or expanding Congress's commerce power.

Its most expansive reading was formulated in *Wickard v. Filburn*, 317 U.S. 111 (1942). In *Wickard*, wheat-raising quotas established by Congress were applied to wheat grown by a farmer for his own domestic consumption. *Id.* at 116. Might this homegrown wheat be counted in the farmer's quota? The relevant constitutional issue was as follows: can wheat grown by a farmer in Kansas, then used by that same farmer to bake bread in Kansas, and consumed by the very same farmer in Kansas, have an effect upon interstate commerce? The answer must surely be no, because the activity occurred only within the confines of the state of Kansas; absent some other enumerated power (of which there was none), Congress could not include the intrastate wheat in its quota system. The Supreme Court held otherwise, using an "effects" based test. *Id.* at 120. In aggregate, domestic consumption would affect interstate commerce because, if all farmers produced homegrown wheat to meet their own needs, then they would thereby not be required to purchase wheat in a sister state. If farmers did purchase wheat in the national market, however, then the national wheat market would not be accordingly circumscribed. *Id.* at 127–28. Farmers might possibly purchase wheat produced in a sister state. Therefore, the aggregate effect on interstate commerce was deemed substantial, albeit tenuous and indirect. *Id.*

Conceding to Congress the power to regulate economic activity that *might* affect trade between the states greatly increased its regulatory authority in areas from banking through product labeling. Those familiar with European Union law on free movement of goods will note the similarity in reasoning between the *Wickard* court's interpretation of the commerce clause and the European Court of Justice's effects test in interpreting the Treaty on the Functioning of the European Union, Articles 28, 110, and 34.

The wide berth of power long given to Congress under the commerce clause has slowly been chipped away at, albeit inconsistently. Most recently, in 2012, the Supreme Court struck down a federal law on commerce clause grounds in its so-called *Obamacare* decision. 56 U.S. at 558. There, the Court constrained Congress from regulating "inactivity," such as the failure to obtain healthcare as mandated by the legislation. *Id.* at 550. This new constraint, namely, that federal law enacted pursuant to the commerce clause cannot create an activity to be regulated but can only regulate an already-existing activity, narrowed Congress's power to regulate under the "substantial connection" category noted above. This constraint added to the Court's assessment of other factors adopted post-*Wickard*, which narrowed the basis for finding whether a "substantial connection" exists. The most critical question is whether the regulated activity is economic or commercial in nature. *See U.S. v. Morrison*, 529 U.S. 598, 610–12 (2000) (discussing factors considered to determine whether an Act of Congress was within its commerce power).

The *Obamacare* decision was a departure from the Court's prior judgment in *Gonzales v. Raich*, 545 U.S. 1, 32–33 (2005), but consistent—at least in the result—with both commerce clause rulings that preceded that decision, namely, *United States v. Lopez*, 514 U.S. 549 (1995), and *Morrison*, 529 U.S. at 613. *Raich* concerned California's Compassionate Use Act of 1996, which permitted the use of marijuana for medicinal purposes if a doctor registered her patient and certified that the patient required the drug to relieve pain. *Raich*, 545 U.S. at 6–7. Federal law, the Controlled Substances Act, however, regulates the use of all drugs in the United States, and excludes the use of marijuana under any circumstances. 21 U.S.C. §§ 801–871 (2000). When agents from the Drug Enforcement Agency seized the marijuana plants of a terminally ill California woman, she sued to overturn the federal law on the grounds that Congress had no power to outlaw the use of marijuana grown and consumed wholly within California. *Raich*, 545 U.S. at 7–8. The Supreme

Court upheld Congressional law on commerce clause grounds, even though the marijuana was grown and used wholly within a single state, California. The Court returned to its earlier understanding of Congress's power under the commerce clause, reviving its position in *Wickard*: Congress may regulate wholly local (intrastate) activities that, if left unregulated, would have an aggregate effect on interstate commerce. Thus, because some drug production and sale occur in interstate commerce, all aspects of the enterprise can be regulated by Congress if the wholly intrastate portions cannot be severed from the interstate and, if in the aggregate, consumption would have some substantial effect on interstate commerce.

Federal power under the commerce clause may also preempt (disallow or displace) state regulation, even where the general purpose of state and federal law is not clearly inconsistent. Preemption primarily occurs in two situations: (1) where federal law expressly preempts state law; or (2) where federal law implies congressional intent to preempt state law. The former focuses on the plain wording of the federal law; the latter involves two methods for ascertaining implicit preemption, the first being field preemption, and the second being conflict preemption. Field preemption may be proper where the federal statutory scheme is so pervasive such that it provides for the reasonable inference that Congress indeed left no room for states to supplement it. Conflict preemption, however, may occur when compliance with both state and federal law is impossible, or where state law creates an obstacle to the accomplishment of the federal law's goals. Where conflict preemption exists, federal law reigns supreme. *See Gibbons*, 22 U.S. at 210–11 (federal law controls); *see also* U.S. CONST. art. VI, § 1, cl.2.

Take, for example, congressional legislation mandating a particular health warning on alcoholic beverages; specifically, all drink containers must have the following dire pronouncement: "According to the Surgeon General, women should not drink alcoholic beverages during pregnancy because of the risk of birth defects." Suppose the New York legislature passes a law which provides that all alcoholic beverages sold in New York may, instead of inscribing the Surgeon General warning, brand their containers with a three-inch graphic of a pregnant woman drinking from a bottle with a red X superimposed over the image. Under the conflict-preemption standard, the New York law could create an obstacle to the accomplishment of the federal goal to explicitly warn of the dangers involved when consuming alcohol while pregnant. If, however, the New York law had merely permitted the graphic in addition to the Surgeon General warning, conflict preemption would be unlikely. Thus, federal law is the "floor"; states may build upon it, but they may not legislate beneath it. *See generally Wyeth v. Levine*, 555 U.S. 555 (2009) (finding it not impossible to comply with both federal and state drug labeling requirements).

Even in circumstances in which Congress has not legislated in a particular area, state law may be struck down pursuant to what is called the "dormant commerce clause." States may not legislate in such a way so as to discriminate against goods or services from a sister state or place an undue burden on interstate commerce. A classic case illustrating the first principle, discriminating against goods produced in another state, deals with, of all commodities, garbage. *City of Philadelphia v. New Jersey*, 437 U.S. 617 (1978). New Jersey adopted legislation that allowed garbage collected within its boundaries to be dumped in landfills in the state, but prohibited out-of-state garbage from being deposited within its borders. The Court held this to be clear discrimination by the State of New Jersey against the State of Pennsylvania, and therefore a violation of the dormant commerce clause, despite New Jersey's articulated environmental protection concerns. However, if Congress determined that it was indeed sound environmental policy to allow states to bar the dumping of out-of-state waste, then it could have and would have so legislated. Absent such action, New Jersey could not exclude Pennsylvania's garbage from being dumped within its borders.

Suppose there is no such direct discrimination in a state law? May it still violate the dormant commerce clause? Take, for example, a Louisiana law that requires that vessels traveling up the Mississippi River through Louisiana be under the control of locally-licensed river pilots.[3] Although interstate commerce is at issue, Congress has not legislated in this particular area. Unlike the "garbage" case above,

---

[3] For an actual case on this issue, *see Cooley v. Bd. of Wardens of the Port of Philadelphia*, 53 U.S. 299 (1851).

there is no explicit discrimination; all boats, those
registered in Louisiana and those registered
elsewhere, are subject to the same rule: locally-
licensed pilots. The dormant commerce clause might
apply, however, even though there is no explicit
discrimination, because the law does in effect protect
local interests: Mississippi River pilots are naturally
more likely to be Louisiana residents than residents
of Rhode Island. In the absence of a valid safety
concern, for example, that the river is sufficiently
treacherous that barges require pilots with
experience in these waters, the regulation should fail.

Notably, state laws that favor state-owned
businesses do not violate the dormant commerce
clause on discriminatory grounds, unlike those that
favor privately-owned in-state businesses (so-called
"economic protectionism"). *Compare United Haulers
Ass'n v. Oneida-Herkimer Solid Waste Mgmt.*, 550
U.S. 330 (2007) (upholding a state law favoring state-
operated waste disposal over out-of-state
competition), *with C&A Carbone v. Town of
Clarkstown*, 511 U.S. 383 (1994) (striking down a
state law on economic protectionism grounds when it
favored a privately-owned in-state business over out-
of-state competitors). State laws that favor state-
owned businesses over out-of-state entities is said to
be within the police power. *United Haulers*, 550 U.S.
at 347.

The Necessary and Proper Clause

The second important clause that has been
construed as conferring expansive power to Congress

is the so-called "Necessary and Proper Clause." This
final clause of Article I, Section 8 permits Congress
"to make all Laws which shall be necessary and
proper for carrying into Execution the foregoing
Powers", that is to say, the enumerated powers. What
legislation might be necessary and proper? Not
surprisingly, the Constitution did not grant Congress
the power to engage in space travel; may Congress
create and fund the National Aeronautics and Space
Administration, an agency that engages in space
exploration? Does the connection between space
exploration and the military render the
establishment of NASA "necessary and proper" given
the constitutional mandate to create a national
military force? Probably.

Consider the more recent establishment of the
United States Space Force through the National
Defense Authorization Act for Fiscal Year 2020 (Pub.
L. 116–92). Under both of the Supreme Court's most
recent decisions concerning the Necessary and
Proper Clause, creation of the Space Force is, at least
plausibly, proper to carry out Congress's military
powers enumerated in Article I, Clauses 11–16. *See
generally Obamacare*, 56 U.S. at 519 (narrowing its
prior holding in *United States v. Comstock*, 560 U.S.
126 (2010), to make clear that federal law is upheld
under the Necessary and Proper Clause only where
use of the clause advances existing authority that is
"a derivative of, and in service to, a granted power").

Ultimately, the broad precedent interpreting the
scope of the Necessary and Proper Clause, set by
Chief Justice John Marshall in *McCulloch v.*

Maryland, remains black letter law: "Let the end be legitimate, let it be within the scope of the Constitution, and all means which are appropriate, which are plainly adapted to that end, which are not prohibited, but consist with the letter and spirit of the Constitution. . . ." 17 U.S. 316, 421 (1819). In other words, the federal law's purpose must be legitimate, and the law must be an appropriate means for furthering that design.

Our Federalism: The Supremacy Clause

Having stressed that the political structure of the United States limits the powers of the federal government, it must be noted that the Constitution clearly accords primacy to federal law. Under the so-called "Supremacy Clause" (Article VI, Section 2), the federal Constitution, treaties, and laws (including executive, administrative, and judicial acts) trump conflicting state and local law. Thus, to return to our example of marijuana for medicinal purposes, once the Supreme Court determined that Congress had the power to regulate the sale of drugs, including marijuana, federal law controlled, and rendered California's conflicting state statute void. *Raich*, 545 U.S. at 33.

While state law cannot conflict with federal law, state law can operate in the same areas, and accord other or greater rights to its citizens than does federal law or the Constitution. For example, the Supreme Court has held that religious freedoms and rights of association, both protected under the First Amendment, are not necessarily violated by certain land-use regulations. *See Village of Belle Terre v. Borass*, 416 U.S. 1 (1974). Despite this, a state may still strike a municipality's land-use requirement as violative of its respective state constitution, even if it comports with federal law. For example, the Michigan Supreme Court has held that its own constitution accorded individuals greater rights than did the federal Constitution. *See Charter Township of Delta v. Dinolfo*, 351 N.W.2d 831 (Mich. 1984). That same court struck down a municipal zoning law governing single-family dwellings, on grounds that it violated the Michigan State Constitution when the law limited a "family" to only traditional nuclear families, and thereby zoned out in effect religious communes. *Id.*

Our Federalism: The Powers of the President

Just as the peculiarities of American federalism can be traced to our colonial heritage, the American wrinkle on separation of powers likewise belies the Founders' wariness of unbridled executive power. Though there is talk from time to time of an "imperial presidency," and the executive is generally the face of American government as projected on the international stage, successive presidents during the second half of the twentieth century were required to come to terms with the limitations that the Constitution has placed on executive power through the allocation of certain powers to Congress and to the courts. The same is, thus far, generally true for the twenty-first century, though the strength of this structure has been tested of late.[4]

The president is clearly the single most powerful manifestation of American government, and the only officer of the federal government that is elected by the entire electorate, albeit indirectly. The president is the only American politician who can claim a mandate from the people of the United States, and presents a stark contrast to the head of government in most parliamentary systems. There is, of course, a quaint contradiction here, because in fact only 538 members of the Electoral College actually cast votes directly for the president. Voters in individual states elect members of the College who are pledged to vote for one or the other candidates for president. Because the number of members of the Electoral College from each state is calculated by adding the number of Congresspersons (which vary by population) and Senators (two per state), smaller states have a disproportionate influence in the Electoral College. The 2000 presidential election illustrated this point. Albert Gore received more votes than did George W. Bush, but the number of Bush's electoral votes exceeded that of his rival. Likewise, in the 2016 election, Hillary Clinton received more votes than did Donald Trump, but did not garner a majority of votes

---

[4] Questions as to the breadth of executive power are before the courts as this edition goes to print; some have been settled—at least for now. *See, e.g., Trump v. Vance,* 140 S. Ct. 2412 (2020) (extending Court precedent, which held that a sitting president is not immune from federal criminal subpoenas, to hold the same with regard to "state criminal subpoenas seeking [the President's] private papers").

in the Electoral College. This peculiarity, undemocratic as it may appear, is calculated to make the president accountable to state government, as well as to the citizenry.

Although the president executes the law, the incumbent's powers are far more expansive. Perhaps the most significant power of the presidency is that he or she appoints a wide array of federal judicial, executive, and administrative officials. Nevertheless, the president's power to fill these offices is checked by the requirement that the chosen nominee be confirmed by the Senate. Take, for example, the federal judiciary. Given the powers of judicial review assumed by the courts, and their broad subject matter jurisdiction, the power to appoint all federal judges (and not merely Justices of the Supreme Court) gives the president significant power to fashion a federal bench that reflects a particular ideological approach to the federal law. The Supreme Court bench in recent years has transformed from a more elderly one to a more "youthful" judiciary. Even with the death of Justice Ginsburg, the members of the Court can hardly be regarded as young: one justice is in his eighties, two in their seventies, and only three are under the age of sixty-five. With a healthy number of elderly justices sitting on the Supreme Court, there is much discussion of this power, given President Trump's objective of appointing justices who share his conservative platform. There is nothing unique in his agenda; President Obama nominated justices with a more liberal cast that did his predecessor or successor.

But, of course, the president is checked by a hurdle, and balanced by a dilemma. The hurdle is that the Senate must confirm nominees. Given the rules of the Senate, it is necessary that a super-majority agree to close debate upon the president's judicial nominee in order to bring the nomination to the floor for a majority vote. Recently, in an effort to mitigate this so called "filibuster," the Senate invoked the so-called "nuclear option" to lower the number of votes necessary to end debate from sixty (or three-fifths vote) to fifty-one, and to move forward with its vote to confirm Justice Neil Gorsuch to the Supreme Court. *See* Matt Flegenheimer, *Senate Republicans Deploy 'Nuclear Option' to Clear Path for Gorsuch*, *Politics*, N.Y. TIMES (Apr. 6, 2017), https://www. nytimes.com/2017/04/06/us/politics/neil-gorsuch-supreme-court-senate.html. The dilemma is that it is often difficult for the president to be quite sure of how the judicial pick will pan out on the bench; the ideological bent of judges (and their positions on particular legal issues) is often uncertain, and once confirmed, federal judges serve for life.

The example of executive dismay with a judicial appointment that is generally cited is that of President Eisenhower. Not known as a liberal, he appointed Earl Warren and William Brennan to the Court, both regarded in retrospect as liberal judges. Indeed, President Eisenhower was said to have regretted his choices. After he was no longer president, Eisenhower *purportedly* said, "I have made two mistakes, and they are both sitting on the Supreme Court," and that Warren's nomination was "the biggest damn-fool mistake I ever made" *See*

William Fassuliotis, *Ike's Mistake: The Accidental Creation of the Warren Court, Columns*, VIRGINIA LAW WEEKLY (Oct. 17, 2018), https://www.lawweekly.org/col/2018/10/17/ikes-mistake-the-accidental-creation-of-the-warren-court.

In addition to appointing federal judges and Supreme Court justices, the president appoints the Cabinet and the heads of federal agencies, so-called "principle Officers of the United States," again subject to the check of Senate confirmation. The foreign relations of the United States are conducted by the Secretary of State; the enforcement of federal law by the president through the Attorney General. Both are appointed by the president with the "advice and consent" of the Senate. In addition, the heads of federal administrative agencies, including the Security and Exchange Commission, the Social Security Administration, and the Commission of Internal Revenue (the head federal tax collector), are all appointed by the president, subject to Senate confirmation. As to "removal" of executive officials, the president can always do so for good cause, subject to statutory limitations imposed by Congress, for example, where the official holds an office where independence from the president is desirable (such as the United States Office of the Special Counsel).

The Constitution empowers the president to conclude treaties with foreign states, checked by the constitutional provision that they be subject to ratification by two-thirds of the Senate (distinguishable from executive agreements, which need no congressional approval). The status of treaties in American law will be discussed in a separate chapter but suffice it to say at this juncture that treaties are accorded the same status as federal statutes: upon ratification, treaties, like statutes, are the supreme law of the land. U.S. CONST. art. VI, § 2. Thus, treaties are deemed to be self-executing, unless by their terms they require implementing legislation. Co-equal status can be a double-edged sword: a subsequently adopted statute that conflicts with the terms of a treaty will repeal the inconsistent provisions of the treaty. Moreover, Congressional enabling legislation can specify that the legislation rather than the treaty is the source of rights and obligations in domestic law. An example of this determination is the implementation of the Berne Convention on Copyright in which Congress made clear that the Convention itself, though ratified, has no legal status in American law. Rather, legislation adopted to implement it does.

The president is also a lawmaker in addition to a law-enforcer. Legislation that has passed both houses of Congress must be signed or vetoed by the president. Both the requirement of assent or dissent is another example of checks and balances under the Constitution. Under limited circumstances, legislation passed by Congress can become law without the president's signature: under Article I, Section 7, the president's veto can be overridden by a two-thirds majority of both houses of Congress. The president can also conduct foreign relations through executive agreements which do not require ratification. Although their status in law is unclear, particularly because they are regarded as an "inherent" presidential power not originating from any express constitutional provision, the ability to make these executive agreements may also allow the president to engage in subsidiary lawmaking in the domestic arena without the consent of Congress in order to fulfill the agreed commitments. Moreover, executive action may be required in exigent circumstances. An example of executive action without the consent of Congress, though not to fulfill an international agreement, is President Truman's seizure of the steel mills during the Korean War, action he undertook because a strike was imminent. Justice Jackson referred to a "zone of twilight" in which the president has the authority to act; unless Congress moves affirmatively to countermand the president's act, its acquiescence thereto is assumed unless the Constitution clearly bars it. *See Youngstown Sheet & Tube Co. v. Sawyer*, 343 U.S. 579 (1952) (Jackson, J., concurring).

The ultimate check on presidential power is removal by Congress through impeachment for "Treason, Bribery, and high Crimes and Misdemeanors." U.S. CONST. art. 2, § 4. The three cases of presidential impeachment, that of President Johnson after the Civil War, and the case of President Clinton in the last decade of the twentieth century, and most recently that of President Trump, have not resulted in removal. The presidential impeachments, particularly the most recent one, illustrate precisely how complex the process is, and why the proceeding is reserved for the most egregious examples of misconduct.

Although there is no specific constitutional mandate that authorizes it, the Supreme Court has extended Congress's power of impeachment to other members of the executive branch. To the extent that the intention of the Framers of the Constitution is relevant, the inference is probably logical; English parliamentary practice recognized impeachment for a wide array of government officials. However, perhaps in response to the difficulty in gathering evidence against executive branch members for misfeasance, and the reluctance on the part of the Attorney General, the chief law-enforcement officer who herself is a cabinet-level executive branch appointee, Congress has created an investigatory mechanism, the so-called "independent counsel." The Attorney General examines initial allegations of wrongdoing by an official, but is required to appoint an independent counsel if, in the Attorney General's judgment, further inquiry is required. Independent counsel then investigates and presents its case to a special panel of federal judges. The independent counsel statute has been challenged, thus far unsuccessfully, on a variety of grounds, including that the process unconstitutionally limits presidential powers and creates an extra-constitutional mode of impeachment.

The Third Branch

No summary of American federalism would be complete without a consideration of judicial review. Most crucial issues raising federalism and separation of powers concerns are ultimately resolved in the federal courts. The delineation of powers between state and federal government, and whether a branch of the federal government has overstepped the bounds of its constitutional authority, are generally determined in the American legal system by federal judges.

Perhaps America's greatest contribution to western jurisprudence—judicial review of legislation—emerged early in the history of the republic in the famous case of *Marbury v. Madison,* 5 U.S. 137 (1803). The case arose when William Marbury sued James Madison, the incoming Secretary of State. Marbury sought a writ of *mandamus,* asking the Supreme Court to order Madison to deliver a commission, signed by outgoing President Adams, which appointed Marbury to the post of Justice of the Peace in the District of Columbia. Without Madison's official delivery of the Commission, Marbury would be unable to assume his post. Madison's refusal to undertake this purely administrative act can be better understood if one recalls that Adams was a Federalist, Madison a Democratic-Republican, and that the commission was one of a number signed in the waning hours of the Adams administration, which was giving way to Jefferson's incoming Democratic-Republican regime.

The landmark case is one of the Court's most noteworthy decisions, and probably would be considered even more so had it decided that judges could instruct cabinet members on the proper execution of their duties. But it did not. Still, in writing for the Court, Chief Justice Marshall exercised both judicial restraint and judicial activism, handing both victories and losses to his co-equal branches while subtly expanding the power of the judiciary. As to judicial restraint, Chief Justice Marshall opined that the Court was powerless to issue the *mandamus* writ (a victory for the executive branch and its new incumbent); the Court's activist bent came to the fore when it held that the congressional statute granting power to the Court to issue writs of *mandamus* was unconstitutional. Article III, the Court reasoned, vests the judicial power in the Supreme Court and assigns original jurisdiction to the Court in particular cases: those affecting ambassadors, other public ministers and consuls, and those in which a state is a party. Having delimited original jurisdiction, Congress had no power under the Constitution to extend it.

Thus, the Supreme Court disclaimed a minor statutory augmentation of the Court's jurisdiction in order to seize a far greater one: the power to set aside statutes enacted by Congress. The Court's logic produced what is perhaps its most famous line ever to be written in an American judicial opinion: "It is emphatically the province and duty of the judicial department to say what the law is." Under the Constitution, judges have the authority to interpret and enforce both statutes and the Constitution. In so doing, judges may find a conflict between a statute and Constitution. When conflict emerges, judges cannot apply such a statute under the Supremacy Clause; rather, "a law repugnant to the Constitution is void." Hence, the *Marbury* Court had no choice but to decline the jurisdiction which Congress was powerless to grant.

The power of judicial review of legislative, and by analogy executive acts, establishes a significant check by the courts on the power of the other two branches. Any judge, federal or state, can set aside an act of Congress, though the ultimate arbiters of constitutionality are the nine justices of the United States Supreme Court. The power to overturn statutes enacted by the legislature raises what Professor Alexander Bickel referred to as the "countermajoritarian difficulty": nine unelected federal officials have the final say as to the constitutionality of legislation enacted by those accountable to the People. ALEXANDER M. BICKEL, THE LEAST DANGEROUS BRANCH (2d ed. 1986). In cases involving a divided Court, where decisions are 5–4, a single Justice wields this countermajoritarian power. Moreover, the power of judicial review is even more significant given the terse language of many clauses of the Constitution. Consider, for example, the so-called "takings clause" of the Fifth Amendment to the Constitution: "nor shall private property be taken for a public use without just compensation." Suppose the local government decides to acquire my house to allow private developers to build a mixed-use urban renewal project. Is that a "public use"? If so, what is the "just compensation" that is required to be paid? Much ink has been spilt by the Supreme Court in determining the meaning of this clause, and indeed many others of the Constitution.

Because it often defines the extent of individual rights granted by the Constitution in the Bill of Rights (the first ten amendments to the Constitution adopted in 1791), Supreme Court jurisprudence is frequently controversial. Perhaps the most noteworthy contemporary example is the abortion issue which the Court has addressed a number of times since its landmark decision in *Roe v. Wade*.[5] Though the standard enunciated in *Roe* has since been narrowed by the Court to constrain states only from imposing an "undue burden" on a woman's access to abortion, a position most recently affirmed in *June Medical Services, LLC v. Russo*, the Supreme Court's construction must be regarded as inventive at the very least. 140 S. Ct. 2103 (2020); *see also Whole Women's Health v. Hellerstedt*, 136 S. Ct. 2292 (2016). Even the most zealous advocate of abortion must concede that the Constitution makes no express mention of the procedure. And finding a right to privacy in the words of the Ninth Amendment, or in the Due Process Clause of the Fourteenth Amendment, that accords an individual the right to decide whether to have a child is likewise a creative reading of the Constitution's text. Yet times change, and the Framers would have been an even more remarkable lot if they anticipated the issues that would exercise their descendants two hundred years hence.

Over time, the Supreme Court has had little choice but to rethink the meaning of the Constitution. Take, for example, racial segregation. At one time, in the late nineteenth century, the Court thought what today would be the unthinkable: that "separate but equal" accommodation for the races was permissible

---

[5]   410 U.S. 113 (1973).

under the Fourteenth Amendment. Later, in the middle of the twentieth century, the Court reversed course, striking down segregated schools in light of acknowledged inequities and the societal harm such separation occasioned.[6]

Conclusion

Non-Americans must be bewildered by America's reverence for this antiquated document setting out the structure of government for the venerable republic. A country of over 330 million people with a president elected by a roomful thereof; a federal government of enumerated powers established over two hundred years ago; all mediated by nine unelected justices of the Supreme Court. A very odd mix indeed. But a government of checks and balances and distinct and separate powers as central themes has survived, and may even have served the nation well. Political power, though articulated by words, is frequently defined by action. Over time, and in particular periods, one branch of the American government has frequently been able to curb the excesses of another. Even the Supreme Court is checked. Though widely regarded as the last word in constitutional interpretation, it is the people, through collective action and at the ballot box, who ultimately decide the meaning of the Constitution.

---

[6] The Court's opinion in *Brown v. Board of Education (Brown I)*, for example, illustrates the societal effect of the "separate but equal" principle enunciated in *Plessy v. Ferguson*, and specifically, that it relegated black Americans to second class citizenship and did not provide full opportunity to contribute to society. *Brown v. Bd. of Educ. (Brown I)*, 347 U.S. 483 (1954); *Plessy v. Ferguson*, 163 U.S. 537 (1896) *overruled by Brown I*.

Amendment of the Constitution, though difficult, is not impossible. U.S. CONST. art. 5.

CHAPTER 4

THE AMERICAN JUDICIARY: GUARDIANS OF THE CONSTITUTION

Introduction

This chapter addresses in more detail the guardians of the American Constitution, the judiciary. It focuses on the federal bench for two reasons. The first is that it is more likely that foreign lawyers will find themselves in federal court rather than in state courts. Second, the two systems, state and federal, broadly parallel each other; once understanding of the federal courts is achieved, it is a simple matter to learn the nuances that separate it from state court systems. That said, lawyers litigating cases in United States courts generally prefer to have the cases heard in federal court, in part because they perceive the level of judging to be far more informed and even-handed.

The Federal Bench in the Constitutional Scheme

Article III of the Constitution created the federal judiciary. Its terms suggest that the Framers intended federal judges to be independent actors. In the first place, Article III federal judges, appointed by the president and subject to confirmation by the Senate, are the only governmental officials who serve for life. The only way to remove an Article III judge is to impeach her for "Treason, Bribery, or other high Crimes and Misdemeanors." This renders Article III judges free to deliver unpopular decisions without the fear of retaliation through removal from office, a practice not unheard of in England in the seventeenth and eighteenth centuries, the colonial period. Second, in order to ensure that Article III judges were free from a lesser means of discipline, the Constitution also provided that the salary of federal judges could "not be diminished during their Continuance in Office." These two guarantees, security of tenure and remuneration, permit the federal judiciary to fulfill its role in the Constitution's system of checks and balances without outside influence and as a monitor of, and sometimes, as observed in *Marbury v. Madison*, as a brake upon, the lawmaking authority of the executive and the Congress. 5 U.S. 137 (1803).

While the judiciary provides a check on the powers of its two co-equal branches, the Constitution has balanced judicial powers by vesting a modicum of control over the bench by Congress and the president. Despite establishing a framework for the federal judiciary and its jurisdiction, the Constitution reserves for Congress considerable leeway in structuring the bench. Article III, Section 1 vests the "judicial Power of the United States . . . in such inferior Courts as the Congress may from time to time ordain and establish." Jurisdiction will be touched on in more detail below. Suffice it to say at this juncture that there are two primary bases of federal jurisdiction: first, cases that arise under the United States Constitution and federal law; and second, controversies "between Citizens of different States." Thus, Congress has created, and has ongoing power to create, additional federal courts. Also, the

Senate must confirm the president's nomination of Article III federal judges after a thorough investigation of their background and a personal appearance before its Judiciary Committee. Finally, Congress sets the budget for the federal court system.

There is also a balance between the federal courts and the president. As noted, the president nominates Article III judges. Since the Constitution gives the federal courts jurisdiction over cases involving federal law, and the executive is charged with law enforcement, both civil and criminal, the Attorney General (the federal government's primary law enforcer) is a frequent litigator in federal court. Moreover, Congress is empowered to create "inferior courts"; these tribunals, courts of specialized jurisdictions including tax, labor law, and social security benefits, are part of the executive branch.

The Federal Court System

There are three levels of Article III courts: District Courts; Courts of Appeal; and the Supreme Court. Unlike some national legal systems, there are no separate courts to entertain the constitutionality of federal law. Each court hears both criminal prosecutions and civil disputes.

Federal district courts are trial courts. They have original jurisdiction to hear most federal cases, that is, those that the Constitution awards federal jurisdiction, and those in which Congress has not allocated to one or another of the specialized courts mentioned above. 28 U.S.C. § 1331. There are 94 judicial districts: some federal districts are coterminous with state boundaries; other states have more than a single district. There are federal district courts in the District of Columbia and in Puerto Rico, as well as in overseas territories, for example, Guam. Trials are conducted by a single judge who makes rulings on issues of law. Trial may be by jury in most criminal cases, in civil cases in which jury trial obtained in England at the time of independence, and for cases in which Congress has provided trial by jury. Interested parties may waive trial by jury, thereby empowering the judge to be the finder of fact, as well as of law.

In every federal case in which final judgment is issued there is a right to appeal to one of the 12 regional courts of appeal. 28 U.S.C. § 1291. The 94 district courts are organized into circuits, and the appropriate appeals court hears cases from its circuit, including in some instances appeals from administrative courts. Congress has created a separate Court of Appeals for the Federal Circuit which entertains intellectual property cases, as well as appeals from the Court of International Trade (trade and customs issues) and the Court of Federal Claims (jurisdiction over federal contracts and claims against the federal government). *Id.* § 1295.

Although appeal to the presiding court of appeals is of right, it must be filed in a timely fashion. The court of appeals reviews the record of the district court (or other trial court). The court sits in panels of three judges, unless the case is deemed of unusual significance, or to rehear cases that have already been decided by the three-judge panel, in which case the appellate court would be sitting *en banc*. Unless it is convinced that the trial court's finding of fact is clearly erroneous, the appeals court accepts the factual record and considers only whether the trial court properly applied the law thereto. If the court requires additional fact-finding, it may remand the case to the trial court. Appellate courts affirm or reverse judgments in written opinions.

The United States Supreme Court sits at the apex of the federal judicial pyramid. It consists of a Chief Justice (*of the United States* and not merely of the Supreme Court because the Chief Justice heads the entire federal bench) and eight Associate Justices. The Court always sits *en banc*. Having limited original jurisdiction (cases between states, for example), the Court reviews cases upon the granting of a writ of *certiorari* petitioned for by a party to a federal case, that is to say, when at least four members of the court decide that the case merits review. The Court docket usually consists of a limited number of cases (about 100 or so per year) in which there is a split in the circuits, different interpretations amongst the courts of appeal on an issue of federal law, or where the parties raise important constitutional issues. The Supreme Court usually sets oral argument for these cases, and the parties and other interested *amicus curiae* (friends of the court) submit written briefs.

A Primer on Federal Jurisdiction

The limits of federal jurisdiction, alluded to above, is a complex area of law. Unlike state court jurisdiction, federal jurisdiction is limited, and both the defendant and the court may challenge the plaintiff's allegation of federal jurisdiction. Simply put, federal courts have subject matter jurisdiction over claims based upon federal law (both statutory and constitutional), and also over controversies between the states and the United States and foreign sovereigns. Important areas of federal jurisdiction include federal crimes, bankruptcy, cases involving the regulation of interstate and foreign commerce, securities regulation, mergers and acquisitions of publicly traded companies, admiralty cases, intellectual property cases, offenses committed on federal property, and, of course, cases challenging the constitutionality of federal law. If the federal judge concludes that federal jurisdiction is lacking, the case will either be dismissed with or without prejudice allowing plaintiff to refile in state court, or directly remanded to state court.

Another important area of federal jurisdiction is when there is so-called "diversity of citizenship" between the plaintiff and the defendant (28 U.S.C. § 1332). The Framers provided for federal jurisdiction in these cases probably because they believed that state courts would favor the claims of their own citizens over those of non-citizens. In fact, many cases come to federal courts when out-of-state defendants are party to a case filed in the plaintiff's state court, and thus petition for "removal" to the appropriate district court on grounds that there is federal jurisdiction.

In practice, then, there is concurrent jurisdiction in many cases between the federal and state court systems: many cases that could be heard in federal court may be heard in state court. Federal juries are drawn from within the entire district, which tends to be larger than state court districts; thus, counsel for a plaintiff with a claim that could go to federal court might decide to file it in state court if counsel believes that a local jury might more sympathetically determine liability and damages. Another reason why a plaintiff might prefer to litigate in state court is that judges may be elected rather than appointed, and therefore arguably favor local interests (and parties to litigation). But taking account of these possible biases, it is possible that an out-of-state defendant may be content to proceed in state court, and not remove a case to federal court. Moreover, a plaintiff raising a constitutional claim need not file in federal court, but may instead proceed in state court.

At this juncture, it may be helpful to list, albeit incompletely, matters that are heard in state courts, absent diversity of citizenship. Most crimes are defined by state law and are prosecuted in state court. Likewise, family law issues (including marriage, divorce, property settlements, and child custody), cases involving rights in land (including landlord-tenant disputes), probate and inheritance matters, private contracts, personal injury claims, and corporate governance issues are also typically subject to state court jurisdiction. When one observes the mix, it is apparent that state courts hear many more cases than do federal courts.

Conclusion

The next chapter outlines the structure of the federal court trial. However, before moving on, first a word on personnel. Unlike the judiciary in some other countries, judges do not follow a particular, structured career path peppered with state-mandated examinations. Rather Article III federal judges are recruited from the practicing bar and from legal academia. With very few exceptions, the federal bench is populated by lawyers of outstanding ability, judgment, and ethical standards.

Because judges are appointed by the president, politics also matters; there is a considerable political cast to judicial appointments. As a general rule, the president consults senators and representatives from his own party, and within the state in which the appointment is to be made, for nomination recommendations. After nomination, the judicial candidate submits details of his or her professional and civic life in writing. Thereafter, the nominee appears at a hearing before the Senate Judiciary Committee, and the Committee votes on whether to bring the candidate to the floor of the Senate for a vote. Sixty votes or three-fifths majority of the Senate was required in order to bring the candidate to the floor for his or her second round of voting (Senate confirmation). However, in 2017 the Senate reduced this requirement to fifty-one votes, supposedly to mitigate opportunity for filibuster. It is also possible that the Judiciary Committee may decline to bring the candidate forward for confirmation.

Recent history suggests that process of appointment of judges is becoming more controversial, because presidents now seek to appoint individuals who share a variety of beliefs about the role of the judiciary in the American constitutional system and positions on particular emotive issues that are before the federal courts. The higher the judge is on the judicial ladder, the greater the stakes. The Supreme Court is, of course, the ultimate flash point because of its position as the final arbiter of the meaning of the Constitution. There is talk about so-called "litmus tests": the president will only put forward judges who will, for example, vote to overturn *Roe v. Wade*; and senators of the opposite side of the political spectrum will only vote to confirm those who would reaffirm the since-narrowed judgment. 410 U.S. 113 (1973). But the late Chief Justice Rehnquist, a formidable historian in his own right, has reminded us in his writings on the history of the United States Supreme Court that we have been here before. Controversy is decidedly not a recent feature of the judicial system of the United States.

CHAPTER 5

THE AMERICAN CIVIL TRIAL: RITUALIZED COMBAT

Introduction

This chapter will sketch the procedure of a trial in federal court. Once again, the federal rather than state courts will be highlighted for two reasons. In the first place, foreign entities (and their lawyers) are more likely to find themselves in federal courts rather than in state courts, because their causes of action generally either arise under federal law, or diversity of citizenship obtains, and the requisite jurisdictional limitations are satisfied. And second, while nuances between state and federal court practice (and amongst courts in the various states) differ, their patterns are strikingly similar. A basic understanding of the federal trial stands a foreign lawyer in good stead to translate knowledge assimilated from federal into state court practice.

A page of history once again is useful, this time in comprehending the fundamental goals and the structure of modern civil procedure in American courts. The Federal Rules of Civil Procedure were adopted in 1938 in response to existing civil practice, modeled on the English pattern, a system that was exceedingly complex. So-called "common law" procedure was governed by the writ system, which mandated particular "forms of action" for different claims, and directed varying modes of pleading, process, and proof depending on the writ selected. Even in its more basic form transmitted to the colonies, and thereafter Americanized, common law pleading and procedure was an arcane art form that set numerous traps for the uninitiated and the unwary. Cases might be won (or lost), not on the merits, but on the skill (or lack thereof) of lawyers well-versed in the esoteric art of pleading.

An Overview of the Federal Rules

While common law pleading gave way to more simplified "code pleading" in most jurisdictions, the Federal Rules are decidedly less complicated than both of these predecessors. The modern system based on the Federal Rules of Civil Procedure seeks to simplify, if not level, the procedural playing field. While no civil procedure system is without complexity, at least to the uninitiated, formality is minimized. In the first place, writs are abolished, so that the procedure, process and mode of proof are uniform, and do not vary depending on the basis of the dispute. Moreover, the pleadings are straightforward. Plaintiff in the complaint and defendant in the answer merely tell their respective stories: plaintiff briefly sets out the basis of the cause of action in a short and plain statement;[1] defendant typically exercises various tools to respond to plaintiff's complaint, often by filing an answer which affirms, denies, or indicates lack of sufficient information to properly respond to an allegation;[2] alternatively, defendant may set out an affirmative

---

[1] FED. R. CIV. P. 8(a).
[2] FED. R. CIV. P. 8(b).

defense that absolves her of liability[3]. In later stages of the process, the facts alleged will be substantiated by evidence, and supporting law will be argued, with finders of fact and law determining the outcome. But the process by which this occurs is not driven by the legal nature of the plaintiff's claim, as it was first conceptualized centuries ago.

Simplification has two virtues. The first is that a perfunctory complaint and answer achieves the primary purpose of the initial phase of process, notice to the defendant of the essential issues of the lawsuit, and plaintiff is apprised of defenses. The system of pleading, therefore, allows the defense at a very early stage in the suit an understanding of the gravamen of the claim against her. That opposing counsel ascertains the basis of the cause of action is obvious, particularly in America's adversarial system. For lawyers on either side to represent zealously the interest of clients, defendant's counsel in particular needs to know the essence of the plaintiff's claim. Having the information to hand, counsel can begin the process of determining whether there is a tenable defense or whether capitulation is advisable. Likewise, if defendant has information that absolves her of liability, conveying it to plaintiff's counsel early on might lead her to advise her client not to pursue the lawsuit further. Given the expense of litigation, encouraging each side to place their cards on the table rather than allowing parties to shield them from preview permits the second objective of the system to function: the efficient administration of

---

[3]   FED. R. CIV. P. 8(c).

justice between the two parties. If the trial is a search for truth, it can more easily achieve that outcome where the procedural system is denuded of the formality that sets traps for the unwary that are unrelated to the merits of the claim.

That said, ours is a legal universe that is imperfect. As the procedural system is described in the chapter, no argument will be made that federal trial practice has fully accomplished all these objectives in the most efficient fashion. The adversarial system in which the judge plays the role of an impartial observer and moderator, rather than an active participant, does place a premium upon the skill of advocates. But the system adopted must also be judged by what it replaced: Anglo-American common law pleading and process. Measured by that benchmark, few would argue that the adoption of the Federal Rules of Civil Procedure was not an advance over the pre-existing system.

Stages of the Trial: Pleading

The system instituted to further these twin goals is comprised of four stages: pleading; pre-trial; trial; and a post-trial phase. In the pleading phase, the parties begin the process of exchanging information relevant to their respective cases. Plaintiff begins the process by filing a complaint in the office of the "Clerk of the Court" in the district court with jurisdiction. Although a modest fee is due, it can be waived if plaintiff can demonstrate need. The complaint need not be detailed. Rather, the complaint typically need only establish the grounds for federal jurisdiction, followed by a "short and plain statement" of the facts which give rise to a legal claim.[4] The complaint must also state the relief sought—monetary damages or equitable relief (*e.g.* an injunction; that is to say, an order that the defendant halt a particular conduct, or perform a particular act).[5] In recent decisions, the Supreme Court has established two principles which govern the factual standard required of a complaint. First, the facts alleged must not make the claim merely conceivable, but plausible, such that the complaint on its face allows the court to draw a reasonable inference that the alleged misconduct occurred. *Bell Atl. Corp. v. Twombly*, 550 U.S. 544 (2007). Second, facts which are no more than "threadbare recitals of law," or legal conclusions, do not suffice to state a claim. *Ashcroft v. Iqbal*, 556 U.S. 662 (2009). Take, for example, the following statement: "My employer discriminated against me based on my sex"; under *Iqbal*, this statement is a conclusory recitation of law and lacks sufficient factual detail to be regarded as actionable by the reviewing court.

Plaintiff must then serve the defendant with a copy of the complaint. Included with that notice is a summons which requires the defendant to respond to the complaint by a particular date, usually 21 days unless the defendant has waived service, in which case a United States-based defendant then has 60 days to answer. In federal litigation, waiver is the preferred form of service because it provides a

---

[4] FED. R. CIV. P. 8(a).

[5] *Id.*

defendant with more time to respond. If a defendant fails to respond within the allotted time, a default judgment will be entered against her. Moreover, "serve" or "service" is a legal term of art. In most circumstances, service is personal, that is to say, the complaint and summons is actually placed in defendant's hand. Because defendant may not be always available or may be a corporate entity, there are exceptions permitting alternatives to personal service, such as certified mail, and rules mandating proper service to legal persons.

Upon receipt of the complaint, the defendant has two choices: to file an answer, or to file a 12(b) motion to dismiss[6]. Taking the last first, a defendant may move to dismiss by, for example, challenging the federal court's jurisdiction over plaintiff's claim. Specifically, the defendant may deny "federal question" jurisdiction, arguing that the plaintiff's claim does not "arise under" the United States Constitution, federal law or a treaty to which the United States is a party. *See Louisville & Nashville R.R. v. Mottley*, 211 U.S. 149 (1908). The defendant may also, or alternatively, challenge the diversity of citizenship between herself and the plaintiff (or that the amount in controversy does not reach the statutory threshold). The defendant may also move to dismiss on the merits, asserting that the plaintiff has not stated a claim upon which relief may be granted. In short, defendant maintains that the facts alleged, if taken as true, do not give rise to a valid legal claim against her. If a defendant's motion is

---

[6] FED. R. CIV. P. 12(b).

granted, then the lawsuit is dismissed. However, if the flaw is a mere technicality, for example, that plaintiff omitted a crucial fact in the complaint, leave to amend the complaint is generally granted. The foregoing examples are just two of defendant's seven primary bases upon which she can move for dismissal at the outset of the pleadings;[7] critically, four of these motions, however, if not raised prior to or in conjunction with the defendant's answer, are lost to her indefinitely and cannot be raised at a later point in the litigation[8].

Rather than challenging jurisdiction through a motion to dismiss the defendant will more commonly file an answer. In the answer, defendant either admits or denies each point in the alleged complaint, or indicates that defendant has insufficient knowledge to respond to the particular details alleged. For example, suppose Buyer under a sales contract sues Seller, alleging that Seller failed to deliver goods in conformity with the descriptions in the contract. Seller would, assuming she believes that she has substantially performed, respond that the goods were indeed in conformity with the contract.

At this point in the proceedings (the answer), defendant-Seller must allege any affirmative defenses she will raise to plaintiff-Buyer's claim or be barred from later asserting them. Suppose, Buyer has delayed filing the lawsuit, and the governing

---

7   FED. R. CIV. P. 12(b).

8   *Id.* 12(b)(2)–(5).

statute of limitations on contract actions has run; the defendant-Seller must raise this statute as an affirmative defense. Defendant may, but is not bound to, allege other defenses; for example, the Uniform Commercial Code recognizes the concept of substantial compliance. Our defendant-Seller might argue that while the goods do not exactly conform to the contract's description, they are sufficiently similar in nature and quality. Substantial compliance would be an affirmative defense to Buyer's claim.

Defendant may also file a counterclaim at this point in the proceedings. A counterclaim arising out of the same transaction is a compulsory one, and must be raised at this time or it will be deemed waived. Suppose our Buyer "covered" Seller's purported shortcoming in performance by purchasing substitute goods from another seller at a higher price. Buyer might seek damages in the amount of the difference between the cost of the goods under the contract and the cost of the substitute goods she purchased from another supplier. In addition to alleging nonconformity, Buyer must counterclaim for the loss suffered by her or she will be deemed to have waived her right to do so in a subsequent lawsuit. The logic that supports the notion that a counterclaim is compulsory is that of efficiency: to allow the court to deal with all claims arising out of the same controversy in a single lawsuit. Additionally, defendant-Seller may, though she need not, counterclaim if she has other claims against plaintiff-Buyer unrelated to the Buyer's claim. Suppose, for example, Buyer has not paid Seller the agreed price on another, separate sales contract; Seller might, but she is not required to, counterclaim for the amount due on that separate contract if it exceeds the jurisdictional requirement. A counterclaim differs from an affirmative defense in that it does not provide the basis for denying plaintiff's claim; rather, it raises separate legal grounds for relief against the plaintiff.

Because the defendant has had an opportunity to dismiss the case on the grounds that there is no legal basis for plaintiff's claim, only, at least arguably, cases in which facts and law give rise to a legal claim will go forward. At this point, the close of the first phase of federal civil litigation, both sides have a sketch of the other side's case. With that knowledge, each side can assess the risk of going forward. If plaintiff's case is weak, she may withdraw it because the potential return (a verdict in her favor with significant monetary damages) is less than the cost of litigation. Recall that in the American system, each side typically bears its own attorney's fees. Likewise, if defendant has a weak case, she may decide to settle in order to avoid increasing costs necessary to litigate plaintiff's claim. Both sides may, of course, agree on a settlement figure.

Pre-Trial Discovery

Having passed through the first stage without settlement, each party begins the peculiar American pre-trial information swap known as discovery. At one time, each side to a civil dispute was required to ferret out evidence necessary to support its case. In many cases, gathering the required facts to support or refute a claim is straightforward. For example, there is no reason why our Buyer cannot interview a third-party to whom she intended to sell the goods under the primary contract to ascertain whether the goods conform to the contract. But consider a products liability case in which plaintiff claims that a design defect led to her injury. Defendant has almost all knowledge of the creation and manufacture of the product under its control. Allowing access to that information levels the playing field between the injured party and manufacturer.

Discovery is therefore essential for both parties to gain access to evidence that might support their respective claim or defense; obtaining evidence includes ascertaining non-privileged information likely to lead to the finding of admissible evidence, even if that initial information itself is not particularly supportive. Of course, producing requested information may be burdensome and costly, perhaps inclining plaintiffs to use discovery as a bludgeon to prompt settlement. Likewise, because trials are public, defendant may be reluctant to reveal a trade secret or provide data that might injure its reputation. Accordingly, discovery requests and conferrals must be proportional to the needs of the case. Discovery disputes (which are virtually inevitable) may force the reviewing court to engage in a balancing test: whether the burden of obtaining the requested information outweighs its likely benefit. Moreover, upon request, judges may look carefully at relevance issues before permitting discovery, and may order the party receiving information to keep the discovered material confidential.

Discovery can be thought of as proceeding in three phases: in phase one, the parties confer and request relevant, general information; in phase two, the parties seek to compel and protect evidence; and the third phase covers potential sanctions which may be ordered by the presiding court. The first phase of discovery is perhaps determinative as to whether the next two phases must follow; if phase one's conferrals and requests progress smoothly, then the need for each subsequent phase is likely unnecessary—but this is rarely the case.

Before proceeding with the details of each discovery phase, it should be noted that a lawyer has an obligation to preserve documents and evidence when litigation is reasonably anticipated or has commenced. This obligation is ongoing; failure to preserve, and destruction of, documents or evidence may result in sanctions against the offending lawyer (see phase three, below). Steps that a lawyer can take to comply with her preservation obligation include issuing a "litigation hold" at the outset of the litigation; or, when litigation is reasonably anticipated, identifying key individuals likely to have relevant, and thereby discoverable, information and communicating to them their duty to preserve; and, because merely notifying others of the preservation duty is insufficient to satisfy it, the lawyer must monitor compliance by such key parties with her established preservation practices. *See Zubulake v. UBS Warburg, LLC*, 229 F.R.D. 422 (S.D.N.Y. 2004).

Phase one of discovery begins with initial disclosures, that is, the conferral of certain information by each party to the opposing side without awaiting a discovery request.[9] These initial disclosures include the names and contact information of individuals who may have "discoverable information": copies or descriptions of documents or tangible items which the disclosing party may use to support her claim or defense, and evidence supporting the estimated damages or relief sought (*e.g.* a plaintiff who seeks $100,000 in damages for medical bills incurred as a result of defendant's alleged misconduct must produce those medical bills in her initial disclosures).[10] A party can also be required to produce documents relating to the lawsuit. If, for example, in our contract case the Seller's manufacturer had informed the Seller by letter that the materials used to produce Seller's goods would be of lesser quality than Seller had a right to anticipate, then Buyer would be able to obtain useful evidence that perhaps the goods may be nonconforming.

Pending opioid litigation provides a far better example. Suppose information possessed by opioid manufacturers suggest that the risks associated with long-term opioid use have been grossly misrepresented. Such information, and the corresponding action (or lack thereof) taken by corporate executives, could provide evidence of the manufacturer's knowledge that consequences such as

---

[9] FED. R. CIV. P. 26(a)(1)(A).

[10] *Id.*

the current opioid epidemic were substantially certain to result. Both would be useful evidence in liability cases. *See, e.g., In re National Prescription Opiate Litigation,* 927 F.3d 919 (6th Cir. 2019).

Initial disclosures are typically followed by oral depositions[11] and interrogatories (a strategically written set of no more than twenty-five non-compound questions requiring twenty-five written answers in response thereto and under oath).[12] Suppose our Buyer knows that Seller had recently switched her products manufacturer. Plaintiff-Buyer might, in an interrogatory, ask Seller to list all product manufacturers hired within the last ten years, and separately, to list the materials used by each, respectively, to produce the goods in controversy. In more complicated cases against corporate entities, interrogatories are useful in trying to determine who in the entity's structure might have direct access to information necessary to prove a case against it. Should those interrogatories be fruitful, the testimony of that witness or individual in possession of pertinent information would be relevant, and the counsel opposing the corporate entity may depose her in advance. Both sides are present at depositions, and the proceedings are transcribed or recorded. The primary advantage of a deposition is that counsel may follow-up on responses made at the deposition, and therefore be better prepared at trial should the deponent be called as a witness. Under certain circumstances, the

---

[11] R. 30(a).

[12] R. 33.

depositions themselves may be entered into evidence at trial if, for example, the deponent is dead or otherwise unavailable to testify. Moreover, counsel might impeach a witness's testimony at trial by showing that statements made in court diverged from those made in the deposition.

Because each party is generally limited to conducting only ten depositions,[13] the discovery tool may be better reserved for individuals who are likely to provide firsthand, compelling evidence; interrogatories, on the other hand, have their strength in leading a party to such deponents, or in supplementing background information. Phase one of discovery may also involve requests for a physical and mental examination of the opposing party so long as that party's condition is central to the controversy.[14]

Phase two of discovery is likely to begin when either or both parties refuse to produce evidence requested in phase one. In such a situation, the refusing party may seek a protective order, or may assert privilege (applicable to communications between privileged persons, such as attorney-client or doctor-patient, made in confidence for the purpose of obtaining or providing advice). A court may grant a protective order to protect a party or non-party from, for example, annoyance, embarrassment, oppression, or undue burden.[15] Alternatively, a court

---

[13] FED. R. CIV. P. 30(a).

[14] FED. R. CIV. P. 35.

[15] R. 26(c).

may compel a party to produce evidence in cases in which that party makes no good faith attempt to satisfy the discovery request, or unjustly objects to any such request.[16] Take a 2014 case involving an Oklahoma jail. *Price v. Leflore Cnty. Det. Ctr.*, No. 13-CV-402, 2014 WL 3672874, at *1 (E.D. Okla. July 23, 2014). The court compelled the jail to produce relevant medical records, as requested by plaintiff, despite the jail's insistence that such retrieval would be an undue burden. The court reasoned that any burden was the result of the jail's faulty retention system and was outweighed by the benefits of production.

The third phase of discovery may arise if, for example, a court sanctions a lawyer for her failure to comply with preservation duties or a court order, or for her refusal to participate in developing a discovery plan.[17] A lawyer may also be sanctioned for frustrating a fair examination of a deponent.[18] A 2014 Iowa case serves as an example. *Sec. Nat'l Bank of Sioux City, Iowa v. Abbott Lab'y*, 299 F.R.D. 595 (N.D. Iowa 2014) *rev'd*, 800 F.3d 936 (8th Cir. 2015). There, an attorney was sanctioned for lodging hundreds of meritless objections during a deposition conducted by opposing counsel. Discovery sanctions are rare, but courts have gone so far as entering default judgment against the offending party if his lawyer's offenses were pervasive. *See Medina v.*

---

[16] R. 37(a).

[17] R. 37.

[18] R. 30.

Gonzalez, No. 08 Civ. 01520, 2010 WL 3744344, at *1 (S.D.N.Y. Sept. 23, 2010).

This summary does not do justice to the extent or complexity of the discovery process. Though burdensome in terms of time and expense, it is efficient in that it allows the parties to the lawsuit to uncover facts that will either support or undermine their case, leading once again to more knowledgeable litigation risk assessment, and possible settlement.

Pre-Trial Motions

Having bolstered its case through discovery, a party may wish to move for summary judgment. Either side may so make the motion, but in practice it is usually the defendant. Unlike in a motion to dismiss, the party moving for summary judgment is permitted to substantiate her factual assertions with evidence. The moving party does not need to produce affirmative evidence but need only establish a basis for granting the summary judgment motion. *See, e.g., Celotex Corp. v. Catrett*, 477 U.S. 317 (1986). To that end, if the non-moving party argues that a material fact is indeed in dispute and thus summary judgment cannot be granted, and if that material fact is one which the non-moving party must prove at trial, then the non-moving party bears the burden of producing affirmative evidence to establish that material fact at summary judgment. Summary judgment will be granted only if there is no genuine dispute as to any material fact, and, on account of the relevant law, those facts lead inexorably to a judgment for the moving party. Federal practice permits partial summary judgment, thereby narrowing the disputed issues by allowing some issues to be removed from consideration in the ensuing trial.

Pre-Trial Conference

Summary judgment having been denied (or partially granted), the trial phase begins. At a pre-trial conference, the trial judge will review the issues of law and fact that separate the parties, hear further motions (particularly those involving the admissibility of evidence) and make a final attempt at settlement. At this point in the litigation, both sides will receive some inclination of the strength of their respective cases by an impartial party, the judge. The reaction of the judge to the evidence exhumed, a jurist experienced in having cases tried before her, may be gauged and may provide some indication of each parties' likelihood of success at trial. The primary judicial chore, reviewing carefully the evidence to be submitted, is rendered critical, largely because of another peculiar American juridical institution: the jury trial in civil cases. It should be noted, however, that most cases that are commenced (filed) are settled at this stage or prior thereto, and do not proceed to trial.

The Right to a Trial by Jury

In federal court, either party may opt for a trial by jury. The Seventh Amendment to the United States Constitution "preserve[s]" this right "In Suits at common law," that is to say, in cases in which jury trial so obtained at the time the Constitution was adopted. The Supreme Court has extended the right to jury trial in federal court by applying it to causes of action arising out of more recently enacted statutory law, if these causes are similar in nature to those that juries would have heard in 1789. Thus, most contract and commercial law cases can be tried by jury, as well as many tort claims.

Of course, American juries must be unbiased. There is a process of selection to ensure impartiality. Pools of potential jurors are recruited by random selection from voter lists of those registered in the individual federal district, an area which may be very large (either geographically or in population). Panels of between six and twelve men and women are selected by lot from the pools of those summoned to serve for "jury duty." During *voir dire*, a process through which lawyers from each side examine potential jurors, counsel for both parties may seek to eliminate jurors from the panel either for cause or by exercising up to three peremptory challenges. As to the former, for-cause elimination, a juror may be excluded from service at a particular trial to ensure against bias, for example, if the juror is related to a party or has already formed some opinion as to the appropriate outcome of the case. Peremptory challenges are likewise permitted to remove jurors whom counsel (or the now ubiquitous and notorious jury consultant) believes may be more likely to be favorable to the opposition. This belief may be based on a myriad of the respective client's social, economic, and demographic factors (as well as counsel's hunches). As noted, each party is limited to exercising a maximum of three peremptory challenges. Of course, jurors may not be excluded on the basis of race or gender.

The American civil jury is the finder of fact. Because the jury should be both unbiased and unknowledgeable about the essence of the cause of action, it must receive its information about the claim through evidence submitted to it by the parties in court. In order to ensure that what is received by the jury is reliable and unbiased, the law of evidence, now largely codified in the Federal Rules of Evidence, (and various state codes) was adopted to offer such protection. The rules, however, need to be applied/ interpreted by judges, and "common law" evidentiary principles still obtain. At trial, each side offers testimony favorable to its legal position, and the jury's pivotal role is ultimately to determine which version of a factually diverse scenario to believe. Again, return to our sales contract. Suppose Seller argues at trial that the goods conform to the contract, and produces a sample which she says she showed to Buyer during their contract negotiations. Buyer contends that the sample produced at trial was not similar to the one she was given prior to the contract formation; Buyer summons two witnesses who testify that they were present during Buyer and Seller's negotiations and that the sample produced at trial is unlike the one provided to Buyer during negotiations. Assume, however, that Seller also has witnesses who testify to conformity. Having heard radically different versions of the transaction, the jury must weigh the credibility of each set of witnesses; perhaps the jury will consider whether any witness stretched the truth out of bias to a side. The issue will be

suggested by counsel in summation, the closing
phase of the trial which occurs after testimony is
concluded. Lawyers present to the jury a closing
argument and may suggest to the jury their version
of the proper conclusions which should be drawn from
the evidence presented. But it is, however, within the
jury's prerogative to render judgment based upon its
own sense of witness credibility.

A crucial fact that the jury must also determine is
the proper amount of damages. Although not entirely
a straightforward determination, actual monetary
loss is generally relatively easy to quantify. Suppose
the cost of cover in our sales contract mooted above
was $100,000. What if the Buyer lost sales, and
assume, therefore, lost $475,000 in profit, because
the goods meant to cover arrived a month after the
initial contract's delivery date? Are lost profits
appropriate consequential damages? And suppose
that our Seller acted beyond the bounds of reasonable
dealing in an unrelated transaction and sold goods to
another buyer knowing that she would not be able to
perform her obligation to Buyer, and therefore
intentionally harm Buyer's commercial reputation
(note that this is not the case in most business
transactions)? Although punitive damages are
unlikely in our hypothetical here, they can be
assessed and awarded by juries in oft-times
staggering amounts when the defendant's conduct is
outrageous, and punishment thereof is deemed
necessary to set an example. Consider the punitive
damages levied by a jury in a recent New York court
case. The appellate court reinstated punitive
damages awarded by a jury against two police

officers, after the trial judge vacated such an award, because the jury could have inferred from the evidence presented at trial that the officers used excessive force against the arrestee. *Cardoza v. City of N.Y.*, 29 N.Y.S.3d 330 (N.Y. App. Div. 2016). The Supreme Court has determined the extent to which such damages are justified as a matter of due process under the United States Constitution.

The Trial

Pre-trial motions and maneuvers completed, the trial itself transpires in unremarkable fashion. Both sides are afforded an opportunity to present their cases in summary form in opening argument. Plaintiff then presents its case by calling its supporting witnesses and introducing the documentary evidence it regards as relevant. Plaintiff's witnesses are examined and then cross-examined by defense counsel. When the plaintiff rests her case, the defense follows on in similar fashion. Judges may also question witnesses, but they do so infrequently in jury trials. As might be expected some judges are more loquacious than are others. Both sides then have the opportunity for summation; counsel for each side summarizes the case presented, attempting to cast their legal theory as the more plausible explanation when admissible evidence is properly considered. The judge then instructs the jury on the applicable law. In our case, the judge would present governing state contract law. The jury would then withdraw and deliberate in private until it reaches a verdict, which in federal court must be unanimous. The jury verdict is most often general: "We find that the defendant Seller was liable and award compensatory damages in the amount of $100,000." In more complex cases, "special verdicts" are rendered; the jury is asked to consider a particular question, "did the manufacturer undertake tests that demonstrated that their product was dangerous to the health of human beings and conceal the results from the public?" The response to a special verdict will ensure that the jury's return was based upon law rather than on perceived notions of a proper outcome. In our contract case, or in the reams of opioid litigation presently in American courts, a jury's conception of justice might direct its verdict (sellers cheat, Big Pharma has deep pockets) rather than its expected function of determining a proper verdict based upon application of law to fact.

The jury's role in the outcome of a civil trial in federal court is not uncontrolled. The trial judge has certain mechanisms to counter a "runaway jury." In the first place, the defendant may, at the conclusion of the plaintiff's case, move to dismiss the litigation on the ground that plaintiff has not presented evidence sufficient so that a reasonable jury could find for the plaintiff. If the judge agrees that plaintiff has not put forward the necessary elements of her cause of action such that there is no case to answer, then the trial is over. On the other hand, if the judge is uncertain, then she may deny the motion until she hears the defendant's case or, if moved for after both parties have presented their case, she may send the jury to deliberate on an outcome. The judge may overrule the jury verdict if she finds that the jury had insufficient evidence to sustain it. Alternatively, the judge might order a new trial, if she believes that the verdict is contrary to the preponderance of the evidence. This judicial prerogative can also be used effectively in cases in which the jury quite reasonably finds for the plaintiff, but awards excessive damages. A judge may order a new trial exclusively on the issue of damages unless the prevailing party agrees to accept a diminished award.

A Mock Jury Trial

Still the role of the jury cannot be discounted as the force that drives litigation. Permit an illustrative digression. A number of years ago, Tulane Law School sponsored a seminar in "Comparative Trial Practice." Two American lawyers argued a hypothetical case in front of a federal district court judge; and two English barristers then argued the same case before an English High Court judge. The facts were straightforward: a middle-aged judge, let's call him Max, was found dead of a shotgun wound to the head; he may have been cleaning the rifle, and it accidentally fired (as the plaintiff claimed), or he might have committed suicide as the defendant insurance company maintained. At stake was $1,000,000. The deceased judge had a life insurance policy in that amount that named his widow, the plaintiff, as beneficiary. But there was an exclusion clause that denied payment in cases of suicide. The American plaintiff's lawyer unsurprisingly chose trial by jury, before whom he paraded the grieving widow, suitably dressed in black, and a number of witnesses including a minister who claimed that the deceased judge had much to live for. Plaintiff discounted the importance of the decedent's crushing personal debt, and the possibility that he had embezzled court fees (and that this peccadillo was soon to be discovered). The defense kept harping on the angle of the wound; one that was not likely, it argued, to have occurred other than by design. Now to the outcome: the American jury found for the plaintiff, bestowing upon her the payout provided in the policy. Contrarily, the High Court judge, perhaps hard-heartedly, denied payment on the grounds that the only plausible conclusion was that Judge Max's wound was self-inflicted. A similar case, one argued to a jury and the other to a judge, yielded a different, but explicable result due to, perhaps, the jury's sympathy rather than its "logic." But one might as easily argue the contrary, that the judge represented the ruling class and had a greater interest in preserving the insurance company's liquidity than in serving the cause of justice.

A Primer on Rules of Evidence

As mentioned above, because the jury is so powerful a determiner of the outcome of a trial, it is essential to vet the evidence that comes before it. The ultimate decision on admissibility of evidence is made by the trial judge, but the objection to evidence as it is presented is usually first made by opposing counsel. Indeed, a trial can seem to the uninitiated as continuing combat between lawyers, each objecting to the admissibility of this or that document or a question posed to a witness. Over the years, a complex law of evidence has emerged, and a brief outline of some of its more salient tenets is useful to understand precisely how it limits the flow of information to the jury that the law deems inadvisable to place at its disposal.

Witnesses may testify only to matters of which they have first-hand knowledge. So, returning to our insurance claim hypothetical, if the now-deceased Judge Max told a witness, let's call her Ms. Lisa, that he was "worth more dead than alive," Ms. Lisa could so testify. But if Judge Max had reflected upon his plight with another witness, let's call her Ms. Wall, who in turn retold this history to Ms. Lisa, then Ms. Lisa could not testify to the substance of the original conversation between Judge Max and Ms. Wall: it is hearsay. Although there are exceptions to the hearsay rule, 29 of them in the Federal Rules of Evidence (which can easily be related in an evidence class in perhaps as many days confounding all listeners), the hearsay rule attempts to narrow the scope of information available to the jury. The hearsay rule also seeks to exclude the admission of more remote out-of-court statements and therefore, arguably, evidence that is likely to be less reliable.

Witnesses are also not able to testify to legal conclusions. While a lay witness may describe the actions and words that our now-deceased Judge Max uttered, she cannot conclude that he intended to commit suicide. An expert witness, on the other hand, may make conclusions consistent with her expertise. An example, forgetting for a moment the protections of doctor-patient privilege, the decedent's physician may, as an expert witness, testify that

Judge Max suffered from clinical depression and was therefore suicidal.

Finally, evidence must be relevant. It must, in the language of the Federal Rules of Evidence, "make the existence of any fact ... more probable or less probable than it would be without the evidence." That may seem like a low standard. Is Judge Max's statement that he is "worth more dead than alive" relevant when applying said standard? What about the following: a witness, the decedent's tailor, is prepared to testify that the judge insisted on him making only black suits; is this morsel of evidence relevant? Does it make the existence of any fact (here, a depressive personality and therefore a suicidal person) more probable or less probable than it would be without the evidence? There are also many wrinkles on the issue of evidence relevance. For example, if our judge were actually convicted of embezzlement, that evidence would seem to be admissible on the grounds that it would make it more likely that he was depressed and suicidal. But it might be too prejudicial, and therefore excluded under the Federal Rules of Evidence. A jury might decide that Judge Max was a "bad" person, and that his wife ought not to benefit by his death. So, while the evidence is "probative," its prejudicial nature "outweighs" its utility.

Appeals Process

Our discourse here has only scratched the surface of the law of evidence. The purpose of this preliminary introduction is to highlight some of the ways that the jury's decision-making process is limited by rules of evidence. After all, it is the trial judge who is the ultimate evidentiary filter: the jury cannot base its decision on evidence which the judge has excluded. Having observed the trial, we may now pass to the final state of the trial process: the appeal.

At the conclusion of the case in federal district court, any "aggrieved" party is entitled to one appeal to the appropriate circuit Court of Appeals; that is, even if a plaintiff wins her case, she may appeal if she did not obtain the relief sought. Although a second appeal may be taken to the Supreme Court of the United States through a writ of *certiorari*, the chances of it being granted in a civil case not of great moment like our contract dispute, and the case heard are remote, unless it raises an important issue on the interpretation of federal law or procedure. The Supreme Court frequently allows appellate courts to construe federal law and intervenes only when there are "splits" among the circuits as to the interpretation or application of a particular statute, so that intercession is necessary to ensure the uniform implementation of federal law throughout the nation.

Generally, only issues of law decided in the trial court are considered on appeal. Unless the appellant argues that no evidence was produced that supports the jury verdict, or that the judge made factual determinations that were clearly erroneous, the appeals court proceeds on the factual record before it. Its task is to review *de novo* instructions of the law to the jury or rulings on the admissibility of evidence.

Error committed must be significant in that it may have affected the outcome and not merely be "harmless."

The appeal process transpires as follows. Upon filing notice of its appeal, appellant is given a deadline by which a written brief supporting the alleged misinterpretation or misapplication of law must be submitted. Appellee, often the party that prevailed below, is given leave to file a reply brief. In particularly important cases, other interested parties may also submit briefs. A date for oral argument before a three-judge panel is set, and lawyers are permitted oral presentations of about half an hour to argue their client's case. Counsel's discourse is often times interrupted by questions from the bench; oral argument frequently approximates a law school classroom, where judges (professors to carry the law school analogy) probe the weaker points in the written arguments submitted by the parties (law students, again to carry the analogy). Thereafter, the judges meet in conference, and vote to affirm or reverse. Often times, a judge is assigned to write the court's opinion, which will, of course, be a useful guide for both lawyers and judges when future cases raise the same or similar issues. Should the judges disagree on the outcome, a dissenting opinion/s can be filed by the judge (or judges) in disagreement. Concurring opinions can be filed if a judge agrees with the judgment, but might differ on the legal grounds offered to support the outcome in the majority opinion.

Conclusion

The pattern of trial in the federal system is calculated to allow disputing parties the opportunity to have it resolved in court according to prevailing notions of due process in the American system of jurisprudence. State court practice is similar, though it differs around the edges. Both systems grind slowly and are costly, perhaps with the hope that the parties will find it more efficient to settle than to litigate; and there are a variety of points at which settlement can be pressed by the judges. Still, everyone is permitted a day in court if he or she so chooses, and to have much of the outcome determined by a jury of "peers."

Some may marvel at how a technically advanced society continues to abide by a centuries-old process through which important decisions are made by juries comprised of lay people such as schoolteachers, truck drivers, doctors and hairdressers (and yes, the odd-law professor and student has been known to serve), etc. A contradiction, perhaps, but to some extent the jury is merely another aspect of democratic decision-making in a microcosm—a single piece of litigation makes law. No doubt it is an imperfect system, but who is to say that the judgments of my former law students (some now judges) would reach a more just result?

CHAPTER 6

CONTRACT AND COMMERCIAL LAW: A PROMISE IS A PROMISE (MAYBE)

Introduction

This chapter covers two interrelated areas of American private law: contract law and commercial law. Contract law governs the formation, performance, and termination of consensual private agreements. It often overlaps with its partner, commercial law, the area of the jurisprudence that governs business transactions. Contract law has had a long and quite complicated development in English courts in the later Middle Ages, and one which was fairly well-entrenched by the time of the American Revolution. Its central tenant was to allow parties to bargain freely, and to award monetary damages for failure to perform a promise; however, under exceptional circumstances, the law might order a party to an agreement to perform it according to the agreed terms. This governing principle still obtains (with some modification) in modern American contract law.

Commercial law developed quite separately from contract law. It governs legal relations between merchants, and in the past, disputes were litigated in a variety of tribunals in England. Because even early commercial agreements were frequently international in scope, it had, at times, a multi-national flavor, the so-called *lex mercatoria*.

Modern American law has merged the two, contract and commercial law, in part through the promulgation of the Uniform Commercial Code (hereafter UCC), adopted in whole or in part by all 50 states. Part of the UCC (Article 2) deals with the sale of goods, which is broadly defined as "all things (including specially manufactured goods) which are movable at the time of identification to the contract for sale." (U.C.C. § 2–105). The UCC, therefore, covers a large swath of contract law. While the UCC applies to the sale of goods and securities, the common law of contracts generally applies to contracts for services, real estate, insurance, intangible assets, and employment. If the contract is for both the sale of goods and for the provision of services, the dominant element in the contract controls which body of law applies. There are other articles of the Code which deal with more sophisticated commercial matters, such as secured transactions (credit transactions in which the lender acquires a security interest in collateral owned by the borrower) and negotiable instruments (signed document in which an individual promises to pay a sum of payment to a specified person or the assignee). Moreover, other statutes, state and federal, govern areas of contract law, for example, consumer protection law and the law governing consumer credit transactions. Regardless of the hand of the legislature, the common law remains well-ensconced in contract law, particularly because of the prestige of successive Restatements of the Law of Contracts (compendia of the common law of contract which articulate basic principles of American law, though they are not themselves law), and venerable treatises by learned commentators (like Corbin and Farnsworth). Thus, the reasoning processes explored in early chapters remain critical in interpreting fundamental issues of contract formation and remedies. Moreover, the general principles of contract and commercial law enshrined in the UCC are sufficiently broad in language to beg judicial interpretation. The UCC has generated a body of judge-made law over time to fill in both the vagueness of, and lacunae in, its provisions. No brief treatment, like the one offered hereafter, can do justice to the richness of American contract and commercial law and its jurisprudence, and this chapter merely aims to provide a background for further study.

Jurisprudential Aspirations of Contract Law

Before undertaking the formidable task of providing an outline of American contract and commercial law, a word first about its aspirations is required. Commercial affairs in modern societies are primarily governed by private agreement. Because most forms of human discourse, words and conduct, are open to various interpretations, contract law is required to provide the legal framework for making sense of commercial dealings when the terms of an agreement reached between parties are subject to dispute. But contract law largely provides so-called 'default rules;" it generally applies only in the absence of terms of clear undertakings stipulated in the contract. As such, contract law, the default provisions, ought to comport with the parties' reasonable expectations and advance certain societal values. As to the latter, perhaps the paramount one in America's *laissez-faire* economic order is to promote freedom to contract. Yet as we shall see, in a number of areas, this principle has been curtailed and perhaps even eroded.

Moreover, other approaches to the law have made their presence felt in the law of contract. A law and economics-minded commentator might argue that the individual rules enshrined in contract law should facilitate economically-efficient commerce. Likewise, business people demand that contract law conform to and further commercially-reasonable conduct. Thus, commercial actors require a law that is fixed and uniform in order to provide a reliable guide that allows them to order their business affairs in a rational fashion; the predictability of law is, therefore, both desirable and essential. Finally, there has long been a deeply-rooted (and perhaps innate) moral dimension to contract; children often remind parents who have reneged on a pledge that "a promise is a promise." In most cases, the law should seek to enforce agreements according to their terms.

Whether contract law actually achieves any or all of these objectives, we can leave to contract law theorists (of which there are many) to debate, and begin to explore what this fundamental area of law actually is, rather than what goals it ought to accomplish.

Contract Formation

Because commercial transactions usually begin with an agreement, we begin our discourse on American contract law by considering the circumstances under which that accord becomes an enforceable obligation in contract law. The common law required three elements for a binding contract to be formed: offer, acceptance and consideration. These elements are elaborated upon in the case law, but only the first two are codified in the UCC.

The UCC creates a distinction between an agreement (the parties' bargain in fact) and the contract (the resultant legal obligation arising out of the agreement), and this discourse will attempt to maintain that distinction. (U.C.C. § 1–201(b)(3)). The most common means by which a contract is formed is through "offer and acceptance." No fixed form for either is required; it is sometimes said that all that is necessary for a contract to be concluded is for the parties to have a "meeting of the minds." (U.C.C. § 2–204). How do minds meet? One party to the transaction, the "offeror" proposes some transaction with sufficient certainty that the other party, the "offeree" understands that all that is necessary for the proposal to become a binding contract is for the offeree to assent thereto.

To be binding, a contract need not be in writing (except if the Statute of Frauds so requires; the UCC has its own version for sales contracts (U.C.C. § 2–201)), nor must all of the terms be immutably fixed. Offers may be informal, and they may be conditional upon the occurrence of an event. Generally, the offeror, as "master of the offer," may revoke her offer at any time before acceptance. Exceptions to this general rule include offers under Section 2–205 of the UCC, so-called "firm offers" extended by a merchant, offers which can be made irrevocable for as long as three months, or those in which a party has given consideration to keep the offer open (a so-called "option contract"), or in which the offeree has in some way relied justifiably upon the offer remaining open.

Although offers are generally accepted by a communication similar to the one used by the offeror to convey the offer, they may be accepted by any reasonable means, unless the offer specifies an exclusive method of acceptance (*see, generally*, U.C.C. § 2–606 on acceptance). Both the offer and the acceptance can be promises to perform an act in the future, a bilateral executory contract. Thus, an offer to sell goods entered into on the 4th of July 2020 to be delivered on the 25th of December 2020 accepted by a promise to pay upon receipt creates a valid contract. Likewise, a contract can be "unilateral," that is, the offeree may accept the offer by actual performance. An example of such contract is a brokerage contract in which a property owner offers to pay a commission to any person who sells her house; procuring the buyer is acceptance of the offer by the broker. With respect to the sale of goods, a buyer may simply send a purchase order to seller: the purchaser (offeror) invites a supplier (offeree) to deliver the goods stipulated therein at the stated time, and for the price specified; delivery of the goods constitutes acceptance of the terms in the purchase order.

In modern commercial transactions, the "offer-acceptance model" of contract formation is frequently an ideal rather than a reality. Modern American contract law has been altered to reflect contemporary practice, particularly with respect to agreements between merchants. Parties to commercial transactions often negotiate orally or through the exchange of writings on the terms of the bargain, and the final product, though a contract, is an amalgam of the agreed terms, rendering it unclear ultimately which party should rightfully be regarded as the offeror. This determination is crucial in contracts for services, not covered under the UCC, as the offeror (by making an offer) grants to the offeree the so called "power of acceptance." In order to create an enforceable contract, the offer must be accepted exactly as offered, without modification, (mirror-image doctrine). However, contracts between merchants, covered under the UCC, are not held to these same requirements, in order to facilitate free flow of commerce. At times, the final stage of a concluded agreement is not reached, and the question may arise as to whether in the absence of a final product, the parties are nevertheless bound to a transaction, the so-called "agreements to agree" or "contracts to bargain." While traditional contract law rejected the binding effect of these inchoate or partial contracts, the modern tendency is to strain traditional doctrine in order to enforce them, at least to the extent of agreed terms.

Another wrinkle on the incomplete contract occurs in "battle of the forms" situations, in which each side to a sales transaction sends the other a standardized or "boilerplate" form with separate, and not uncommonly, inconsistent sale/purchase terms. If the sale goes forward, but a dispute thereafter develops regarding some aspect of performance, and the terms in dispute are covered differently in the competing forms, a court may have to decide which party's term prevails. UCC Section 2–207 has recently been revised to allow contract formation even in cases in which the acceptance has additional or different terms from the offer. Additional terms are regarded as a proposal for an addition to the contract. They become part of the contract, if it is between merchants, unless the offer expressly limits acceptance to the terms of the offer, or the terms material alter those in the offer, or the offeror has already objected to the additional term or does so in a reasonable time after receiving notice from the accepting party. In achieving its objective to preserve bargains, the UCC also provides that actions, "conduct by both parties which recognizes the existence of a contract", will establish a contract even if the writings are insufficient to create a contract. (U.C.C. § 2–204(1)). Accordingly, the terms of the contract consist of those upon which the parties have agreed, plus any supplementary terms, so-called "gap-fillers," incorporated in Article 2.

Consideration

For agreements to be binding, American contract law generally requires there to be "consideration" for the exchange. Perhaps oddly, the UCC does not specifically require it for a contract for the sale of goods to be binding. Nevertheless, it is regarded as a fundamental component of a contract. The requirement is sometime said to separate gratuitous promises from those in which the parties exchange, or promise to exchange, something of value to each other. Consideration is a term best defined by example. Ponder the following two hypothetical cases: Professor West promises to give you an A on your exam; Professor East promises to give you an A if you always attend class. In both cases, you attend class, but receive a D; in which hypothetical might you prevail in an action for breach of contract? The first promise by Professor West is purely gratuitous; but in the second, where Professor East demands that you must go to class, there is consideration. If you do attend, you have done something—performed your promise according to the terms of the bargain. The requirement of consideration separates purely gratuitous promises (and therefore those with less commercial implications) from those which probably are more serious commitments worthy of enforcement, because in the latter, each side has undertaken to act in exchange for an act of the other party.

Usually, the consideration for an agreement is apparent by its terms, for example, the contract price for the goods. Suppose Buyer has paid the price for the goods; if the Seller refuses to deliver the goods, and Buyer seeks damages, relief should be granted. The performing party has suffered a detriment and has received no benefit in return. The more difficult cases are those in which the contract is executory, that is to say, neither side has performed, and one side decides to renege on the performance of the promise. Contract law is faced with a different issue. Not having performed, how might the non-reneging party suffer a detriment so as to demand the benefit of the bargain? Nothing has passed from one party to the other; no detriment has been suffered by a party. Courts were originally reluctant to award damages in such cases.

Enter commercial reality: judges began to recognize that under particular circumstances, a party could also suffer injury where there had been no performance on her part if the facts of the bargain suggested that the agreement was supported by "consideration." Consideration then became a legal conclusion: executory contracts were enforceable if there was consideration; they were not in its absence. But consideration also had to be defined in law. Consideration sufficient to support a contract varies and continues to be a complex area of contract law. The Restatement, Second, § 71(2) regards that an agreement is supported by consideration if the offeror's promise was bargained for and given in exchange for performance or a promise of performance by the offeree. In reality, one can envisage consideration as a gate-keeper regulating which contracts are enforceable: if the court believes that the bargain should be upheld, it can find consideration for a bargain; if it does not wish to enforce a bargain, it can conclude that consideration for the promise was lacking or inadequate.

Promissory Estoppel and Unjust Enrichment

Arguably, then, there is some element of reliance that underpins the doctrine of consideration. One is entitled to rely, that is to configure its acts upon the other party's future promised performance where there has been a bargained-for exchange. But even where there is no consideration, the common law as proclaimed in the Restatement, Second, § 90, allows a party to enforce a promise if she has reasonably relied on the promise. If in our examples above, you enrolled in Professor East's class because of her promise, and thus acted in reliance of her promise, even though unenforceable, East may be required to perform the otherwise unenforceable promise based upon the principle of "promissory estoppel." Your reasonable reliance (though I would not recommend such a course) converts the unenforceable agreement into an enforceable one.

Finally, contracts can be created when a party undertakes an act which confers a substantial benefit on another party. For example, in the absence of an agreement, if a merchant delivers goods to you and you retain them, but refuse to pay on the grounds that you never so promised, the law may require your payment to the merchant in the amount of the reasonable value of the goods in order to avoid your "unjust enrichment."

Contract Interpretation

The doctrines of consideration, promissory estoppel, and unjust enrichment provide the doctrinal basis for enforcing promises, regardless of whether there has been a formal offer and acceptance. Now that contract formation has been observed, contract interpretation and enforcement may now be addressed. It is axiomatic (and therefore simplistic) to relate that a contract will be enforced according to its expressed terms. Above it was noted that a contract need not be in writing, except if the type of contract is within the modern iterations of the 1677 English Statute of Frauds. Examples of contracts within the Statute of Frauds are those for the sale of real property, and those which are to be performed more than one year after their making. UCC Section 2–201 (which applies only to the sale of goods) also isolates other particular types of contracts and renders them unenforceable (though still valid) unless their terms are reduced to writing and signed by the party against whom enforcement is sought. Yet the UCC relaxes the requirements of the required writing: it need not be set out in formal terms. Moreover, it need not be perceived by the parties as the contract; a signed letter or memorandum, even one executed after the contract has been formed, is sufficient.

If a contract is in writing, the written terms are evidence of the bargain, and oral evidence of terms not reduced to writing are generally excluded, though consistent additional terms can be added. The theory that supports this limitation, the parol evidence rule (U.C.C. § 2–202), is that the writing manifests both the final and the best evidence of the terms of a contract. Moreover, the doctrine of merger assumes that all terms discussed prior to the writing have been integrated into the document, and any terms excluded have therefore been abandoned by tacit agreement of the parties. Like many other common law "rules," the parol evidence rule has numerous exceptions, particularly if a party can persuade the presiding judge in a lawsuit that the words used in the contract are ambiguous, and that extrinsic evidence (the testimony of witnesses or consideration of other documents) ought to be admitted to assist in interpreting contract terms.

In addition to the terms expressed, the contract may be expanded to include other sources to assist in the interpretation of the obligation of the parties. In particular, there are three: the parties' prior dealings; their own understandings about the terms of the contract, the so-called "course of performance"; and trade practices. When a dispute between parties over performance comes before the court, the judge may imply terms consistent with these extrinsic (because they are outside the four corners of the expressed agreement) sources of law. (U.C.C. §§ 1–303, 2–208).

Likewise, time honored legal maxims assist in interpretation. For example, ambiguous terms are construed against the party that drafted the agreement. Or the Latinism "*expressio unius exclusio alterius*:" in a list of items in a contract, only those items specifically mentioned are included; non-inclusion implies exclusion. Finally, both parties are assumed to have a duty to perform in good faith, a vaguely articulated principle which includes "honesty," and "fair dealing." The contract's terms will be interpreted accordingly.

Moreover, contract law implies certain terms in agreements unless these provisions have been expressly excluded. A good example comes from the law of warranties under UCC Article 2. In contracts for the sale of goods, absent terms to the contrary, the seller, who is a merchant, warrants that the goods be "merchantable" (U.C.C. § 2–314), and under certain circumstances, that the goods be "fit for the particular purpose" for which the buyer intends (U.C.C. § 2–315). Likewise, seller warrants legal title to the goods. Each of these terms has been elaborated upon in the common law, in individual disputes, and ones with differing factual contexts. (U.C.C. § 2–312)

Contract Performance

Interpretive issues may also arise regarding performance. Failure on the part of one party to perform consistent with its contractual obligations, is a breach of the contract, and entitles the other party to a remedy. But breach occurs only when performance is due, so a threshold interpretive question may often be: when is the proper time for performance of contractual obligations? Although the contract may stipulate a time for performance, and therefore render this issue straightforward, the duty to perform may also be conditioned upon the occurrence (or non-occurrence) of an event, or upon the performance or the partial performance of the other party. The buyer, for example, may condition her obligation to purchase on securing adequate finance, a circumstance not uncommon in a variety of commercial transactions from real estate to the purchase of airplanes. No duty to perform in the buyer or seller ripens until the occurrence of the condition, although the party obligated to seek financing is likely required to act in good faith to borrow the required sum. Likewise, some conditions expressed in the contract may be regarded as technical, or non-material, allowing a party that does not abide by them nevertheless to compel performance by the other party. Take, for example, a delivery term. Suppose the contract contains a written requirement that a seller give the buyer written notice two days before shipment. Seller telephones notice of the delivery date a week before. Is such a failure to abide by this explicit provision as written material? Probably not. Failure to give notice may be breach of a material term, but non-adherence to the means of communication stipulated is probably not critical, and a technical, though not material, breach.

Most agreements require performance by both parties, and a party may believe that her own performance is not required until all or part of the other party's performance has occurred. In contracts for the sale of goods, this question often does not arise, because delivery of the goods and payment of the contract price often will occur more or less simultaneously; the buyer of goods becomes obligated to pay the price under Article 2 of the UCC § 2–507 when the seller "tenders" delivery.

However, consider a contract for the performance of services, and therefore one not governed by Article 2. In the absence of agreement to the contrary, if I contract with your university to lecture on American law for five one-hour classes for a fee, the university (absent agreement to the contrary) is not obligated to pay the compensation until the lectures are delivered. Payment is conditioned on my performance, and because I must perform first (absent agreement) there is an element of risk for me in the transaction: the university may default on its payment.

In contracts to be performed over a long period, however, a specified amount may be due at particular points in the course of performance, and failure to pay the stipulated sum in a timely manner is a breach. In my lecturing hypothetical, the university and I may agree to a payment of one-fifth of the total fee after each lecture. Unless my first lecture is substandard, the university is obligated to pay me when the service is provided. If it is not of reasonable quality, the university may claim that they have no obligation to pay, and that I am in breach. They may also decide that inadequate lectures are a material breach, and decide to terminate the contract, not allowing me the opportunity to deliver my remaining lectures. In addition, they may sue me for damages occasioned by my breach, but I might be able to claim a lesser amount, the reasonable value of the inadequate lectures. If, however, the "product" is serviceable, and I am not paid, I am entitled to sue for breach. Because the university's breach is a material one, I may decide to terminate my obligation; not only may I claim my first payment, but as we shall see, I am probably entitled to some measure of damages even for the lectures that I never delivered. If I suspend (rather than terminate) my performance under the contract, and the university subsequently changes its mind, and decides to honor its commitment, it can "cure" by so informing me and making its payment. But it must do so before I give notice of termination.

Excuses for Nonperformance

American contract law also recognizes certain excuses for performance. For example, in a contract for the sale of goods, one or more of its terms can be voided (and the obligations thereunder terminated) if an individual term or the entire contract is "unconscionable." Once again, we visit a legal word of art in contract law that has been elaborated upon by judges. Unconscionable contracts are unfair contracts, often, though not exclusively, found in transactions involving consumers. Along with unfair contract terms, some underlying evidence of deception by a party to the contract or inequality of bargaining power is usually required for the contract or a provision in it to be considered void.

This modern American concept of unconscionability (U.C.C. § 2–302) is an extension of traditional contract law grounds for avoiding a contract in whole or in part. As noted above, American contract law, as an offshoot of American capitalism, generally assumed a *laissez-faire* approach to bargaining between parties: freedom of contract was the norm. Parties were required to live with their bargains, good, bad or indifferent. But, avoidance of a contract (the unilateral termination thereof) was permitted in a few circumstances.

Consider mistake, where one or both parties contracted based upon a misapprehension of a material fact; relief would be granted if so doing would not place too great a burden on the other contracting party. Likewise, freedom to contract presupposes willing parties to a deal; thus, coercion and duress are grounds for which contracts could be set aside at common law.

Misrepresentation, a tort in American law, might also provide grounds to avoid a contract. Whether the deception must be active, such as a fraudulent statement, or whether silence in circumstances in which there may be a duty to disclose particular information that might disincline the other side to contract is sufficient, may depend upon the nature of the parties' contractual relationship. Courts are now more inclined to find duties to disclose material facts that might have a bearing on the terms contract or its performance.

Finally, when unforeseen circumstances at the time the contract is formed render performance impossible or impractical, a contract may be avoided in whole or in part. The key to invoking this rule is foreseeability. Generally, freedom of contract requires parties to a contract to take steps to protect themselves against changed circumstances where the contract requires performance in the future, particularly where a party should have realized such occurrences might transpire. For example, assume an increase in the price of oil. Delivery companies, for example, Federal Express, who have contracted with customers to charge a fixed price for their services, based upon cheaper fuel costs, cannot avoid the contract merely because the deal made is no longer profitable; commodity price fluctuation is foreseeable, and protective terms should have been included in the contract or otherwise hedged against. But if there is an embargo on oil exports, and the delivery company is unable to secure fuel, performance may be excused; arguably the embargo is "unforeseeable," and performance under the contract is "impossible." The embargo might be regarded as *force majeure* and performance might be excused. The line between impracticability and impossibility is a thin one. Suppose some oil is available, but the price is very high due to the embargo. The unforeseen circumstances do not render performance impossible, oil can still be purchased, but the cost is prohibitive. The "just" outcome here is not clear-cut. Neither party can be expected to hedge against circumstances that could not have been foreseen at the time of the contract; yet granting relief to the delivery company merely shifts the burden of the loss to the other equally "innocent" party. And foreseeable is a slippery term: in the modern world, is there any calamity which might occur that a vigilant counter-party could not conjure?

A timely example is the performance issues that have arisen due to the COVID-19 pandemic which rages as this volume is being written. It has occasioned a decline in oil prices which may have made the performance of oil supply contracts unprofitable on the part of the buyer, or the economic recession may reduce the buyer's need for the commodity and disincline buyer to take delivery of unneeded oil. Was the pandemic foreseeable? If so, at what time? Ultimately the application of *force majeure* is about risk allocation. One ought not to shift the burden of loss to the counter-party for foreseeable calamities. That said, it begs the question of precisely what events are foreseeable.

Remedies

A contract has been created, and there is no excuse for performance. We now consider more directly remedies for non-performance. The basic principle which drives the remedial calculus is "to place the non-breaching party in the same position that she would have been in had performance occurred." Money damages are the norm, because they can usually achieve this end. Unlike in American tort law, "punitive damages" are rarely awarded in contract cases. Indeed, it may be efficient at times to breach a contract. Return to my lecturing contract: suppose after I promised to lecture to your university, I am subsequently asked to serve as an expert witness on American contract law at a trial. My compensation for testifying is triple the amount agreed upon with the university. I cannot do both; if the university can secure a suitable alternative at twice the fee I charged, and I am liable in damages to them for the difference in their costs, are not both parties (the university and me) in at least in as good a position as they would have been in had I performed? My conduct may be "immoral," and it is certainly unprofessional, and there may be consequences to my reputation for the breach, but the non-offending party has been made whole; and contract law should be content with the resolution and not punish me pecuniarily for my bad manners.

Of course, in some contracts there may be certain additional interests that require protection. Three have been isolated by the Restatement of Contracts: expectation, reliance, and restitution. Consider again my hypothetical contract for lectures. Suppose shortly after having concluded the contract, I began to write lectures, and the week prior to the date of my appearance at the university, the dean informs me that they no longer require my services: they are in breach. My expectation interest is my fee, the sum that I would have received had the university not breached and allowed me to perform the agreed service. But there are also other potential damages. Assume that I made plane reservations which were non-refundable, or I produced a snazzy handout at my expense to illustrate my talk. These are expenditures made in reliance of the contract; I could also claim these costs as damages. Finally, suppose my lectures were part of a larger comparative law program, and I could prove that my name on the program contributed to enrollment in the advertised course of study, that the university actually received some benefit from the contract that they breached. I might be able to claim "unjust enrichment": that the breaching party nevertheless received a benefit from a contract which they repudiated.

While my straightforward hypothetical sketches three interests which have been injured, the more complicated the contract, the greater the difficulty in calculating appropriate compensatory damages for each interest violated. Even my simple hypothetical raises some questions. For example, suppose I received all three of the above articulated measures of damages, would I have been made whole, placed in the same position that I would have been in had the university not breached? Perhaps the calculation we rehearsed has made me just a little bit "too" whole; after all, I did not have to spend the days lecturing. I could have earned some money doing something else. Accordingly, the agreed contract price might be offset by the value of my recouped time.

Generally, the party who alleges a breach has the burden to prove that the damage suffered was a consequence of the breach, and that the damages were reasonably foreseeable at the time of breach. A claim for lost profits raises the latter issue. In the famous case of *Hadley v. Baxendale* (contract law's *Pierson v. Post*, because no American law student gets a degree without coming to terms with the late delivery of a crankshaft to drive a millstone to crush wheat into flour), potential profits during the period of the delay in delivery were held not to be foreseeable. *Hadley v. Baxendale*, 9 Exch. 341, 156 Eng. Rep. 145 (1854). Why were they not? Surely the carrier had heard the adage "Time is money." But exactly how much money would be lost for the delay? Was the amount lost foreseeable at the time of the contract?

Finally, in assessing damages, modern contract law has placed an obligation on the innocent party to mitigate damages. In my hypothetical case, assume the university intends to breach. Once so informed, I would have some obligation to seek an alternative lecturing post, or another way to occupy my time in a gainful manner. The disappointed contractual party cannot always sit on his haunches and expect to collect damages from the breeching party. The obligation to mitigate is efficient: if I can recoup some of my losses by obtaining another position, is it not mutually advantageous to the parties, and to the economy in general, that I work for another rather than stand idly by and collect the contract price for not engaging in productive labor?

Another possible remedy that would place me in the same position that I would have been in but for the breach would be to require the university to perform, a remedy known as specific performance. While contract law was being developed in one branch of the English royal courts, the common law courts, Common Pleas and King's Bench and later Exchequer, the Court of Chancery was also intervening in contract disputes. Typically, the chancellor would take cognizance of a contract dispute only in cases in which the remedy at law was inadequate. And because equity considered done that which ought to be done, the chancellor would order a party to keep his promise, the remedy which has come to be known as "specific performance." The traditional example of a circumstance in which specific performance may be ordered is in contracts for the sale of real property. Because the law regarded each parcel of land to be unique, monetary damages for nonperformance could not be regarded as adequate. The only remedy that would be suitable would be to order a conveyance.

In contracts for services, specific performance is usually not ordered. In our case, the chancellor might order the university to allow me to lecture. But, of course, as we have seen, my remedy at law is adequate (indeed perhaps even more than adequate), so my case is probably not suitable for an equitable remedy. Suppose, however, I am not a mere law professor, but rather Mick Jagger of the Rolling Stones, and I have agreed to perform at your university's concert hall, and then renege? Mick is, as we all know, unique, and even though damages might be sufficient to compensate the innocent party, would it be possible to secure an injunction requiring him to perform? Unique though he may be, courts are generally reluctant to order specific performance in contracts for services.

Commercial contracts frequently contain clauses that set out in advance the damages for breach. Consistent with the underlying policy of contract law, to permit freedom to bargain, such liquidated damage clauses are generally enforceable. But, again, consistent with limitations on freedom to bargain, if the amount so specified is well beyond the actual damages incurred so as to be regarded as punitive, they will not be enforced. Similarly, contract provisions that greatly limit damages may also be regarded as unenforceable.

An Introduction to Commercial Law

Having sketched the basics of American contract law, our attention may now shift to interrelated aspects of law clumped together under the term "commercial law." The UCC itself highlights the interrelationship between contract law and commercial law in its introductory comment, which is paraphrased here. Commercial transactions generally begin with a contract for sale, but that sale may also include a payment in whole or in part by check drawn on a bank. Ultimately the check will be negotiated and pass through the banking system for collection. The purchase may be financed over time. Part of the purchase price may remain unpaid and be subject to some form of security interest in the goods. The goods are either shipped or stored and are covered by a bill of lading, warehouse receipt, or both. Alternatively, the entire transaction may be undertaken pursuant to a letter of credit. While a full treatment of issues arising out of complex commercial transactions is beyond the scope of this introduction to American commercial law, a discussion of some of the UCC's more important principles follows.

Payment

An important aspect of any commercial transaction is the mode of payment by the buyer. Payment may be made by "cash" or by "credit," as the parties so agree by contract. Payment for a cash sale is due upon tender of delivery, and unless the seller has contracted only for a cash payment, it may be made by "any manner current in the ordinary course of business." (U.C.C. § 2–511).

Payment in cash sales is frequently made by check (buyer's order to its bank to pay seller or another party named as payee), wire transfer, or letter of credit. Unless the check is certified by the bank, payment by check is a risky proposition for the seller, because if the buyer has insufficient funds available in its account, the bank will "dishonor" (refuse to cash) the check. Should this occur, the seller is then in a difficult situation, because in the usual case, seller will receive notice of dishonor after seller has delivered the goods to buyer. Although in the event of non-payment, seller does have recourse against buyer for either the money due or the goods, seller has possession of neither, leaving a costly lawsuit as seller's likely recourse. (U.C.C. § 2–702).

This dilemma has led sellers to prefer wire transfers, in which payment is made at the time of delivery. Buyer's bank sends funds in buyer's account to seller's bank account. Upon acceptance of the transfer by the seller's bank, the seller has a legal right to the funds. These transfers are governed by Article 4A of the UCC.

Finally, although no cash changes hands, payment by a commercial letter of credit, governed by Article 5 of the UCC, has a similar end. Instead of buyer's own funds being paid over to seller, buyer arranges with a bank (the issuer) to pay over an amount specified in the letter of credit (usually the purchase price) to the seller. The letter of credit also specifies particular terms under which the issuer becomes obligated to pay the seller, usually when a document of title or a bill of lading has been presented to the buyer or its bank. If the documents strictly comply with the terms of the letter of credit, the issuer must pay the seller regardless of whether the goods conform to the contract, (U.C.C. § 5–103(d)). This so-called "independence principle" facilitates credit transactions; the issuer is a neutral party to the essence of the transaction, and buyer's recourse in such a situation of non-conformance is against its contracting party, the seller. Thus, in a letter of credit transaction, a buyer does assume the risk of having made payment for non-conforming goods.

Transactions on Credit

It is not unlikely in commercial transactions for the seller to extend credit to the buyer for some specified period. The extension of credit can be either secured on the goods or unsecured. Seller takes a greater risk in unsecured credit transactions, because it cannot reclaim the goods back in the event of buyer's default on payment. Seller must sue buyer and obtain a judgment in order to repossess the goods by an officer of the court, a time-consuming and expensive process. Thus, sellers prefer secured transactions. But the reality of the marketplace drives the availability of credit, its costs, and its terms: credit terms vary depending upon the relative strength of the bargaining parties.

When buyer is extended credit by seller, the sum owed is considered by the UCC as a "receivable." Receivables are classified as either accounts, instruments, or chattel paper. Accounts are sums owed by buyer to seller which are not evidenced by an instrument or chattel paper. So, unless the buyer has executed a separate writing which specifies either seller's right to payment (a negotiable instrument) or the seller's right to payment secured on the goods (a security interest), seller's only recourse is to collect on the account. (U.C.C. §§ 3–104, 9–201). Because sellers often borrow on their receivables, they are more inclined to choose the latter two financing options; the more secure the underlying transaction between buyer and seller is, the easier it will likely be for seller to transfer the obligation to a third-party on advantageous terms.

Negotiable Instruments

A seller, then, may require buyer to execute a negotiable instrument which represents the extent and terms of the credit arrangement. A negotiable instrument is an unconditional promise to pay, so the sum specified is due to the seller at a time stated (or on demand) regardless of whether there is some underlying dispute over the performance of the contract. These instruments are "negotiable" because they can be transferred in the ordinary course of business to third parties. A good faith purchaser (one who has no notice of defects) of the negotiable instrument, a "holder in due course," can demand payment on the instrument even if there is some outstanding claim that the issuer (buyer) could raise against the payee (seller). (U.C.C. § 3–302). While this rule may seem harsh to the buyer, it facilitates the free flow of commercial paper, thereby arguably reducing the cost of borrowing. While merchants can negotiate their own terms, and thus the buyer can protect its own interests, the consumer of goods is not believed to be in a similar situation. Federal law has abrogated this so-called "holder in due course" doctrine in consumer transactions.

So concerned is the UCC to facilitate the transfer of negotiable instruments that two further characteristics of them have been written into the law. The first is that the transferor who endorses a negotiable instrument may be liable to pay the transferee if the obligee defaults. When the original payee of the negotiable instrument, payable to the payee's order, transfers it to a third party, it "endorses" the note. If the obligor under the note dishonors the note (fails to pay), the holder may seek payment from the endorser, unless it is endorsed "without recourse." (U.C.C. § 3–415). Second, transferee of a negotiable instrument essentially warrants its legal validity, and in particular, guarantees that the note is not forged or altered, and that the obligee is not insolvent.

Secured Transactions

While requiring buyer to execute a negotiable instrument to facilitate transfer of the underlying receivable, seller still has no recourse against the goods that were the subject of the transaction unless the seller retains a security interest in them: a right that allows seller to claim back the goods or other collateral from the buyer without commencing a legal action. Sellers prefer these so-called "secured transactions." The collateral for the transaction may be real property (in which case the real property is said to be subject to a mortgage and is covered under the land law of the jurisdiction in which it is located), fixtures (property which is affixed to real property such as the gas boiler or hot water heater in a home), and most forms of personal property. The collateral may also be the property of a third party.

Some vocabulary is required to understand Article 9 of the UCC. It deals exclusively with secured transactions created by a contract or other agreement: the "security agreement." The creditor, be it a lender, seller, supplier or other provider is called the "secured party;" the "debtor" is the borrower, purchaser, or other user of the property subject to the credit transaction. Either the debtor or the creditor can take possession of the collateral; the debtor "pledges" the collateral to the creditor by either delivering it to the creditor, or by allowing the creditor to retain rights to possession for as long as debtor is not in default of payments.

Secured transactions can be undertaken at every level of the chain of sale from supplier of components to manufacturer to end-user. For example, a common method for a dealer to finance inventory is for her to obtain goods on credit from a supplier (or a financial institution) with the debt secured on the stock purchased. When the inventory goods are sold to consumers, the buyer takes free of the security interest, but the creditor retains a right to the proceeds of the sale. (U.C.C. § 9–203). Likewise, end-users themselves may finance their purchases through a secured transaction with the dealer; the "chattel paper" generated by the sale to the consumer is also a proceed of the original secured transaction. Even though the account or chattel paper generated by the sale to the end-user is security for the original sale of the inventory, it may also be used as collateral by the middleman. Article 9 encourages the circulation of "chattel paper," by according priority to the subsequent creditor. This policy permits free circulation of chattel paper and encourages the original creditor to consider purchasing the note generated by the retail sale to protect its interest.

Financing of commercial transactions is also encouraged through the recognition of the so-called "floating lien." (U.C.C. § 9–204). A single arrangement can provide for both present and future financings. Secured interests may be obtained by the creditor in a broad range of collateral, including property that has yet to be acquired by the debtor. Future advances by the creditor may also be covered by the agreement. (U.C.C. § 9–323). The transactions are cross-collateralized so that a default by the debtor on one transaction allows the creditor to claim collateral secured by all transactions. This so-called "revolving credit arrangement" allows the creditor holding the "floating lien" to have priority over creditors who subsequently make loans secured on the same collateral, unless the loan is "purchase money financing," an arrangement that allows the debtor to acquire new assets. (U.C.C. § 9–324).

In order to be protected against purchasers or other transferees of the collateral, the secured party must undertake steps to perfect the security interest. (U.C.C. § 9–312 *et seq.*). Perfection is usually accomplished by filing a financing statement in a central governmental office, usually that of the

Secretary of State in the jurisdiction where the property is located. The need for perfection is particularly necessary if the debtor becomes insolvent. Unless perfected, the collateral will pass with other unsecured property to the trustee in bankruptcy instead of the secured creditor. Without perfection, the creditor may find itself in a similar position to an unsecured creditor, and not receive the full value of the outstanding debt.

Should the debtor default on its obligation, the secured party may either sue the creditor for the debt, or else take possession of the collateral. The defaulting party can use self-help, and seize the collateral, if such an action can be managed without a breach of the peace. The creditor may keep the collateral or sell it at a public or private foreclosure sale, so long as the debtor is notified of the sale. (U.C.C. § 9–610). Likewise, junior secured creditors must be informed of the sale. Any value received in a sale by the creditor that is in excess of the debt is paid over either to the other secured creditors or to the debtor. The creditor must conduct the foreclosure sale in a "commercially reasonable" fashion, in accordance with standard practice amongst dealers who trade in the particular type of property concerned.

Consumer Protection Law

Having discussed the UCC's provisions on contract, negotiable instruments and secured transactions, our attention can turn to a final area of commercial law: that governing consumer protection.

Over the last half-century considerable legislative intervention has limited the ability of lenders to employ sharp practices in securing consumer loans. The laws in this area are a combination of state and federal initiatives. Federal law governs "Truth in Lending" and many other areas of credit protection. The Truth-in Lending Act (15 U.S.C. § 1601 *et seq.*) does not fix interest rates, states do; rather, its goal is to require the lender to make clear to the borrower the actual cost of credit. To that end, the law requires a common vocabulary in describing finance charges. For example, the real cost of borrowing must be disclosed and be denominated the "annual percentage rate" (APR) which includes a variety of hidden charges which increase the cost of the loan, and not merely the lower notional interest rate. The law requires lenders who loan funds to homeowners on the security of their home to inform them that they are entitled to rescind the agreement if they do so within three days of the transaction. If they fail to inform them of this right, the period of rescission is extended to three years.

Credit cards have also been regulated by federal law, the Credit Card Accountability Responsibility and Disclosure Act, (Pub. L. No. 111–24, 123 Stat. 1734 (2009)). Credit card issuers can no longer send out unsolicited cards. Cardholders are liable for only the first $50 of unauthorized use. A procedure has been set up to permit credit card holders to question charges on their cards. While an alleged billing error is being investigated, the issuer may not restrict or cancel the account, nor may it undertake legal action to collect the disputed charge. Debit cards, however, are governed by a separate set of rules.

Consumer credit data is also protected by law. The Fair Credit Reporting Act (15 U.S.C. § 1681) promotes the accuracy, fairness, and privacy of information in the files of consumer reporting agencies. It restricts the type of information which can be accumulated in a credit file and limits their use. Certain types of information may not be kept by credit reporting agencies. Moreover, the law accords individuals certain privacy rights, as well as the right to demand to see their credit reports, and the ability to challenge the accuracy of the information held therein.

State law may even go further than federal law in protecting consumers. A uniform law, the Uniform Consumer Credit Code, was proposed and revised, but has not been adopted in a majority of states. However, all states have enacted laws that protect consumers. For example, states have extended the right to rescind consumer transactions, have limited certain contract terms, and have prohibited a variety of fees regarded as unfair contract terms.

Conclusion

From freedom to contract, American law has moved towards the protection of parties to commercial transactions, particularly those whom the law regards as having less bargaining power. While this transition is most visible in consumer transactions, some UCC provisions also protect merchants. Courts may set aside contract terms between merchants as "unconscionable," and terms like "good faith" and "fair dealing" in the context of commercial transactions have tempered freedom to contract. The balance between parties seems more strained in the area of security interests, where the law favors creditors over debtors. But, arguably, the efficiencies that the system of secured transactions engenders can redress the balance, because debtors are given freer and cheaper access to the credit that is so vital in contemporary American society.

CHAPTER 7

AMERICAN TORT LAW: VENERABLE COMMON LAW ON THE EVE OF REFORM?

Introduction

The law of torts determines whether, and to what extent, individuals can receive compensation from others for injuries sustained to their persons and to their property. Torts are civil wrongs, so the law of torts (like contract) is private law. The general remedy provided by tort law is that of monetary compensation: damages paid by the tortfeasor to the injured party, remuneration calculated to reimburse a tort victim for losses sustained. To some extent, the damages equation mirrors that of contract. Of course, there is no agreement or expected performance. Therefore, the remedy is not to put the party in the same position as she would have been in had the counterparty performed. Tort remedies are calculated to make the injured party whole: in the same position she would have been had no tort occurred.

Tort law is generally state law, and it is largely, though not exclusively, common law. Thus, the law that we shall explore in this chapter may vary by jurisdiction, though specific local differences are usually modest in scope: the details, the nuances, rather than broad principles, change as state lines are crossed. Like other areas of the common law, American tort law evolved over the centuries from the English common law; indeed, the process of evolution began long before there was an America. Torts or trespasses to persons and property (as they were denominated in the past) emerged early in medieval English courts. The common law of torts, like the common law of contracts, was received into American law after independence, and then "Americanized," largely through litigation, and thus by judicial consideration, interpretation, and invention.

Tort Law Reform

A number of preliminary points need to be made before the broad outline of tort law can be addressed. The first, and the most crucial, is that American tort law is presently under siege. Many on the right of the current political divide regard the magnitude of damages awarded in tort cases, particularly in the area of products liability, as gravely injuring the economic performance of key areas of American industry and undermining its international economic competitiveness. Because few non-American jurisdictions award such hefty compensation, foreign producers are not liable to pay the additional cost when they do business outside the United States. Accordingly, it is argued that the sums levied against producers and awarded to private individuals for pecuniary losses (usually for pain and suffering and as punitive damages) sustained go well beyond the amounts required to redress the economic loss suffered by the injured party.

Two examples can be offered. Recently 22 women brought a case in Missouri against Johnson and

Johnson alleging that their famous baby powder caused ovarian cancer. The jury awarded each woman plaintiff $550,000,000 in compensatory damages and then added over four billion dollars in punitive damages. An appeal is underway. Similarly, Bayer AG has recently set aside between 8 and ten billion dollars to compensate those whom it is believed contracted non-Hodgkin's lymphoma from the use of its garden weed-killer "Roundup."

Payment of those claims will not drive either of these multinationals out of business. But in some instances, it has. Asbestos litigation over the last three decades has already bankrupted the industry, arguably preventing deserving asbestosis victims' adequate compensation, because those who secured their judgments first exhausted the industry's coffers with excessive awards. These lofty settlements have been facilitated by class action lawsuits where similarly situated claimants bring a single action to redress their loss. The effect of class actions is to lower the cost to sue per individual claimant incentivizing, perhaps, frivolous litigation. That said, there is a benefit to the class action; in some cases, the reckless companies could not be pursued without plaintiffs joining together.

One particular genre of tort litigation that is controversial is medical malpractice. The cost to the medical system is significant. Physicians are said to abandon the practice of particular medical specialties (for example, obstetrics), because malpractice insurance premiums are so high that they cannot earn a living. Malpractice insurance is costly, it is argued, because lawsuits against doctors are common, and expensive. A particular concern of advocates of "tort law reform" is the award for "pain and suffering": the non-economic loss sustained by a tort victim due to an injury that was suffered from a dangerous product or ineptly performed medical procedure. They decry such awards as unnecessary, speculative, and outrageous in magnitude. The federal government has intervened and placed a $250,000 cap on non-economic damages for medical malpractice claims.

Another example of the work of these "demonic" trial lawyers, and the ongoing battle with politicians, is hailstorm litigation in Texas. After over 5900 lawsuits had been filed in relation to hailstorms, litigation allegedly drummed up by trial lawyers, the Texas Senate introduced a bill to limit the financial damages to insurance companies. Other states have enacted damages cap laws that limit the amount of non-economic damages that may be awarded for a loss.

Like most political issues involving the law, there is another side to the sketch of modern American tort law drawn by the exponents of reform. The defenders of the current system counter that a longstanding imbalance between businesses and individuals is merely in the process of being redressed. Prior to the last half-century, American products liability law (and medical malpractice law) was decidedly favorable to the manufacturers (and to the doctors). Trial lawyers, the responsible party for the current situation (the devil incarnate—at least so the political right would argue), worked long and hard, re-weaving the common law to protect individuals from dangerous products (and incompetent doctors). While the costs of jury verdicts to the producers of dangerous products are no doubt high, so they should be; deterrence is a longstanding basic principle of American tort law. Those who engage in conduct without due regard to its effects on others must be economically sanctioned. Tort law should strive to strike a balance between the under-compensation which promotes risk-taking by manufactures and developers of new products, and the over-compensation that drive costs beyond sums that can effectively be sustained by businesses. A just equilibrium is indeed a difficult one to strike, but earlier generations got it wrong; modern law probably needs some readjustment. Which side will ultimately prevail in this debate is at present uncertain, suffice it to say that current American tort law will not be passed to the next generation of lawyers intact.

Links Between Criminal Law and Tort

A second important point to consider in understanding tort law is the relationship (or lack thereof) between tort and crime, the law of torts and criminal law. Wrongful acts can be either tortuous or criminal or both. Because the burden of proof is higher in criminal cases, a person prosecuted for a crime, and thereafter (or simultaneously) sued in tort can be acquitted of the crime, but required to compensate in tort. The infamous O. J. Simpson case (as do the more recent cases where police have disproportionately killed Black men) provides an example of this pattern. Simpson was acquitted of 2 counts of murder for the deaths of his wife and her friend in a criminal court but found liable for her wrongful death in a civil court. In criminal cases of murder, proof beyond a reasonable doubt is required for a conviction, but in a civil case of wrongful death, proof by a preponderance of the evidence results in tort liability. The policeman whose acts culminated in the death of Eric Garner in 2014 in New York City was not charged by a grand jury with a criminal offence. He was also not charged with federal civil rights violations. Nevertheless, the city of New York paid nearly $6,000,000 to Garner's family to settle a potential claim for the tort of wrongful death.

The Link Between Contract and Tort

In addition to the link between crime and tort, there is a connection between contract and tort. Both areas of the law establish legal duties to act or to refrain from acting. But duties in contract law (be they expressed or implied) emanate from agreements. Tort law operates in the absence of (and sometimes in addition to) agreements. For this reason, tort law remedies may frequently be broader than those in contract. Contract law, for example, rarely awards the punitive damages that obtain in tort. Thus the cigarette smoker who sues in tort is arguing that breach of a duty to inform of the dangerous nature of the product known to the producer at the time of sale is negligent or reckless conduct, rather than a breach of some implied obligation in contract derived from the fact of the sale of the product to inform customers of the dangerous nature of cigarettes.

The Moral Dimensions of Tort

As the above discourse suggests, there is an economic argument that underpins American tort law. There is, however, a moral as well as an economic component to the American law of torts. Certainly, the objective of tort law is to compensate for injury caused by the acts of others. But it is the "unreasonable" conduct of the tortfeasor that gives rise to civil liability. By implication, then, tort law sets acceptable guidelines for human conduct and for the treatment of fellow human beings (and their property rights), and then economically sanctions those individuals who do not adhere to them.

Traditionally, American tort law has been divided into three categories based upon the conduct of the actor that gives rise to liability: intentional torts, negligence, and strict liability. Though interlaced to be sure, each of these branches of tort law is usually studied individually. Because torts in which the actor's conduct was "intentional" are both the most straightforward, and least subject to modern wrinkles, we begin with the variety of wrongs categorized under the rubric of intentional torts, before casting a glance at the other types of torts.

Intentional Torts

Intentional torts raise two threshold questions. The first is the requisite state of mind for the actor's conduct to be regarded as "intentional;" the second is what interests are protected from intentional invasions by others. These interlinked issues will be explored. But it must be conceded that tort law is more nuanced. For example, if we meet in an elevator, you in front, me in the rear, and I lean over and tap your shoulder, have I committed a tort—a battery—an unconsented touching of your person? Perhaps. Surely I intended to touch you, and I did; and I did so without obtaining your consent. Not sure? Try this. Suppose, after discussion over drinks, we differ on the relative wisdom of the American law of torts, and I punch you. A battery? More sure?

To recount the obvious, how do these two examples differ? In the first case, a tort was probably not committed because of two possible reasons. The first is that a battery requires some "harmful or offensive contact." Such actionable contact is determined by an objective test: what a reasonable person would believe violates prevailing social standards of acceptable touching. Secondly, if you enter a crowded elevator, you may have given implied consent to being jostled about, my touching you arguably being of the same nature as the contact to which you impliedly consented. And before I am held liable for the tort of battery in our barroom brawl, much more evidence of what actually transpired must be introduced, because there are defenses to battery; perhaps you were striking me, and my act was one of self-defense.

Returning to the question of requisite intent for intentional torts, the focus is upon the state of mind of the actor. The general requirement for an act to be regarded as intentional is expressed as two of three alternatives: that the actor must willingly intend to act, and know that her act will cause harm; or else she must engage in reckless actions, those that a reasonable person would understand that an injury would be substantially certain to arise from her conduct. The classic example of the distinction is the person who discharges a bullet from a loaded gun. In the first case, she points a gun at the head of the victim, and pulls the trigger; in the second, she is cleaning the gun, and ineptly she jostles the trigger, firing the gun, and a bullet hits the victim in the head. In the first case, her act is intentional; in the second, it may be reckless.

Suppose, in the first case, however, she maintains that she had no intention to cause harm. Because the actor has the only direct evidence of her intent, and may be unwilling to admit to either required state of mind, the finder of fact, the jury or judge, may draw conclusions from surrounding circumstances. Given her actions, our shooter's testimony strains credulity; and a jury would likely find her conduct "intentional."

Likewise, whether the conduct in the second case is reckless will also be determined by the fact-finder: would a reasonable person understand that the handling of a gun in such a fashion would probably result in discharge and injury; did the actor know that discharge and resultant injury was substantially certain to occur? Perhaps not; perhaps she was negligent (acting without due care and attention), rather than a person who was acting intentionally or recklessly.

Thus, whether the actor intended to commit the act in question is an issue of fact. The conduct required varies with the tort. There are three intentional common law torts: battery, assault, and false imprisonment.

Battery

Return to both our elevator and our barroom brawl. In each case, my acts may constitute a battery. But the act committed must be harmful. Actual contact to the person of the victim usually must be proved, though extensions to body (including the space around an individual—the so-called "extended personality" doctrine) also count, so if I am carrying a spear and it, rather than my hand, touches you, I have committed the battery. One need not be holding the harmful instrumentality. Poisoning food that leads to illness may also be a battery.

Likewise, the conduct, though it must be harmful, need not be violent. The casual contact in the elevator might be a battery, if it was somehow harmful. Moreover, my conduct need not be the exclusive cause of the injury. If, for example, I happened to touch an open wound on your shoulder, and somehow it became infected, because, for example, my hands were dirty, my conduct would be harmful. I might be liable even though I was not responsible for the initial wound, and my act was harmful only because of the special circumstance. One takes one's victim as one finds her—the so-called "eggshell skull" doctrine. Harm arising from a physical invasion of the body need not be physically injurious to be actionable;

bodily contact in particular areas may be sufficiently objectively "harmful or offensive" to incur liability.

Simply because liability in tort is found, do not assume a significant payout. Compensation and liability are separate issues. One may be liable for battery, but if the damage to the person is minor, the jury may award token compensation.

Assault

Assault is another intentional tort, and is frequently (though not always) present when a battery occurs. In assault, the offensive contact is not the touching *per se*, but the reasonable apprehension of it by the victim of the potential battery: the victim is aware that some bodily harm might occur. Thus, in our hypothetical barroom brawl, if it commences (as brawls frequently do) by threatening behavior, for example, I shake my fist at you, I may have committed an assault. But whether my act is an assault depends upon context. If my otherwise threatening behavior is between friends, and done in jest, it probably is not reasonable for you to believe a battery is imminent. In such a case, no assault has been committed. Likewise, if we are enemies, but I am at the other end of a rather lengthy the bar, the threat of bodily harm does not appear to be sufficiently imminent to constitute an assault. But should I be in proximity, in reach, an assault has likely been committed. Even if you are far stronger than am I, and likely to emerge unscathed from fisticuffs, the threat may still be sufficient to constitute an assault, even if you are too brave a lad or lass to be seriously alarmed.

Assault, however, requires actions and not merely words. Future or conditional threats are likely not to be regarded as sufficient to constitute an assault, because the harmful or offensive contact apprehended must be imminent. The speaker must possess the present ability to act on his or her threat. Therefore, menacing statements alone are insufficient to constitute an assault, unless the means to carry out the threat exist. Thus, my statement, "I'll club you to death," is probably an assault only if I have a club (or similar instrument) in hand.

False Imprisonment

Another common law tort that is committed against the person is false imprisonment. It occurs when an individual is intentionally confined against her will. The psychic trauma occasioned by the detention itself is said to constitute the harm suffered. All that is necessary for a victim to prove false imprisonment is to show that the unwarranted confinement is the result of an act or omission by another, either by the use of force or the perceived threat thereof. The individual must be aware of the confinement, but the length thereof is not relevant. Any gradient of time is sufficient. For example, suppose a shopkeeper suspects you of shop-lifting, and escorts you to her office where she calls the police. Even if you have not tried to leave, you are probably falsely imprisoned if you reasonably believe that you are unable to do so. Because shoplifting is so prevalent in America, shopkeepers have strongly lobbied to reform the common law exempting them from civil liability in false imprisonment. Thus, in most jurisdictions they are allowed to detain a suspicious person if there is probable cause to believe that she was shoplifting, the so-called "shopkeeper's privilege"—the ability to detain for the time necessary to investigate the conduct in question.

Trespass to Real Property

In addition to these three intentional torts to the person, the common law recognized intentional civil wrongs to a person's property called trespasses. The most significant were trespasses to land, wrongs which were occasioned generally by a physical entry. Rights in property were regarded as sufficiently important to warrant protection even in cases in which the intentional intrusion was incidental or accidental. No damage to the property need be demonstrated for a trespass to be found; the physical intrusion was held to be sufficient to render the violation actionable, though the magnitude and the injury to the owner's interest in land might be considered in assessing appropriate damages.

For it to constitute a trespass, the invasion need not be a physical intrusion by a person; he or she need not make actual physical contact with the land. A trespass may occur when an individual causes smoke or other pollutants to cross a property line. These acts may give rise to actions in tort for a private nuisance: intentional, knowing or reckless invasion, physical or otherwise, of a person's property interest, somehow interfering with its use and enjoyment. Even blocking the sunlight by a neighboring property owner or the impeding of the flow of water downstream by an upstream landowner might be considered trespasses at common law. Indeed, modern environmental law has developed in part from the common law of trespass, and new actions were created to ameliorate some of its shortcomings.

Modern technology has increased the types of invasions that might be actionable, for example drone over-flights, and has required some rethinking of the concept of what constitutes an actionable invasion of land, a trespass to real property.

Trespass to Personal Property

Where an individual carried away personal property, the chattels of another, a trespass was also committed. The common law provided two different forms of civil actions (in addition to possible criminal penalties) in cases in which a person intentionally carried off the goods of another. If the owner sought the value of the property taken from the individual who interfered with it, she maintained a cause of action in conversion; however, if she sought the return of the property itself, the action was one in replevin. Having abolished the common law forms of action, modern law allows an owner whose property is taken by another to sue and to select whichever remedy she prefers.

Transferred Intent

Intent, as noted, is a frequent element of torts. However, for conduct to be actionable, the requisite intent to commit a tort may be transferred from the intended victim to another. Suppose I throw a punch, intending to hit Mike, but my aim is off and I end up hitting John instead. Although I did not intend contact with John, the doctrine of transferred intent allows John to sue in tort: the requisite intent to strike John is satisfied by my intent to hit Mike.

There are four instances in which the doctrine of transferred intent may be invoked. First, like the example above, intent can be transferred from the intended victim to an unintended victim. Second, intent to commit one tort can be transferred to the actual tort committed. For example, suppose I simply intend to scare or threaten Mike: my attempt to wave a fist in his face in a threatening manner, but I actually make contact with his person. Although I only intended to scare Mike (assault), I actually end up committing a battery on him. The third instance in which intent can transfer, is a combination of the first two, different tort and different victim. For instance, I point a gun in Mike's direction, fire at his feet trying to scare him, but miss and the bullet hits John. Finally, intent can be transferred from things to persons. Suppose I intend to damage property but instead injure a person. Generally, intent to damage property or chattel will not transfer to the intent required to commit a tort against a person. The logic for not accepting transfer is that the moral culpability required to commit damage against property or a chattel is not the equivalent of the moral culpability required to commit damage to another person. However, the injured party may still have a claim under negligence, which we will discuss later in this chapter.

Another wrinkle in the issue of intent is the so-called "disjunctive intent." Let's say I see a group of people, and decide to throw a rock into the group, not particularly interested in whom it hits. In this case, no matter whom the rock makes contact with, the intent element will be satisfied.

Defenses to Intentional Torts

A variety of defenses were available to the actor in each of these intentional torts: consent, self-defense, and necessity. Our survey begins with consent; no tort was committed to the person of an individual if she agreed to the harmful conduct, either expressly or impliedly. Thus, if an individual agreed in advance to being battered or possibly physically harmed by the acts of others, for example, boxers in the ring, fans sitting down the first base-line in a baseball game, no cause of action would lie in battery for punches and foul balls that struck and injured the person. Consent can be expressed: surgery would be a battery; hospitals, therefore, routinely require patients to sign consent forms. Or it can be implied: skittish about foul balls, buy a seat elsewhere in the stands.

Likewise, self-defense is a defense to an intentional tort. To claim self-defense, the force used must be commensurate with the threat perceived, so if at our barroom brawl, I raise my fist first, you cannot take out a pistol (Hollywood films to the contrary) and "fill me full of lead." Only such force that is "reasonable" under the circumstances, and necessary to avoid the harm, are permitted. Self-defense also applies to defense of property, and the same limitation of reasonable force applies. Deadly force at common law would not be permitted to defend property. However, some states have passed statutes to allow its use. In Texas, one can use deadly force not just to protect a person, but also to protect personal property, including to "retrieve stolen property at night," during "criminal mischief in the nighttime" and even to prevent someone who is fleeing immediately after a theft during the night or a burglary or robbery, so long as the individual "reasonably" thinks the property cannot be protected by other means. This law has been the basis for not pressing criminal charges against individuals who shoot and kill suspected car burglars, and an individual suspected of stealing copper wiring from a car. It is worth noting that some other states authorize the use of force to protect personal property, but not deadly force. Other states have by statute permitted deadly force to defend one's home from intruders. Even in states that require a person to retreat from the threat of imminent harm before defending themselves, a person can often use deadly force against someone who unlawfully enters their home. This rule, also known as "the castle doctrine," allows people to defend their homes against intruder through lethal force. Even in states without such laws, a jury might be disinclined to assess damages against a person defending herself against an intruder who is shot while "trespassing" upon her property, regardless of the law's niceties.

Finally, necessity: in very limited situations, a person may intentionally injure the person or the property interest of another, usually in order to avoid a greater harm to person or property. Thus, if you are sunbathing on the railway tracks, believing them to be disused, and the "train they call the City of New Orleans" (immortalized in song by Arlo Guthrie) is bearing down on you, and I decide to lift you up and dump you on the railway siding, breaking your arm in the course of my heroic act, I can claim a defense of necessity should you be sufficiently ungrateful to sue me in tort for your injury.

Necessity can also be claimed when property is damaged, again in order to prevent greater loss. So, firemen may in fact burn down your house or yard in order to slow the progress of a conflagration, thereby destroying your property, if they deem it necessary to protect the property of another. Reasonableness counts in applying the necessity defense (and indeed all other defenses) to a particular factual circumstance that is raised in an individual case. The jury will be instructed on the law by the judge, and will use their judgment to determine whether the specific context should excuse the harmful conduct undertaken.

Negligent Torts

Let us turn to a second type of tort: negligent torts. Many more negligent torts are committed than are intentional torts. Cases in which negligent conduct is alleged in order to find tort liability run the gamut from straight-forward automobile accidents and slips and falls on banana skins to the more complicated medical (and legal) malpractice and injuries in the workplace. What ties these disparate cases together is that the law has established a duty of care in an individual undertaking an act, and the actor's conduct (either in the form of an act or an omission) does not measure up to the established norm.

Simply put, the plaintiff must allege and prove a duty in another person, a breach of that duty, and a causal connection between the breach and the injury sustained. Examples? Landlords have a duty to maintain common areas in apartment buildings. Your landlord knows that a common stairwell has steps in need of repair but does not fix them. You slip, fall and break your leg. The landlord is liable for damages. Another common example: the driver who fails to stop at a red-light and thereby crashes into an innocent passerby. Duties also arise in the professional context. Suppose I am a practicing lawyer, specializing in the drafting of last wills and testaments and I agree to craft your estate plan for a fee of $1,000 (giving rise to a duty of care). My paralegal types out the provisions, you sign, and I alone witness your signature. Most states require two witnesses for a will to be valid (your will execution is a breach of duty), a fact that you later discover. Your will is invalid. You die. The expressed beneficiaries under the will do not take and suffer pecuniary loss (causal connection and injury) and sue me for malpractice for the loss of their inheritances.

Suppose the error is discovered before death. An attorney has a duty to use reasonable care (a standard that may be established by the testimony of expert witnesses) in the preparation of documents relating to her practice. That duty is breached when the attorney fails to do so by omitting a crucial legal requirement; until you discover the blunder, your will may be invalid due to my error, and your financial affairs in disorder. Even if the omission is rectified, malpractice has been committed. The extent of the loss suffered is a question for the jury, which will assess your damages.

A medical malpractice drama may also be sketched. A surgeon removes your appendix, and you thereafter feel a sharp pain in the region; she has failed to retrieve her scalpel: duty of care (furnish competent medical services); breach (the offending instrument); causal connection; the injury (the "stabbing" abdominal pain).

Duty of Care

The hypothetical cases given illustrate (and were so intended to highlight) egregious cases of a breach of a duty of care. But given the variety of acts individuals undertake, precisely how may this duty be defined in the abstract, to apply to this concept to a veritable plethora of human conduct? Take an automobile accident. First, the simple one: the driver of a car is licensed and drives through a red-light, knocking you down while you are in a crosswalk. Duty of care breached?

Probably, but let us change the facts slightly to make the case more interesting: suppose there is no stoplight and you are crossing at a corner, and the driver is observing the speed limit, but it is dusk, and regrettably, just does not see you. Duty of care breached? Not all collisions can be attributed to driver error. The driver may not be liable, if, for example, you cross against the light and stop in the middle of a street, and she is traveling at an appropriate speed, but cannot avoid striking you.

Consider: the duty of care is one of reasonable care. The law does not require individuals to be saints; rather that individuals constantly undertake a series of rudimentary cost-benefit analyses. The sort of caution demanded by tort law is that of a person who assesses the risks involved in undertaking particular conduct; considers the possible ramifications of her conduct; and then balances both with the costs of altering her conduct to avoid the risk. Not an easy task to undertake in day-to-day activity.

Of course, this prudent person, this cautious individual, our mythical reasonable human being, is an ideal construct. That said, this "reasonably prudent person" standard is the one broadly applicable to individuals in undertaking the various burdens of everyday life. Yet the standard is not invariable. In particular cases, individual circumstances may demand higher duties of care, such as is the case with respect to professionals, our doctor and lawyer. Younger people and the disabled may be required to meet only a lesser standard in accordance with their age or infirmity. The marketplace may also set the standard of reasonable care. In the past, industry practice once established a benchmark; but more recently regulatory legislation has established the requisite duties for industrial and commercial actors, usually at an elevated level.

While the duty of care is a legal standard established by law, it is the jury which decides whether the defendant's conduct constitutes a breach. Instructed by the judge on the standard of care in law, the jury cobbles together its particularized application of that norm in the sanctity of the jury room, thereby imposing liability or absolving individuals thereof.

Breach

Once a legal duty of care is established, the plaintiff must show that a breach of that duty has occurred. To do so, a plaintiff will show what the appropriate duty of care was and how the defendant's actions failed to reach that standard. In general, the burden of proving a breach of duty falls on the plaintiff. However, in limited circumstances, a plaintiff can shift this burden to the defendant, to prove that they did not breach their duty of care. This is the doctrine of *res ipsa loquitur*. There are three requirements that must be shown before the shifting of the burden of proof transpires. First, it is only available in instances where the mere fact that the accident has occurred, is evidence of negligence. Classic examples are two trains, owned by the same company collide or a barrel falling out of a second-floor window. Neither could occur without some negligent action. Second, the instrumentality of harm must be within the exclusive control of the defendant. As is the case with the two train cars owned by the same company and by the barrel falling out of a window, which couldn't have happened on its own. Lastly, the plaintiff must be a passive victim. Imagine the scenario of walking down the street minding your own business, when all of a sudden, a barrel comes tumbling out of the sky and strikes you. Another example is in the medical field, where a patient, unconscious during surgery, wakes up to later discover that the surgeon's scissors have been left inside her body. This clearly could not have occurred without the surgeon's negligence, the scissors were within the exclusive control of the surgeon, and the plaintiff was unconscious: a completely passive victim. The breach of duty on the part of the defendant-actor in each case is presumed; the burden to disprove falls to the defendant-actor.

Causation

In addition to demonstrating the duty and its breach, the plaintiff in a negligence claim must prove that the defendant's conduct was a cause of the accident and was indeed the "proximate" cause. Often this requirement is a difficult one for the plaintiff to establish. Accidents may occur due to a single cause or to the unhappy combination of factors. Take a man who slips on a banana peel outside my shop, falls breaking his leg, and sues me. Is the plaintiff's slip and fall due to my negligence (breaching the duty to keep the sidewalk clear of

potentially dangerous obstacles) if I offer evidence
that the plaintiff was overweight, carrying a stack of
packages, and had recently imbibed a pitcher of
martinis? Perhaps he would have tripped anyway.
After all, others, presumably, navigated the peril in
the street, and avoided slipping on the offending
object.

In addition to being the *de facto* cause of the injury,
the defendant's breach of duty must be the proximate
cause of the loss suffered. An intervening act
undertaken by a third-party might mean that
defendant's breach of a duty owed was too remote a
cause of the injury to assign liability. For example,
should the failure on the part of the shopkeeper
whose store fronts the sidewalk be held accountable
for your slip and fall on the banana skin on the
publicly "owned" concrete path? Was the
shopkeeper's failure to remove the banana peel the
proximate cause? Who else may be to blame? After
all, it was the banana farmer who actually produced
the offending fruit; would it be fair to require her to
compensate our victim? And consider the culpability
of the wholesaler and retailer of the fruit who made
the banana available to a consumer? How about the
purchaser, and the person who dined on the fruit, and
who inadvertently (or not) dropped it on the
sidewalk? Should the city have employed more staff
to clean the sidewalks? Did any of the above have a
duty of care; and was the breach of that duty the
proximate cause of the slip? Likely not.

There is an economic efficiency argument to
proximate cause as a benchmark for tort liability: it

promotes enterprise. By holding liable generally only the individual whose act was the most likely cause of the injury, the law allows others whose conduct may have contributed indirectly to the ultimate outcome to continue their economic activity without financially contributing to the loss suffered by the injured party.

There is, as usual, a countervailing consideration. The drawback to holding responsible only the individual whose act was the proximate cause of the injury, is that this rule narrows the field of those potentially liable to pay compensation; the fewer the potential defendants, the more likely it is that the injured party will find herself faced with a judgment-proof tortfeasor.

Contributory Negligence

Thus far we have hypothesized negligent acts in which the victim's conduct is without fault. The common law generally did not provide relief if the victim's own negligence in some way contributed to her injury. This position is consistent with tort law's view that there is generally a single proximate cause of an injury. If some act committed by the plaintiff was also a factor in causing the injury, perhaps the defendant's conduct was not proximate. Might the plaintiff's intervening act render the defendant's negligence less blameworthy? And would awarding damages somehow compensate her for an injury that she had a role in causing? This rule on contributory negligence barred recovery for those victims whose own careless acts might have *contributed* to the injury. Having done so, should not the defendant's liability be limited?

More recent rethinking of the common law has tempered the rule that the victim's contributory negligence bars her recovery. Instead, the plaintiff's conduct has a bearing on her ability to recover damages awarded, and their extent. In some states, a quantitative approach is undertaken; the awards match the jury's percentage reckoning of comparative fault. Thus, if the jury finds that the incident was 40, 50 or 60 percent due to the plaintiff's fault, the award is reduced by that value. Some states only permit recovery in cases in which the plaintiff's negligence is apportioned at less than half.

Multiple Parties

This emerging notion of comparative negligence requiring percentage assessments of fault is also applied in cases in which there is joint and several liability, that is to say in situations in which there is more than a single negligent defendant. The plaintiff may bring her action against any defendant whose conduct was a substantial factor in causing her injury and collect the entire amount of compensation from that defendant. It is up to the defendant so charged to seek contribution from other tortfeasors, in rough proportion to their comparative fault. This rule allows plaintiff to select strategically her defendant, with the goal of wringing a more financially advantageous award or settlement from the chosen defendant. In some states, this rule has been altered, rendering a defendant liable to pay only that percentage of the award that is attributable to her fault. In these jurisdictions, it is the plaintiff rather than the defendant who suffers a loss if one of the tortfeasors is judgment-proof.

Strict Liability

Our discourse has jumped ahead to damages. Before focusing on that issue, we should consider the third circumstance that gives rise to tort liability, a number of situations in which intent and negligence are not factored into the liability equation: strict liability torts. At common law, certain acts were regarded inherently dangerous, say the storing of explosives, that those who undertook such conduct which resulted in damages were per se liable. Keeping a dangerous animal might also give rise to liability in instances in which it injured a person. At common law, however, there was no tort liability for harm caused by a defect in the product purchased by an individual. Recourse was limited to remedies in contract, even if the product sold was negligently produced, and an ensuing injury was reasonably foreseeable.

Strict liability has been extended in current law to hold product manufacturers responsible without proving fault for damages suffered due to design defects, manufacturing flaws, and for providing inadequate safety information or incomplete or imperfect directions for use. Finding tort liability without proving an intentional or negligent act is a rather more recent development in American law.

While the emergence of strict liability for defects in products aided the consumer because she no longer need to prove how a sophisticated piece of machinery failed and whether producing it in such a manner was negligent, a hurdle had to be overcome for the consumer to prevail in products liability cases: the waiver, or limitation of liability provision in the sales contract. Let us explore the context in which doctrine developed: through the case of *Henningsen v. Bloomfield Motors*, a useful one, because it illustrates the links between contract and tort. *Henningsen v. Bloomfield Motors*, 161 A.2d 69 (N.J. 1960). The plaintiff was interested in purchasing a new automobile as a Mother's Day gift for his wife. After shopping around, his heart became set on a shiny new Plymouth. A "Purchase Order" was prepared by the dealer on a printed form which included one paragraph in small print in which the generous husband (as the purchaser) acknowledged that he had read the terms of the agreement contained on both sides of the form, and agreed to be bound by them. On the reverse side of the "Purchase Order" was found eight and one-half inches of fine print (fondly called, in American legal parlance, "boilerplate") which included "Paragraph 7." The paragraph read as follows:

"It is expressly agreed that there are no warranties, express or implied, made by the dealer or the manufacturer ... except as follows:"

What followed was a warranty on the part of the dealer and manufacturer of "a vehicle free from defects in material or workmanship" but this warranty was one of limited duration in fact 90 days or 4,000 miles, whichever occurred first.

In addition to the temporal limitation, the obligation under the warranty was limited "to making good" the defect. The boilerplate further excluded any other warranties expressed or implied. The car was delivered, and about two weeks later an accident occurred in which the spouse was injured, and the car was "totaled." The damages were so extensive that it was difficult to determine precisely which working parts, if any, were defective. However, the manufacturer was prepared to repair the car or give the owner a replacement vehicle.

At first glance, it would appear that there was a case in tort; the accident likely occurred because of the manufacturer's negligence. And by this time the rule precluding tort remedies in products liability cases had been altered. Moreover, the injured party need not prove precisely what part in the automobile actually malfunctioned; strict liability pertained to injuries caused by any defect in the automobile. But what about the contract; was it not a waiver of liability for damages, except the express promise to "make good" the defect? Arguably, the manufacturer and dealer would not be liable for injuries caused to Mrs. Henningsen (or indeed any other losses suffered), because both parties had agreed to limit the manufacturer's liability.

The court, however, refused to recognize the waiver, and allowed recovery for the injuries sustained. Thus, product liability was strict if the producer put into the stream of commerce a dangerous product, and the consumer could not waive the manufacturer's tort liability by contract. The case, then, was a crucial one in both the law of tort and of contracts as they pertain to dangerous products that cause serious injury.

Damages in Tort

Like contract damages, the basic result that tort law hopes to achieve is to make the injured party whole, to be in the same situation that she would have been in had the injury not occurred. And like most abstract formulations of law, this principle is more easily stated in the abstract; the particulars are far trickier to elucidate. In introducing the chapter, reference was made to the disquiet amongst some commentators on the current state of the monetary extent of available damages in tort. Their position is not without some merit regardless of one's ideological stripe.

Let us now consider at least some types of harms that command compensation in tort law, remembering of course that recoveries are largely case-specific. Regardless of the tort committed, the plaintiff receives her actual damages. Whether it is our barroom brawl or a slip and fall, a workplace injury (though in America such injuries are usually covered by state-sponsored Workers' Compensation Insurance) or an automobile accident, the plaintiff receives her medical expenses and her lost earnings. Because the defendant takes her victim as she finds her, the tortfeasor may pay a higher price if her victim has an "eggshell skull," if for some reason the injury sustained is greater due to some individual particularity: the hemophiliac who bleeds to death when the brawler punches her in the nose. Likewise, a negligent driver who injures a senior partner at a Wall Street law firm instead of a mere law professor to such an extent that she misses a month of work, is liable to reimburse the practicing lawyer at her decidedly more exalted hourly rate rather than the professor's more meager one. Should either lawyer die due to negligence, the heirs may also be able to claim the present value of future earnings, much greater (sadly) in the case of the lawyer than the law professor.

Tort damages can go beyond compensation to include the much derided "pain and suffering," and may also include punitive damages. The latter usually requires a flagrant breach of a duty of care and outrageous, even criminal or quasi-criminal, conduct, an act or course of conduct that ought to be punished. Likewise, repeated tortuous acts suggesting a wanton disregard of the cumulative consequences, and those committed knowing that serious damage may occur are more likely to attract punitive damages. The over-compensation awarded to the plaintiff is justified on the grounds that a heavy penalty will deter others from following a similar path. "Pain and suffering" payments compensate victims for losses that go beyond lost wages and medical expenses. Compensation is awarded to redress losses; these damages assess the cost of the injury to the quality of a victim's life, and not merely to her purse.

Damages may take other forms depending upon the individual tort committed. Damage to property as well as to the person is compensable. Commercial interests are also protected by tort law. For example, the pecuniary loss of business which may occur due to misrepresentation or fraud, common law torts, may attract significant damages. In addition, defamation is a tort; libel and slander, injury to one's personal and professional reputation, can occasion pecuniary damages. So if one goes around falsely deriding your professional reputation as an attorney, proclaiming "He embezzles from his clients," you may be able sue for lost income if you are honest and upstanding. While historically some statements were *per se* defamatory, truth is a defense to actions in defamation, and to prevail in either of these torts, the plaintiff must demonstrate that the statement was false. Greater latitude, however, is permitted for political speech, because of First Amendment guarantees.

Conclusion

To conclude, we have observed in this sketch of tort law the manner in which American society allocates risks of injury, and how it developed a regime for the compensation for losses. Not all injuries are compensable in tort, but for those that are, the measure of damages may be generous and include non-economic losses. Moreover, from a legal culture that did not recognize liability for injuries sustained in the use of a defective product, American tort law (though its particular nuances may vary state-by-state) now generally imposes a standard of strict liability for defective products that cause damage to the person and/or property. The result may often be to increase the development and testing period for products to minimize the potential that a defective product will engender a lawsuit.

Yet even with these precautions, recent events in the drug industry, for example the questions raised about the safety of Vioxx or opioids, prescription drugs for pain, makes one wonder whether tort law's protective umbrella effectively shields the public from dangerous products. On the other side, there is the issue of cost, and the simple hard fact that compensation payments drive up the price of products. Perhaps tort law in America is asked to do too much, and the debate over its future must be more extensive than the current one: the much-mooted greed of the plaintiffs' bar. Fashionable though attacks on them may be, curtailing the right to a cause of action in tort cannot be sufficient to remedy the deficiencies in the law. After centuries of internal reform, the common law of torts may require more than the mere piecemeal reform that has transpired in the last century.

CHAPTER 8

AMERICAN PROPERTY LAW: PLENTY OF OLD WINE IN BOTH NEW AND OLD BOTTLES

Introduction

Of property, Sir William Blackstone, the eighteenth-century commentator on the laws of England, proffered that nothing captures the imagination of people as the sole dominion that individuals exercise over land and goods. The drive to acquire rights in property (sometimes referred to quaintly as the "bundle of sticks" that constitutes ownership) also inspires contemporary Americans. But the "ancient" law of property (the old wine) has evolved and increasingly consists of limitations on the use of property, particularly land, as it does on protecting the exercise of rights therein. From *A to Z* (*a*ir quality standards *to z*oning), recent trends in land law more frequently concern restrictions upon its use and enjoyment (the newer bottles) than they do on the protection of rights, or dominion, therein (the older bottles). Thus, as absolute as private property rights should be in *laissez-faire,* free-market America, the primacy of property rights unfettered by regulation is less pervasive than is widely imagined.

A few examples can be offered to make my point. Let's assume I own a residence on a one-half acre lot. Suppose I decide that I could maximize the value of my land by building a miniature nuclear power plant in the backyard of the house. Regulatory law will restrain me, as well it should. But consider even more modest commercial aspirations, like a convenience store or a video rental shop (if they still exist in the age of Netflix and other purveyors of internet streaming content). Such a contemplated use will be subject to zoning regulations, and in my current single-family residential neighborhood, it would not be permitted. Moreover, even in the absence of a zoning plan, private agreements known as servitudes might restrain my proposed non-residential use, thereby limiting the development rights of myself and my neighbors. Even in the absence of such land-use agreements, the common law of nuisance might permit nearby landowners to contain the noxious uses of property by others. Likewise, as the residents of an historic district in New London, Connecticut recently discovered, municipal government may decide to acquire (condemn is the legal term of art) privately-owned property for its own use or even use by a private developer. *See Kelo v. City of New London*, 545 U.S. 469 (2005). Such governmental action is subject to limitations contained in the Fifth Amendment to the United States Constitution: the project contemplated must be a "public use" (it must confer a general public benefit) and the condemning governmental authority must pay the owner "just compensation."

As the above sketch suggests, American property law is multi-faceted. It regulates rights in personal property, as well as in real property. Recall how the remnants of the fox were disposed of by property law in *Pierson v. Post*, namely, that possession is obtained by satisfying the requirements of capture. 3 Cai. R.

175 (N.Y. 1805). In addition, property law mandates the form that intergenerational transfers must take for individuals to create "estate plans" which will pass their wealth, both real and personal, to their legates or beneficiaries, and in lieu thereof property law stipulates the pattern of succession to wealth upon the death of its owner. Finally, property law governs the way in which ownership attaches to creativity, be it in the form of words or inventions or distinctive marks. But before delving into its mandates, let us begin with a consideration of one of its most basic principles: the distinction between possession and ownership.

Possession and Ownership in American Law

Each spring semester, with boring regularity, I begin my first property class by wandering up the aisle of the lecture hall into the second row (the first is generally vacant), and surreptitiously tuck a student's property casebook under my arm. A few minutes thereafter, I ask the class to whom the book belongs. With little dissent, it is agreed that the book is the property of the student whom I so deprived of her casebook. But when I ask the aggrieved student to prove that the casebook is hers, she will usually say, "I wrote my name in the book," or "I briefed the case in the margin," or "Here is my receipt." While I agree that each response provides some evidence that the casebook is hers, I argue that none are conclusive. If I cross her name out and insert mine, does the book become my property? What if I brief the next case in the margin? And the receipt: that merely shows that she bought *a* property casebook, and not necessarily *the one in question.* My point is a simple one: with respect to most items of personal property, all that one who has paid good money for an item can prove is "possession" rather than ownership. Only with respect to personal property that passes through documents of title, for example, an automobile, can ownership be proved. A "Certificate of Title" registered by the state division of motor vehicles has a fifteen-or-so digit vehicle identification number printed on the official form, which is also emblazoned in some obscure place on the car; and ownership can be proved by a match of the numbers. Likewise, one can prove ownership of securities which have registered numbers, now largely electronic. But cars and securities to the contrary, all that one can generally prove with respect to personal property is this legally protected right we call "possession," and that, in fact, suffices in most cases where some cunning law professor tries to deprive a diligent student of *her* casebook.

Anglo-American common law accords a possessor a right as against all but the "title holder" or "true owner," and protects the interest of the prior possessor (my student in the hypothetical) against a subsequent possessor (me). If you thereafter lifted the book from me, I could bring an action for its return, even though I do not own it. This notion of a hierarchy of rights in personal property was articulated in the case of *Armory v. Delamire*, which came before the Court of Kings Bench in 1722. 93 Eng. Rep. 664 (1722). The facts are as follows: A chimney sweep's "boy" (probably the small lad who actually climbed the chimney, brush in hand, and did the dirty work) found a ring on a public street; he took it to a goldsmith for appraisal, and was informed by the goldsmith that it was worth three half-pennies. The clever lad reckoned that the ring was worth more, and demanded it back; the smith duly returned the socket, but without the valuable jewel. The sweep brought an action in trover (a common law form of action to recover property, initially for a loss that was subsequently found, but by the eighteenth-century, for property entrusted to a third party by a lawful possessor) seeking the return of the jewel. In order to maintain his action in trover, the sweep had to allege that he had a right in the jewel superior to that of the smith, an allegation that the smith denied. But the court held for the sweep, according him a right as finder as against all but the true owner. While he could not maintain that he owned the jewel, his possession was deemed lawful; and though he transferred the ring, and surrendered possession to the smith, the sweep's right was sufficient, indeed superior to the smith, which allowed him to demand its return from the smith. In modern legal parlance, the sweep "bailed" the ring, that is to say, the sweep voluntarily turned possession over to the smith, with the understanding that he could demand its return without having to prove his ownership.

Once again, we can observe in the judgment the economic efficiency woven into the common law of property. Protection of possession is essential to facilitate transactions in a commercial society. Imagine having to prove ownership each time you wanted to retrieve property handed over to another. One would think twice about taking clothes to the dry cleaner, or a computer to a repair shop. Were these "bailments" not protected, a sophisticated system of registering each item of personal property would be required, and one in which the underlying costs would likely exceed the ultimate benefits. Moreover, according the sweep's right as a finder encourages honesty; he may be prepared to admit to his finding of the ring if he knows that he would have his right protected as against all but the owner or a lawful prior possessor. And if the sweep retains a right to possession, the property is more likely to be returned to the owner, since their paths had once crossed. Don't you retrace your steps when you have realized that you lost something? And isn't the ring worth more to its owner, due to accrued sentimental value? Though non-transferrable, this subjective worth attaches to many items of personal property: the watch my parents gave me when I graduated from law school.

Adverse Possession

Possession is also protected with respect to land, and sometimes to the extent that peaceful possession by an individual may, in certain circumstances, be protected as against a titleholder. Once again, I offer an example. Suppose that I have decided to retire in California and purchase a small island off the coast. Alas, retirement is a long way off, at least twenty years. I am too busy to visit my island paradise, but I regularly pay the property tax bill in a timely fashion. My law school dean, the man who runs the place, on the other hand, has far more time on his hands than I do; he learns of my uninhabited paradise, and decides to spend his weekends there. He even builds a modest abode on the premises, erects a boat house to store his small, but impressive, yacht, and constructs a pleasant dock from which he whiles away his endless summer days fishing.

Twenty years thereafter, retirement is upon me. I return to my island; astounded to see him comfortably ensconced. I order him off. He refuses. I bring an action in ejectment (another of those now-obsolete common law forms of action in which an individual with a greater right in property seeks to oust one with a lesser). He argues that my claim is barred by his "adverse possession." He will allege that he used the land for a period stipulated by statute (of varying terms by jurisdiction, but generally about ten to twenty years). Having failed to take legal action to eject him, or otherwise interfere with his use during the statutory period, he argues that my claim is barred. To prevail, the dean must demonstrate that his use of the land was *open*, not concealed; *continuous*, regular and without interruption; *exclusive*, not in conjunction with my use and that of others; and *adverse*, typically with the intent to claim as his own depending on the jurisdiction. If he can do so, he will prevail. The right to possession in my forgotten island is with him. Since I had title and cannot eject him because the statute of limitations to bring an action in ejectment has passed, he can bring an action to quiet title in him. Voilà, the island is now his property and not mine. If, however, the dean fails to establish any one of those requirements, then he has not perfected his adverse possession, and title to the island remains with me.

While adverse possession sounds like little more than theft, American law has long protected the occupiers of land against the claims of others. After all, one may argue that much land in America was "adversely" possessed from Native Americans (though extensive research indicates far more hostility was exercised to secure the transfer of native lands than that which is typical of an adverse possessor today). In a frontier society with little formal recordkeeping, possession might be protected for the same reason that my student's right in her casebook was recognized: what greater interest can be demonstrated without a viable paper record?

Yet law need not be a captive of its past. Why grant title by "theft" in modern America where ownership is recorded? Why indeed. Once again, an economic efficiency argument can be offered, even if it does not generally persuade most of my students. Adverse possession, it is argued, provides a carrot and a stick. The carrot is to reward a person who, like my dean, actually uses the land productively; the stick is to deprive owners like me who do not monitor their land of their right. After all, if within the period of the limitation against actions provided by law (again, usually ten to twenty years) I bothered to go to my island, and attempted to assert my rights by ejecting the dean (or even giving him permission to remain until I retire, so to preclude his possession from being "adverse" and thereby negating his fulfillment of an essential requirement to a finding of adverse possession), then adverse possession would not be perfected. Ought we to protect the interests of one who cares so little of his land and monitors its use so casually?

Real Estate Transactions

Like my students who never quite buy into the concept of adverse possession, you will no doubt be relieved to know that most Americans actually purchase land rather than poach it from others. Land transfers are governed by state law. Most real estate transfers require financing regardless of whether the property is residential or commercial. The purchaser-borrower "mortgages" the property to the lender. "Ownership" in the property differs according to two theories of mortgage. In most states, title is held by the buyer (otherwise known as the "lien theory"), subject to a security interest (the lien) in the lender. Once the loan is repaid, the lien is removed. However, if borrower defaults, lender may foreclose on the lien and gain title to the property. In other states, the lender has title (commonly referred to as the "title theory"), and borrower has the equity of redemption (the amount of the loan principle that borrower has repaid). Once the mortgage is paid, the lender conveys title to the borrower. However, if borrower defaults, title remains with the lender, and the lender must restore the equity of redemption to the borrower.

When buyer and seller reach agreement on the price, lawyers draft a written contract for sale which integrates the terms of what generally begins as an oral agreement to purchase the real property. Buyer's lawyer is responsible for "searching" title and must satisfy herself that the property is unencumbered, except as to outstanding loans that will be repaid out of the purchase price at "closing," the point at which title will be transferred from seller to buyer. Buyer's lawyer must also satisfy herself that seller has "marketable" title, and that she has the power to transfer the property in question. A deed is then prepared (usually by buyer's lawyer) which transfers title from seller to buyer (or to the financial institution holding the mortgage in so-called title states—see above). Of course, many real estate "deals" are decidedly more complex, with corporations formed to own the land, and others created to develop it. Moreover, because development is often subject to land-use regulation, a requirement that planning permission must be obtained for a proposed use may be inserted in the contract for sale as a condition precedent for proceeding to closing.

Eminent Domain

Another way in which property is acquired is through eminent domain, a power of government recognized by the Fifth Amendment to the United States Constitution. Suppose the city decides that the current airport runway is insufficient for projected air traffic. The optimal tract of land for the new runaway is owned by several individuals. While the city might decide to negotiate with each owner to purchase their property separately, the price will probably rise once the owners learn of the runway project. Moreover, the last person to sell may be able to "hold-out" for an even higher price, because the city's plans have advanced, and without her property the entire project might have to be scrapped. The power to compel private owners to transfer their land is, therefore, a very powerful card in the city's hand, permitting it to undertake development of its infrastructure without purchasing the property to accomplish it at inflated prices.

The exercise of eminent domain is pursuant to the so-called "takings clause" of the Fifth Amendment: ". . . nor shall private property be taken for a public use without just compensation." Each cluster of words has a defined meaning in "takings" jurisprudence of the United States Supreme Court.

Let us begin by exploring the constitutional limitation that private property be acquired only for a "public use." Though the term maintains some ambiguity, the Court has typically deferred to the police power of the state or municipal legislature in determining whether a project constitutes a "public use" under the Fifth Amendment. Generally, a project is within the ambit of the legislature's police power if it prevents a harm to the public and thereby promotes the health, safety, morals, or general welfare of the public. *See Haw. Hous. Auth. v. Midkiff*, 467 U.S. 229 (1984); *see also Berman v. Parker*, 348 U.S. 26 (1954). However, it is not necessary for the land taken through eminent domain to be used directly by the government, for example, to build a post office, a school, or city hall. Rather, a private developer may persuade the legislature that an urban renewal project or an office building would sufficiently benefit the locality's tax base and/or the local economy by providing jobs. Thus, such a project would qualify as a "public use."

Having determined that the land's contemplated use is within the mandate of the "public use" requirement, the condemning authority and landowner should try to reach an agreement on the value of the private property interest acquired, the constitutionally required "just compensation." The landowner will be paid the fair market value of the land at the time of condemnation. This figure is frequently articulated as the amount that "a willing buyer would pay a willing seller" for property acquired.

But, of course, the seller is not always (in fact is not usually) a willing one. If, for example, the property has been in the family for generations, a house or a farm may have sentimental value to its owner; the current owner would never contemplate a sale at any price, but certainly not at a market value that does not include some additional payment for this added personal value. Likewise, a business might have been established on the premises for generations, and therefore have accumulated "good will" (a strong customer base). In neither case will the landowner receive compensation for these components of value. In the first place, they are regarded as too speculative; and second, the condemning authority is not "acquiring" the good will (it is probably not going to operate a similar business on the land), nor is government interested in somehow making use of the "sentimental value."

Thus, in many situations, the property owner does not walk away from a taking in the same position she would have been in before the exercise of eminent domain. Rather, her just compensation is simply the fair market value not of what she has lost, but only of value that the government has acquired. This process may seem harsh in specific situations, but businesses must deal with a wide array of risks; the liability that its property may be the subject of eminent domain is merely one further possibility against which a prudent business-owner must hedge.

Land Regulation

Government has the ability to regulate land use in order to ensure that it is not exploited in such a way so as to harm the public. This authority, too, is within the government's police power, and its operation has raised a fundamental conundrum for American jurisprudence. One cannot do better than to express it as did Justice Oliver Wendell Holmes in the well-known case of *Pennsylvania Coal v. Mahon*, 260 U.S. 393 (1922). On the one hand, Justice Holmes realized a need for government regulation and the possibility that it could diminish land values. He wrote that "Government hardly could go on if to some extent values incident to property could not be diminished without paying for every such change in the general law." *Id.* at 413. Government, therefore, need not compensate the owner for every reduction in value occasioned by some public act. It is possible that a regulation of land use that might reduce its underlying value to the owner might be permitted under the "takings" clause without triggering a need for the payment of just compensation. Yet, and this is the conundrum, some regulations diminish the value of land too substantially and thus warrant that just compensation be paid to the affected owner. Holmes reasoned that, in such a situation, there exists "[a] danger of forgetting that a strong public desire to improve the public condition is not enough to warrant achieving the desire by a shorter cut than the constitutional way of paying for the change." *Id.* at 416. Striking the balance between permissible regulations which need not be the subject of compensation and those which trigger such a need has led to a lengthy series of cases in which the police power justification for a regulation is challenged by a private landowner, and if it is deemed valid, whether the loss to the landowner is too great to be borne without compensation from the public purse.

A good example of this "balancing test" is the case of *Penn Central Transport Co. v. City of New York,* 438 U.S. 104 (1978). The facts are as follows: the railway owned Grand Central Station in New York City and sought permission to build an office tower "cantilevered" above it. The magnificent edifice had been listed as an historic landmark, and pursuant to law, the Landmarks Preservation Commission had to approve any changes to the structure. Two sets of designs were offered to the commission seriatim, and both were rejected. The railway sued, arguing that the law was not a valid exercise of the police power, and if it was, then the denial of the permit to build either building "went too far," triggering the need for just compensation.

The Supreme Court held that the amenity's legislation was a valid exercise of the police power; historic buildings were a component of a city's spirit and soul and might therefore be protected. As to the issue of whether the railway should receive compensation, the Court held first that the government did not occupy the railroad's land (if it did, then existing jurisprudence would always require the payment of just compensation[1]), and secondly, the railway's primary expectations for the property (its investment-backed expectations) were not thwarted by the denial of the development permit: they bought the land for a railway terminal, and they could still use it for that purpose. Clearly, the Court believed that a private landowner need not be compensated for lost value if the land cannot be exploited to its highest economic use; there is no intrinsic property right protected by the Constitution to achieve the greatest return from land. Yet, the Court was unable to do any more than suggest that the balance would continue to be one that had to be struck within specific contexts.

---

[1] Note that the "extent" of the invasion (the trespass) is indeed relevant to determine what is just compensation; *de minimus* invasions, such as placement of an indiscrete telephone cable along the roofing of one's home, may require only nominal damages. *Loretto v. Tel. Manhattan Catv Corp.*, 485 U.S. 419 (1982). Note also, that the "extent" of the invasion is not, however, relevant for determining whether a permanent physical occupation constitutes a taking—any permanent physical occupation of real property is a taking for purposes of the Takings Clause, even a telephone cable on the roof of a building—it is a trespass eviscerating one's right to exclude to others from one's property. *Id.*

This uncertainty has led to a myriad of cases in which landowners have claimed that some limitation on development diminished to too great an extent the value of their lands. The *Penn Central* analysis meant that the determination of when just compensation must be paid would be made on an *ad hoc* factual basis. Many cases followed trying to work out precisely when investment-backed expectations were thwarted. In response to requests for development permits or the like, a planning authority (usually a municipality or city council) often conditions approval on calculations of harm that the project will create for the public, frequently, environmental degradation. Suppose a landowner applies for a permit to build a house on beachfront land. The planning authority is prepared to allow the development for a beachfront home provided that the landowner creates an easement in the public along the property near the sea which connects a public beach to the north with one to the south, ostensibly so as not to obstruct the current public view thereof and to also provide a pathway for public access between the two parks. Does such a condition constitute a per se taking? An easement is a permanent physical occupation of a landowner's property—it is a "trespass" thereupon—so here, the conditioning of construction on the dedication of an easement suggests that a so-called "trespassory taking" has indeed occurred.[2] Does it require just compensation, similar to a physical taking? Return to our "bundle of sticks," and a landowner's desire for

---

[2]   *See* case cited *infra* note 5 and accompanying text.

sole dominion over his property. Here, our landowner would have to concede his right to exclude (a principle purpose of the Takings Clause) beachgoers from traversing his property on the easement.

The Supreme Court has held that such concession cannot be coerced; more precisely, the property concession demanded must bear a relationship to the harm the development occasioned. The test's threshold question asks whether the condition imposed advances the same interest that would otherwise allow the government to deny the developer's permit outright. Specifically, the condition must have a close nexus to the original purpose for which the permit could be denied. Suppose that our landowner's permit could be denied for the purpose of protecting public view of the sea, which is visible to the public when driving by landowner's property No close nexus would exist between the purpose served by the municipality's concern (public access to the beach), and the original purpose for which denial of the permit could be justified (public view of the beach). Though the municipality's condition would advance *some* government purpose (public access to the beach), it would not advance the *same* government purpose justifying denial outright (public view of the beach); it is therefore an unconstitutional condition absent just compensation. *See Nollan v. Cal. Coastal Com.*, 483 U.S. 825 (1987).

If a close nexus exists between the harm caused and the exaction, however, courts then turn to whether the concession to be made is roughly proportional, in nature and extent, to the impact or harm that the proposed development would cause. Humor a slight change of facts in our beachfront hypothetical: suppose that the purpose justifying outright denial of the permit was not to protect public view, but instead to prevent flooding from rainwater runoff; further suppose that the municipality conditioned the landowner's permit on creating a pathway to the beach for drainage purposes, but one that the public could traverse. Even if the condition survived the close nexus requirement, is the interference with the landowner's right to exclude proportional to the harm that his beachfront development would cause? Likely not. The easement indeed could exist for drainage purposes without eviscerating the landowner's right to exclude. In other words, the landowner's proposed development would not interfere with access to the beach and therefore the nature of the concession (the pathway— the loss of right to exclude) and the extent of the concession (permanent transfer of beach access from landowner to beachgoers) is not proportional to the actual harm that would result from the landowner's development. Recall that the resulting harm was only proper rainwater runoff. Accordingly, the planning authorities' easement condition would be unconstitutional absent just compensation because, as Chief Justice Rehnquist so bluntly put, "public burdens, . . . in all fairness and justice, should be borne by the public as a whole [and not by some people alone]." See Dolan v. City of Tigard, 512 U.S. 374 (1994). If the municipality wants to create a public pathway to the beach using landowner's property, then the municipality (the public) should pay for it.

Zoning

Regulations like those seeking to preserve historic buildings are particular types of "targeted" zoning laws. In addition to these specialized regulations, many American cities have developed comprehensive zoning plans that create separate land-use districts. The logic of zoning is not that there are good or bad uses of land, but merely that non-conforming uses (for example, homes and factories) should, to the extent possible, be isolated from each other. Thus, a city may determine that in order to maximize the attractiveness (and therefore the value) of residential land, it will create areas in which only single-family houses on half-acre lots can be erected. These residential districts are frequently attached to, or are surrounded by, multiple-family dwellings, which in turn may be adjacent to commercial districts. Industrial uses are permitted in outlying areas of the municipality. This comprehensive plan allows the city to provide higher levels of required services in the areas in which they are needed: schools are located near the residential areas; police protection is more present in commercial areas; sophisticated fire-fighting equipment marshaled in the industrial areas. The deployment of public tax dollars is targeted, and therefore arguably more efficiently expended.

Because zoning may diminish the value of land in the hands of its owner, use restrictions are subject to the police power. Thus, cities must employ zoning in order to prevent harm to the public, namely, the economic and social costs incurred when areas undergo unplanned growth. Although cities have tried, zoning ordinances cannot be used to insulate a city from constitutionally protected (but oft controversial) free expression, such as adult bookstores,[3] erotic dancing, or the like.[4] Similarly, cities cannot use zoning to exclude racial minorities from residing within their borders. Some state courts have rejected community zoning plans that do not provide opportunities for housing for the poor. *See generally NAACP v. Mt. Laurel*, 92 N.J. 158 (1983) (invalidating a township's zoning scheme when it thwarted reasonable opportunity for people of varying economic means to live within its boundaries).

On balance, zoning laws have allowed communities that have adopted these comprehensive plans to order development in a more rational fashion. Zoning laws have set improved construction standards for new buildings, preserved historic

---

[3] *But see City of L.A. v. Alameda Books*, 535 U.S. 425 (2002) (upholding an ordinance regulating crime as a secondary effect of adult bookstores, or porn shops, to mitigate decline in surrounding property values).

[4] *Compare City of Erie v. Pap's A.M.*, 529 U.S. 277 (2000) (upholding an anti-nudity law, and inadvertently establishing a roadmap for zoning ordinances to constitutionally regulate adult clubs by regulating nudity on grounds that its mandate for "pasties" to be worn by exotic dancers was merely a *de minimus* intrusion on an activity not inherently expressive nudity), *with Schad v. Borough of Mt. Ephraim*, 452 U.S. 61 (1981) (striking down an ordinance banning all live dancing with in the municipality).

edifices and districts, and protected environmentally sensitive areas. Although some landowners may find their parcels of less value because a proposed use is not permitted, zoning regulations are sufficiently flexible to permit "variances" when circumstances require deviations from the plan (ironically, though, this other side of the coin can present new concerns of decreased property value because a previously circumscribed use is now, indeed, more widely permitted). *See e.g., Vill. of Arlington Heights v. MHDC*, 429 U.S. 252 (1977) (validating concerns raised by single-family homeowners regarding decline in property value if a variance permitted multi-family housing in the buffer area near their homes). Compensation may be provided when the regulation too greatly diminishes the value of a particular parcel.

Environmental Regulation

Although not generally studied in a course in property law, the wide array of statutes adopted since the growth of concerns over the environment have greatly impacted the use of property by landowners. Both state and federal laws have been enacted, and the enforcement of these laws is the responsibility of either state or federal environmental protection agencies. Because economic development generally has some environmental impact, these concerns have long been subject to a delicate, if not always definable or realizable, balance. The concept of "sustainable development" should be a goal of those who create and enforce environmental law. As a matter of policy, environmental law has the difficult task of achieving its goals in a manner least likely to impede private uses and therefore values of land.

Federal law sets both environmental policy and pollution standards. The National Environmental Policy Act (NEPA) establishes the broad goals of environmental protection. It requires that an Environmental Impact Statement be produced in conjunction with the federal Environmental Protection Agency (EPA) when proposed federal action may affect the environment. Thus, a variety of projects that require permits through the federal government, such as airports, military complexes, or highways, must be accompanied by an assessment of their environmental impact. NEPA has been a powerful weapon in the arsenal of environmental interest groups, because it has been interpreted to allow a private right of action to curtail development that has been instituted without the production of an adequate impact statement.

Other federal environmental laws set discharge standards, such as those for air (the Clean Air Act) and water pollution (the Clean Water Act). Federal law likewise manages both the dumping of hazardous waste (Resource Conservation and Recovery Act) and the clean-up of toxic waste sites (Comprehensive Environmental Response Compensation and Liability Act). The use of pesticides (Federal Insecticide Fungicide and Rodenticide Act) and the manufacture of chemicals (Toxic Substance Control Act) are also the subject of federal law.

State law provides an important component of environmental regulation. A number of states have adopted comprehensive environmental laws, and some impose stricter standards than federal law. Local government, through building codes and safety regulations, also addresses environmental concerns. Finally, tort law (state common law) has been used to provide remedies for individual injuries occasioned by the unleashing of hazardous materials into the environment. One particular area of common law, the law of nuisance (itself a branch of tort law), is particularly useful for redressing damages occasioned by environmental pollution.

The enforcement of environmental law has long been politicized, though it must be said that America owes its early environmental legislation to a Republican, President Richard Nixon. Likewise Republican, the Trump Administration has clearly ramped back the enforcement of existing environmental law, doing away with a number of Democratic Obama-era executive orders dealing with the environment. The ebb and flow of enforcement has always been related to the executive branch's enthusiasm for environmental protection; the length of time it takes to complete impact studies has, among other things, left the current occupant of the White House unenthused with the process. Accordingly, the future of environmental law in the United States awaits the outcome of the 2020 election.

Nuisance

Sic utere tuo ut alienum non laedas was a maxim established by the common law to govern the manner in which landowners should exploit their property. Likewise, this maxim "do unto others . . ." (do not use your property in such a way so as to impinge upon another's enjoyment of her property), spawned a corollary, "first in time, first in right," permitting those who initially exploited the land to continue to do so, even if the conduct interfered with a neighbor's subsequent use of her property. Some exceptions to the "first in time" rule were established, particularly if the property's use was one of those deemed in law to be "noxious," but its dictates largely informed the American law of nuisance until relatively recently.

While there were complications that arose in individual cases that made the application of these simple concepts problematic, there was a certain efficiency component to the rule of "first in time," a doctrine that was attractive in a developing economy. Individuals could exploit their land in an economically beneficial manner, either agriculturally or commercially, with the assurance that their investments would be protected against the nuisance claims of neighbors who subsequently arrived.

The entitlement that "first in time", granted however, had drawbacks in a rapidly developing society because it tended to "freeze in" existing property uses, even when a subsequent employment of that property might be more efficient. Suppose, for example, a "feed lot" for cattle is established in the prairie miles from an urban area in 1950. Thereafter, as the city grows in population, residential development progresses towards the feed lot. By the year 2000, residential lots are now adjacent to the feed lot, and cannot be sold; or if sold, the operation of the feed lot becomes a health risk to the neighbors. If the land is worth $500 an acre as a feed lot, and worth five times that as residential lots due to urban sprawl, it seems "efficient" for the feed lot to move, rather than to remain and limit the growth of the residential areas. *See e.g., Spur Indus. v. Del E. Webb Dev. Co.*, 494 P.2d 700 (1972) (finding it efficient for hundreds of head of cattle to be relocated after flies and odor flowing therefrom had a noxious and costly effect on nearby residential development). But if "first in time," is strictly enforced, it would allow the feed lot to continue operations regardless of the implications on neighboring land, except if it is deemed a noxious use: that is, a use often found to endanger public health, as determined by whether others can smell it, taste it, or hear it. If, of course, the alternative use is so much more valuable than the feed lot, the equitable result might be for the residents and the developer to "buy out" the feed lot, or at least pay the costs of moving the operation out to the prairie.

Modern nuisance law has established a different theorem for determining liability. As might be expected, it is decidedly more complex. Because nuisance law is part of the law of torts (civil damage to property), it is found in the Restatement of Torts, Second sec. 821 *et seq*. While not all courts (or legislatures by adopting it as law) adhere to it, the

Restatement view is the "majority" rule and is two-fold: one is liable in nuisance if, one, her conduct is an intentional interference with the use and enjoyment of another's private property interest; and two, that interference is unreasonable. "Unreasonable" is, of course, a malleable concept. The Restatement defines the term by referencing two decidedly economic balancing tests: the first is whether the gravity of the harm of the actor's conduct outweighs its social utility; the second asks whether the harm is serious, and the actor can continue her enterprise, but compensate the neighbor for his losses.

Much ink has been spilt on these two balancing tests. If the harm caused is great, why should it be permitted, even if there is some pressing greater societal value to the conduct? Arguably, the law should require that enterprise or the government to pay the economic costs to the unhappy neighbor. Similarly, how efficient can an enterprise be if it can only continue its operations without paying the full social and economic costs suffered by neighbors?

Regardless of its potential shortcomings, the Restatement test is probably an improvement on earlier nuisance law. It permits consideration of a wider array of circumstances in order to determine which competing use of land should continue, and if so, whether one side or the other ought to make some contribution to the losses in value that might be suffered by neighboring property owners due to development. After all, while nobody wants them in their own backyards, modern society demands goods produced by a wide array of farms and factories. Commercial property is similarly critical to our economy; likewise, hospitals and prisons must be located somewhere. Nuisance law attempts to allocate more fairly those costs between landowners who hold different aspirations for their property.

Estates in Land

Return now from the regulation of property to the classification of interests in real property. The system has, like much of the common law, a dose of logic, though it may not seem so to the uninitiated. It is another area of the law in which a page of history is of *some* assistance in understanding *some* of its fundamental principles. When it was initially contrived in the century or so after the Norman conquest of England in 1066, it created a paradigm for landownership: all land was "owned" by the Crown and granted out to others who "held" land of the King. These sets of legal principles comprise what subsequent generations called the "feudal system." A holder of a fee (an absolute interest in land) from the Crown might "subinfeudate," that is to say, he might grant some or all of his holding to another. In this fashion, landholding descended vertically from the Crown in the form of a ladder, with some men holding of the Crown (usually quite important ones or the Church), and others holding of one of these intermediate or "mesne" lords. The ladder could have many rungs, with steps even for unfree peasants who worked the land.

Why does anyone want to hold land? Then, as now, it has value. Picture yourself as a landowner in medieval England. You can use the land, live on it, farm it, or otherwise commercially exploit it yourself; alternatively, you can rent it out to others. You may also want to realize its market value by selling it to another for a commodity or the medieval English form of cash. Assume that you have both a spouse and family. When you die, you may want it to pass to your spouse and/or to your children. To accomplish that end, land should be alienable and descendible.

Early on, the common law responded to these demands. Ownership of land could, like the land itself, endure forever. An estate that so lasted was called a "fee simple absolute," and required particular words to be created: Tulaneacre (a hypothetical estate) to Sir Nigel (a hypothetical grantee) "and his heirs." This interest was alienable (he could transfer it to another), descendible (it could pass to his heirs if he died holding it without issuing directions as to its descent), and, under certain circumstances, devisable (he could will it to another). The system also recognized lesser estates. In particular, an owner of land like Sir Nigel, who would not live forever, might determine to whom and in what manner his property should pass upon his death. Accordingly, the law allowed the creation of other more limited interests—those that might endure for a finite period, for example, the lifetime of an individual. The law also allowed an owner to lineup successive interests, one after another.

For purposes of an example, suppose that Sir Nigel, an elderly landowner, decided to make a gift of one of his landed estates, Tulaneacre, to his eldest daughter as a marriage portion. His mind is that she should have the land for her life, but upon her death, it should pass to his younger daughter forever (he likes her better, but she is at present too young to marry and he fears that he might not live to her union), if she survives her elder sister; if she does not, then he would like the estate to pass to his heir male.

What does this grant indicate about the common law system of estates? The system permits grants to be of limited duration (the life interest in his eldest daughter), to take effect or to terminate on the occurrence of an event (the gift to the youngest daughter is conditioned on her survival to the death of her sister), and even be limited to take effect to persons uncertain at the time of the transfer (his heir male).

Let us rehearse why such an "estate plan" was fashioned. Because his elder daughter was certain to die and her estate limited to her for life, the property would certainly pass from her. Upon the death of the elder daughter, possession would pass to the younger daughter or to the heir male, depending upon whether the younger daughter survived her sister. There is also another wrinkle; the identity of the individual who might take the estate at the death of both daughters was uncertain at the time of the grant. While an individual had presumptive heirs during his life, one's heirs were ascertained only upon death. Thus, the final interest created fashioned an estate in a person who, at the time of the grant, was not ascertained.

By manipulating these interests, the common law system of estates allowed landholders considerable flexibility to transfer and to transmit land to the next generation. But, of course, the law knew bounds. Both the types of present possessory and future interests were limited: the common law recognized only a few distinct types of estates in land. Whether a landowner could accomplish a particular design for the future of his land depended upon whether he could string together the recognized common law estates in land. What follows is a sketch of the system, and a discussion of why the categorization undertaken generations ago has continuing relevance.

The system of estates, as we have seen in our example, permits the creation of present possessory interests and future interests. Present possessory interests are those which give their holder the right of immediate (current) occupation. The present possessory interests that appear most frequently are the fee simple absolute and the life estate. It was of critical importance in the past to grant land "to Sir Nigel *and his heirs*," if one intended that the grantee's estate endures forever and be alienable, descendible, and devisable. In the absence of such "magic words" (*and his heirs*), courts might assume that a lesser interest was intended, and that only an estate *for life* was created. There was also an estate called a "fee tail" (limited "to Sir Nigel and the heirs of his body"); though once inalienable by statute, the bar on transfer, as a practical matter, disappeared by the sixteenth century and for all intents and purposes, the fee tail has since ceased to exist.

However, it is the "future interests" in property that were (and still are) the most important because, by using them, a landowner could control the destiny of his estate after his own death. Our example of Sir Nigel's gift on his daughter's marriage illustrates such future interests. The most straightforward one (and not illustrated in the hypothetical) is called a reversion. It is defined as that estate which remains in the grantor after he has made a grant: so, if Sir Nigel limits Tulaneacre to Roundhead for life, and makes no further transfer, the estate "reverts" to Sir Nigel on Roundhead's death. Possession returns to Sir Nigel, or to his heirs should Sir Nigel predecease Roundhead (or, if he wishes, to another to whom he has transferred the reversion by deed or will). In the hypothetical grant, no reversion is reserved, because Sir Nigel granted a fee simple absolute to either his youngest daughter or his heir male upon the death of his eldest daughter. The property cannot return to Sir Nigel or his heirs.

In addition to this retained future interest, the common law system of estates also recognized transferred future interests: the remainder and the executory interest. A remainder is a transferred future interest that takes effect upon the natural termination of a simultaneously created estate. When Sir Nigel limited Tulaneacre as above, two remainders were created: one in the younger daughter; the other in his male heir. These remainders are called contingent remainders because the enjoyment of the interest as a possessory estate may or may not occur. Contingent remainders are limited to uncertain persons: to Sir Nigel for life, then to his eldest surviving daughter (who will not be ascertained during Sir Nigel's lifetime). Contingent remainders can also take effect upon uncertain events, like in the original grant in which there are two: the first to the younger daughter who must survive until her sister dies, and the other, to the heir male whose interest becomes possessory only if she does not.

But remainders need not be contingent; it may be vested: to Sir Nigel for life, and upon his death to Lloyd Bonfield and his heirs. I have a vested remainder in fee simple absolute: it is limited to take effect to a certain person (me) and to take effect upon an event certain to occur (Sir Nigel's death).

The other type of transferred future interest is an executory interest: a transferred future interest that does not take effect at the natural termination of a simultaneously created estate. Suppose Sir Nigel wanted to encourage his younger son, Wilfred, to follow him to the bar (that is to say, to become a barrister!): "to my son Wilfred if he is called to the bar." The estate remains in Sir Nigel until Wilfred is called to the bar; if he is not, then at Wilfred's death and the death of Sir Nigel, the property reverts to Sir Nigel and passes by descent to his heirs.

The recognition that one might control the disposition of land during and indeed after one's life by the manipulation of future interests was a useful one. It enabled a landowner to fashion "estate plans," individualized strategies of inheritance that might be tailored to particular circumstances: to encourage his son to become a lawyer (or not); and to provide for a child if she survived to a particular event. But there were bounds. The most important was the temporal limits placed on the power to manipulate contingent future interests in the course of the seventeenth and eighteenth centuries. The judge-made "rule against perpetuities" set an outer boundary for the control of the so-called "dead hand" of the grantor over the disposition of property at "a life in being plus 21 years."

Inheritance: Wills and Trusts

This discourse on estates in land has been largely historical, but its purpose is not solely antiquarian. It set the stage for the modern law of inheritance in the United States. While the estates in land system has continued vitality, that is landowners can create a series of present and future interests in land as in previous centuries, most wealth in America is held as personal property, rather than as real property. While there are patterns of succession to property directed by law in each state, property holders are free to determine to whom their property should pass by gift made during life or at death by will. In all states except Louisiana (which adopted a modified version of the French *Code Civil*), a property owner is free to disinherit his or her children and a spouse. The spouse, however, may have a right in most states to "elect" against their deceased spouse's will (a modern version of common law dower and curtesy—

rights that a spouse had in the land of their deceased spouse at common law), and receive a stipulated proportion of the deceased spouse's estate. In some states, those which adhere to the community property regime, earnings are allocated to the non-earning spouse as received, so there is no need to protect a spouse from disinheritance. The spouse has already received a payout.

While disinheritance of children in America is possible, most parents do not in fact desire to exclude their children. Rather, they may wish to regulate the time, and the manner, in which parental wealth passes to the next generation. An example: suppose I have a 21-year-old daughter. Were my wife and I to meet our end today, we would not want her to inherit our property in the equivalent of "fee simple absolute": most parents and estate planners recognize that a young person coming into a tidy sum at a tender age would not be able to manage it effectively. Moreover, should she marry, and like many a contemporary union, should it end in divorce, her ex-husband in some states might be able to claim a share of the property that she inherited from us.

To protect her from herself and a hypothetical rapacious spouse, we might prefer to create a trust, which would grant her only the income interest in the property until she was in her early thirties, and allow her full control over the property at say, 35 (when asked at what age the distribution should occur, my estate planning buddy Ken Weiss remarks tongue-in-check, "I like to get them through their first divorce!"). In my will (or if I prefer during my life), I can create a trust which vests legal title in the trust property (the trust corpus) in a trustee (the manager of the property), and the beneficial ownership of the income in my daughter until she reaches the age of 35. In order to infuse more flexibility into the arrangement, I can give my trustee the "power to invade the corpus" in favor of my daughter for specific purposes, for example, for her further education, or perhaps for a down payment on a house. At age 35, the trust may terminate, and the remaining trust corpus might pass to my daughter (hopefully past her first divorce) subject now to her complete control. If I were wealthier, and with a more complicated family circumstance, then I could create a longer lasting trust instrument. Three generations of Joseph P. Kennedy's descendants (now deceased Mother Rose, sons John, Bobby and Ted—plus their sisters, and the vast array of grandchildren, the most famous being Caroline and John-John) were and continue to be supported by a trust he created in the mid-twentieth century.

Trusts can be easily drafted and administered with little formality. For some property owners, they are not necessary. Wills are easily made by those with less grandiose designs or pocketbooks. States differ in determining the requirements for will validity. In about half the states, a will may be holographic (handwritten and unwitnessed). Other states do not permit holographic wills, and require all wills to be attested, usually witnessed by two competent persons. Still others only require that a will be signed by the will-maker and notarized. Finally, a few states permit electronic wills.

Landlord-Tenant Law

Governed by property law rather than the law of contract, landlord-tenant law has undergone a considerable transformation in the last quarter of the twentieth century. Because the common law did not recognize leaseholds or terms of years as estates in land, regardless of their length, a different body of law developed around this interest in property than the one that governed estates in land.

As it emerged, this body of legal doctrine treated tenants rather harshly. Leases are comprised of mutual promises: the landlord's promise to make the land available to the tenant, usually for a particular time span (though tenancies at will were recognized—ones which could be terminated by either side by giving notice to terminate) in return for the tenant's promise to pay the rent. These two covenants were regarded at law as independent, so, if either side failed in an obligation under the lease, the other party was nevertheless still required to perform and sue for the losses occasioned by the breach. This notion of independent covenants was eventually modified by allowing a landlord to evict a tenant who defaulted on the rent. As we shall see, other more tenant-friendly exceptions have been created.

Moreover, the landlord's obligations to tenant were initially very limited. Absent expressed provisions in the lease, the landlord only covenanted title (that she had the legal power to make leasehold estate), possession (that she did not make a competing estate in the same property), and "quiet enjoyment" (that she would not interfere with the tenant's use and enjoyment of the leasehold). In addition, because the tenant was held to be purchasing the use of the leased premises for a term, the tenant was, absent agreement to the contrary, usually held responsible for repairs to the leased premises during her period of occupation.

Significant alterations have been made in the last quarter-century to this body of law both by statute and the common law. In particular, the landlord's implied covenants have been extended to include one of "habitability" for residential accommodation in most states, and one of "suitability" for commercial premises in some states. Particular remedies for breach of these warranties have been fashioned by the courts and by state legislatures to facilitate enforcement of these warranties by tenants, including the right of tenants to terminate the lease prior to the expiration of the term, to demand a reduction in the rent, or to undertake the repairs or remedy defects and deduct the charges from the rent. Recall that the obligation to repair was allocated to the tenant. Responsibility for repairs now usually lies with the landlord because the average tenant is unlikely able to undertake repairs on his or her own behalf. Allocation of the repair obligation to the landlord (who is in the business of owning leased property) is sensible because the landlord can probably undertake repairs more efficiently than a tenant who seeks only a place of business or residence. Even if the tenant of residential property moves out before the end of the term, the landlord is deemed to have an obligation to mitigate damages, to re-let the premises, and to deduct the payments received from the subsequent tenant from the rent owed by the defaulting tenant.

Intellectual Property

Property law does not merely allocate rights (and limit them) in wild animals or to land, it also governs the way in which ownership attaches to the creative processes, be it in the form of words, inventions, or distinctive marks. Perhaps no aspect of property law has seen as much recent interest as has intellectual property law: copyright, patent, and trademark. Intellectual property law in the United States is largely federal law because the Constitution (Article I, Section 8) grants to Congress the power "To promote the Progress of Science and useful Arts, by securing for limited Times to Authors and Inventors the exclusive Right to their respective Writings and Discoveries."

The clause has been interpreted to grant to Congress the power to confer monopolies upon those who create intellectual property. But it is a power with a limitation: Congressional protection must be calculated to "promote the Progress" in the arts and sciences. In short, the mandate is to further learning and the development of products and processes that are both novel and useful. The protection granted to individuals who produce intellectual property is part of a bargain between the innovator and the public. Authors and inventors have the exclusive right to exploit their work, but only for a finite period, after which the fruits of their labors belong to the public at large; in other words, after the period of monopolistic exploitation, they enter the public domain.

Copyright

Copyright protects "works of authorship," creative expression in almost any medium. While literary works, novels, plays, poems, and even academic writings like this Nutshell, spring immediately to mind, copyright protection has been extended to almost all art forms including the visual, and to recordings, computer programs, and even architectural works. Copyright protects forms of expression; facts or ideas themselves are not protected, but their expression may be, for example, reducing your unwritten lyrics to a recorded studio album. Likewise, copyright extends only to original and creative works. Mere work product is not always protected; for example, the compiling of the phonebook's yellow pages cannot be copyrighted, because it lacks the so-called "creative spark" that is necessary for the expression to promote the useful arts.

Moreover, as technology advances, questions have arisen as to who exactly qualifies as an author; does a work produced by artificial intelligence qualify for federal copyright protection, or is protection limited strictly to works produced by the human mind? *See* Sarah Ligon, *AI Can Create Art, but Can It Own Copyright in It, or Infringe?*, THE LEXIS NEXIS PRACTICE ADVISOR JOURNAL (Jan. 2, 2019), https:// www.lexisnexis.com/lexis-practice-advisor/the-journal/b/lpa/posts/ai-can-create-art-but-can-it-own-copyright-in-it-or-infringe. The Copyright Act itself does not so expressly define "authorship" (but it does suggest that the author be human by defining "anonymous work" as one in which "no natural person is identified as author," and by making reference to an author's widow). 17 U.S.C.S. § 101 (LEXIS through Pub. L. 116–155). The U.S. Copyright Office has also not plainly addressed the issue, but it has rejected as copyrightable "works produced by a . . . mere mechanical process." U.S. COPYRIGHT OFFICE, COMPENDIUM OF U.S. COPYRIGHT OFFICE PRACTICES § 101 (3d ed. 2017).

Copyright right protection commences at creation, and strictly speaking, filing is unnecessary (though it is prudent to do so because it creates a public record of the work and substantiates the claim of copyright). The term was extended by Congress (and the Act upheld by the Supreme Court in *Eldred v. Ashcroft*, 537 U.S. 186 (2003)) to seventy years after the author's death for works produced after 1977. 17 U.S.C.S. § 101. Works created earlier have a ninety-five-year term, as do "works for hire," those which are produced by employees in the course of their duties, with the intellectual property owned by the employer. The author or owner of the copyrighted material has the exclusive right during the period to exploit the work, including the right to reproduce it, make copies, prepare derivative works, or in the case of visual works, perform it or arrange for its display. Further protection is accorded to visual artists under the Visual Artists Rights Act, which accords artists rights similar to (though perhaps not as extensive as) the moral right of artists in European Union law. 17 U.S.C.S. § 106A (LEXIS through Pub. L. 116–155).

Even during the copyright period, the public may make some, albeit limited, use of the copyrighted material. For example, others are permitted "fair use" of the copyrighted material during the copyright period. Though an amorphous concept, first developed by the courts and then codified by Congress, the "fair use" doctrine allows criticism and comment on copyrighted work and permits it to be used for teaching and scholarship. But there are limits to "fair use," particularly with respect to photocopying. Some of the rules may seem somewhat contradictory: while an individual student can reproduce a few pages of copyrighted material on a photocopying machine without violating the author's rights, commercial reproduction for the classroom is not permitted.

Once a copy of copyrighted material is sold, the copy belongs to the purchaser, and the owner of the copyright cannot prevent resale. This "first sale" doctrine is similar to the "exhaustion of rights" doctrine that obtains with respect to patents and trademarks. Copyright holders cannot bar parallel imports. If the copyright holder places the work in circulation in both America and abroad, she cannot prevent imports of the copyrighted work sold by distributors overseas from being sent back into the United States. This is the case even if they were sold abroad at a discount, and the import can be sold at a lower price than copies that were originally destined for the American market.

Both damages and injunctive relief can be sought for copyright infringement. Copyright holders must prove that there is "substantial similarity" between the two works. Though intent to infringe is not necessary, the copyright holder usually must demonstrate access to the copyrighted work. The copyright holder need not show verbatim appropriation of expression. With works of fiction, the reproducing of general themes is not sufficient, but the use of similar plots and characters can constitute infringement. Although the issue of whether the similarity is actionable is one for the finder of fact, recourse to the expert testimony of professionals is useful in order to provide context within the particular "useful art." This is particularly the case where computer programs or algorithms are at issue.

Patent Law

The process for securing a patent is more formal than that for obtaining copyright. American patent law requires the inventor of "any . . . process, machine, manufacture or composition of matter, or any . . . improvement thereof" to file an application with the United States Patent and Trademark Office in Washington, D.C., delivering a description of the patentable invention. The claim must set out the patent's innovative aspect, and each application is examined to determine whether the proposal submitted is both "new and useful." Almost anything, both a process and its result, including certain software programs, may be the subject of a patent. However, business plans and processes are controversial. The Supreme Court has recently addressed the issue of patent eligibility. If the application is "directed to" the law of nature, a natural phenomenon, or abstract idea, then the invention may not be patentable and requires then determining whether the application has a so-called "inventive concept." *See Alice Corp. Pty. v. CLS Bank Int'l*, 573 U.S. 208 (2014), *and Mayo Collaborative Ser. v. Prometheus Lab'y, Inc.*, 566 U.S. 66 (2012).

The requirement of utility is often a straightforward one: the invention must provide some benefit to potential users. The issue of novelty may be more complex; it may arise when an invention is a modification or alteration, an improvement, of an existing patented process or product. Should the examiner reject an application for any reason, the applicant has the right to review. She may respond to reservations raised by the examiner, or amend her application to explain the invention with additional specificity. A second opportunity to submit is permitted, and after that rejection, there is recourse to the Patent Office's Board of Appeals, and ultimately to the Court of Appeals for the Federal Circuit.

American patent law protects the creator—the inventor of the concept—and one may apply for a patent even before having produced a completed working model of a device. Such an inventor has priority, even over another who has subsequently produced a working model, so long as she continues to work diligently on reducing her novel concept to a model.

In common with copyright law, patent law strikes a bargain between the inventor and the public: she has the exclusive right to exploit the invention herself or license others to do so for a term, presently a nonrenewable 20 years (design patents are 15 years), from the date of filing, after which the patent becomes a part of the public domain. Because it can be used by the public after the expiration of the term, the patent application must set out a description of precisely how to make and use the invention, so others may exploit the process or product it after the term expires.

The patent holder may sue others who infringe upon her patent by marketing the process or product without her license. Both injunctive relief and damages can be obtained. Moreover, a patent holder may ask for a declaratory judgment, asserting that a product or process is covered by her patent, and/or that another patent should be re-examined because it was issued for a product or process that was insufficiently distinct from her existing patent. Often this type of dispute results in a cross-licensing agreement between the parties.

Trademark

The final form that intellectual property assumes is trademark. Trademarks are distinctive words or symbols (or combinations thereof) that identify a specific item with a particular producer: the word

"Coca-Cola" or "Apple": Coke's distinctive script or the characteristic partially-munched apple that graces your computer, tablet, and phone. Likewise, a phrase like British Airways' (undocumented and improbable) claim to be "The World's Favorite Airline," can be trademarked. Or even the phrase "Tulane University of Louisiana." And who can forget McDonald's Golden Arches.

The logic that supports trademark law differs from that of copyright and patent. Instead of rewarding those who engage in the creative processes, trademark law seeks to quell consumer confusion regarding the origin of largely comparable products. Consumers often rely on a qualitative association between an item and its producer (Coke makes tasty soft drinks; Apple, user-friendly tech; McDonald's, a good burger). When other makers use similar words or symbols to describe their product, the consumer may be deceived into believing that she is purchasing the preferred product when she is duped into buying one from the inferior competitor. By vesting a specific producer with a property right in a mark, trademark law minimizes the risk of confusion between competing products by making it more difficult for second-rate producers to "pass off" inferior products as those of superior quality.

Of course, there is another side to trademark law. Trademarks are valuable property, and the subject of considerable investment in time and money. Manufacturers spend millions on advertising to create brand recognition, to fashion a close connection between their product and its mark. In the absence of trademark protection, without allowing the producer exclusive rights to exploit the association between product and mark, interlopers (like our interloper Mr. Pierson) rather than those who expend labor (like our huntsman Mr. Post) would profit (or poach) from the investment. The point, I trust is made, even if the analogy is obscure.

The key to triggering all forms of trademark protection is the concept of "distinctiveness." Frequently, trade names are made up and bear little connection with the product; take for example, "Exxon". Alternatively, they may be fanciful: Apple and its MacBook. Trademark protection extends further than names and symbols. "Trade dress," the "clothes" worn by the product, and the image conveyed by its packaging and presentation, as well as displays, may be protected. Likewise, mere descriptive words or clusters of words that acquire a secondary meaning because they are strongly associated in the mind of the public with a particular product designation may be trademarked. Virtually every American child has snacked on zoologically-shaped cookies "dressed" in a red box depicting merry animals in a circus-like fashion called "Animals Crackers," the plain treat remains ready to be devoured.

The extent to which trademarks confer exclusive rights to exploit is generous. After all, the original developer of the fast-food giant just happened to be a chap named McDonald. While it may be easy to comprehend why I cannot dress-up like Ronald McDonald, and peddle burgers, surely there is a fellow out there who has unfortunately been so named by his parent. Ought trademark law permit him to don a clown suit and sell burgers? What about toys? Or computers? Without doubt he can use his own name to sell computers. But while toys are associated with "Happy Meals" (a trademark and trade dress), a ban on Ronald McDonald's toy store probably goes too far in depriving a person of his right to exploit his own name. Fast food, however, is another matter: many gents named Ronald McDonald would have an incentive to form food service corporations to exploit the originator's concept. Perhaps the compromise is to permit surname use but require our competing Ronald to issue a disclaimer.

To play on another mark, trademarks (like diamonds—or so their peddlers would have you believe) are forever. It is only when distinctiveness is lost, or when the owner ceases to use the mark, that the trademark disappears; aspirin, for example, can no longer be trademarked.

Like copyright, trademarks need not be registered to be protected by law (mere "use in commerce" is sufficient), though it is prudent to do so. The United States Trademark Office in Washington, D.C., receives applications and determines whether the mark meets the distinctiveness standard and does not too closely resemble existing registered marks. Applications that are rejected are subject to administrative appeal (Trademark Trial and Appeal Board), and eventually, judicial review (Court of Appeals for the Federal Circuit). If approved, a certificate of registration is produced, the trademark is published in the Official Gazette of the Trademark Office, and after five years of use, the trademark is incontestable for as long as the holder continues its use. Without registration, the common law of trademark only protects the mark in states in which its holder does business. Registration, however, entitles the trademark holder the right to exclude use of the mark by others nationally, preserving the ability to market the product more widely under the trademark. Thus, registration protects future expansion of the marked product into other geographical areas. It also assists in demonstrating that a trademark has achieved a secondary meaning.

Trademark infringement cases can be brought in cases in which a competitor's use of the trademark or a similar mark has created a likelihood of confusion between her product and the mark. The burden of proof can be satisfied by recourse to consumer surveys. Both damages (lost sales) and an injunction against further use of the disputed mark may be obtained.

Conclusion

Like the American law of property, this sketch has ranged widely. Property law creates rights and defines their extent. This process can best be illustrated in the case of intellectual property rights. But property law also creates limitations. In our consideration of real property, we observed that, while the law establishes private rights, much property law (common law, statutory law, and the

Constitution) curbs its exploitation thereof. While nothing may indeed capture our imagination like property, whether our dreams will come true is heavily dependent upon whether they are consistent with a vast body of regulatory restrictions which themselves are delineated by property law.

CHAPTER 9

AMERICA'S BUSINESS IS BUSINESS: AND BUSINESS LAWYERS GOVERN THE SHOW

Introduction

The law governing the formation and regulation of business entities attempts to strike a balance between facilitating economic development and protecting the public's interest in promoting responsible external conduct and internal governance by business entities. Current events (most notably the financial crisis of 2008–09) have suggested that the law has not always achieved these aspirations. High corporate officials now reside in state and federal prisons in significant numbers, convicted of criminal acts which have occasioned staggering financial consequences to innocent employees, shareholders, and perhaps most notably, to the public at large. While the names of Enron, Worldcom, Lehman Brothers, and Bear Stearns, all now defunct, spring to mind, those of an earlier generation may recall the near-economic disaster that was the Savings and Loan crisis of the 1980s. Yet, the last quarter of the twentieth century and the first decade of the current century did not witness the "invention" of business scandals; those of us alive in the eighteenth century (or law students with a historical bent) may recall the South Seas "bubble," an event of striking similar financial consequences for those who invested in shares in the first quarter of the eighteenth century.

Each set of corporate and individual misdeeds is (and continues to be) blamed on a combination of human greed and inadequate governmental oversight of the marketplace. This has therefore spawned regulatory acts to remedy perceived shortcomings, the much-discussed Sarbanes-Oxley Act being perhaps the most recent American foray into remedial legislation. Likewise, the advent of the Consumer Financial Protection Bureau constituted in the Obama Administration proclaims on its website that one of its core missions is: "Rooting out unfair, deceptive, or abusive acts or practices by writing rules, supervising companies, and enforcing the law."[1] Much concern both in America and in the European Union is to make corporate governance more responsive to the needs of shareholders and other stakeholders, including workers and the general public.

But these acts by the government frequently seem to resemble a juridical Maginot line, retroactively focused to fight the last war, rather than proactive, to fight the next. That said, a dose of realism is required: after all, government's resources for oversight of business activities can stretch only so far. Other actors in the business community may also have additional regulatory services to provide. An example is business education which is not immune to criticism of its own. Some perceive that the personal ethical shortcomings of corporate leaders ought to be attributed to an inadequate moral bent, leading several commentators to place the blame on

---

[1]   https://www.consumerfinance.gov/about-us/the-bureau/.

the failure of business schools to infuse more
discussion of ethical values into a curriculum
otherwise laden with practical training in business
combat. Business school professors probably regard
such suggestions from law professors as misplaced,
and perhaps rightly so, lest law professors be held
accountable for the transgressions of wayward
lawyers.

Indeed, lawyers are virtually omnipresent in the
whirlwind of business dealings. They figure
prominently in establishing business entities, and in
assisting in their smooth functioning. Business law
includes a variety of specialties: corporate, securities,
antitrust, and labor and employment law. Each will
be addressed separately, but we start by considering
the various forms that business entities may assume,
through the eyes of a hypothetical young lawyer
embarking upon a "business plan" for her practice.

Forms of Business Entities: "Non-Corporate Forms"

Modern American business entities are organized
in one of four ways: as sole proprietorships; as
partnerships, either general or limited; as
corporations; and more recently, as limited liability
companies. Eventually, the differences (sometimes
mere nuances, but at other times significant
distinctions) between these various forms will be
discussed individually.

But let us begin with a practical exercise. Imagine
yourself as a young lawyer about ready to begin the
practice of law. In selecting the form that your

practice will assume, what factors spring to mind that might govern your choice? Money is always a good place to start; let us suppose that capital must be raised in order to rent office space and furnishings, to purchase some leather-bound books to impress clients, and to employ a clever legal assistant. Income begets taxes; what is the most tax-efficient entity form for your enterprise to assume? But suppose you have sufficient capital, yet wish to limit your financial exposure, lest the law truly not prove to be your calling: do you want to shield some of your personal assets from potential business creditors? Moreover, perhaps you want others to participate in the practice. If you decide to include outside investors in the enterprise, how will the governance of the entity be arranged? Perhaps the simplest form is the best, given your current limited aspirations. But are you certain? As we begin to discuss business entity forms, these issues and others will emerge and be addressed.

Forms of Business Entities: Sole Proprietorship

If ease of formation and management is paramount, then a sole proprietorship may be the business entity form selected. The sole proprietor has complete control over the management of her business, because the business is, in law, not regarded as a legal entity distinct from that of the owner. She is personally responsible for all of the business's debts, and may retain all of the profits for her personal use, or she may determine to plow some or all of her proceeds back into the business's working capital. And why not? In law, it is all her money. Likewise, for tax purposes, the business's expenses, and its permitted tax deductions, are reported on the sole proprietor's individual tax return. Of course, she may hire others to do some or all of the work, including the management of the enterprise, but they are "employees," and not "owners" of the business.

Other advantages include lower transaction costs and no requirement to draft or file documents to start up the enterprise. However, some local ordinances require an individual "doing business" under a particular name to register that fact to avoid misunderstandings with suppliers and customers. This allows the public to know the individual who is the responsible person for a business when its name is not merely that of the proprietor.

Forms of Business Entities: Partnership

Suppose, for any number of reasons, you decide to include another in your enterprise, other than as an employee. To add another person or persons, a partner or partners, requires some type of an agreement or understanding (tacit or otherwise) between or amongst the proposed participants, and one legal form that the parties can select as a partnership. A partnership combines many of the advantages of a sole proprietorship, while adding additional individuals who may contribute capital and expertise to the enterprise. Once again, in common with sole proprietorships, transaction costs are low; there is no need for a written agreement, and no public filing requirements (save as mentioned

above for sole proprietorships) are necessary. With
two major exceptions (considered below), all
partnership terms are subject to negotiation and
agreement between or amongst the partners. An
understanding, either expressed or implied from
conduct, is sufficient to create a partnership, and any
of the gaps in the agreement as to the form and the
operation of the entity are filled in by relevant law,
the Revised Uniform Partnership Act (RUPA), in
force in all states except Louisiana, which has not
adopted the act in its entirety, but provisions of
Louisiana law governing partnership are similar to
that of the RUPA.

Partnerships are created when individuals make
initial contributions to the business in cash or in kind
and agree to share profits. Equality of interests,
while frequent, is not required. The agreement may
provide that the value of each partner's input differ
in form and monetary value. Likewise, partnership
profits are presumed to be distributed equally, but
the agreement can specify a particular percentage
draw. Absent agreement, losses are allocated to the
partners in the same proportion as are profits. Once
again, it is the agreement that controls, and this
flexibility allows maximum tax efficiency, enabling
partners to allocate profits to the partners who pay
taxes at the lowest rates, and assign the losses to
those partners most able to utilize the deductions, if
they so choose. Similarly, management of the
partnership is shared on an equal basis, unless the
agreement provides otherwise by delegating duties
and powers to a single party, or by establishing
weighted voting. But the undertaking of a single

partner acting in the name of the partnership will bind the entity, and the other partners, regardless of whether she has the authority to do so under the partnership agreement.

The two non-waivable provisions of RUPA go to the very essence of a partnership. The first is that partners, like sole proprietors, must remain jointly and severally liable for the partnership's debts. One cannot be a partner without assuming the economic consequences of business failure. The second is that each partner owes to the other partner or partners a fiduciary duty, a bond of loyalty, and must always deal in good faith in areas of partnership concern. Thus, it is axiomatic that a partner must always act in the business's collective best interests, and not for her own individual gain.

Partnerships end when one of the partners dies, voluntarily withdraws from the partnership, or enters into bankruptcy. At the death of a partner, her estate may demand that the partnership be terminated, and its assets distributed. However, the partnership agreement's terms will prevail over this default rule. A partnership agreement may specify that a cash payment be made in lieu of liquidation. Likewise, voluntary withdrawals may be limited by agreement, allowing the remaining partners to continue the business while negotiating a buy-out of the partner's interest. Frequently, there is the need to renegotiate financing provisions, and the withdrawing partner may be liable for losses incurred if she acts inconsistent with the obligations specified in the partnership agreement.

Thus far the partnerships discussed have been general partnerships, with each partner assuming unlimited liability for the partnership debts. Partnership law permits limited partners, sometimes called "silent partners," who risk only the assets that have been committed by them to the partnership: this arrangement bestows upon them a degree of limited liability. They are "silent," because they have no "say" or control over management. In essence, silent partners are tantamount to investors who fund the project. Returning to our law firm hypothetical, a lawyer might band together with others of the same ilk in a general partnership, establish initial contributions, assign management roles, and establish a partnership draw with respect to profits. If, however, it was necessary for someone to put forward additional (or total) financing, one might seek merely a limited partner to bankroll the enterprise. Like a general partnership, taxation of the limited partnership can be allocated in a tax-efficient fashion. Frequently, (and perhaps perversely or at the very least counter-intuitively) limited partners sometimes join precisely because they find the losses often occasioned in a newly-formed business attractive: they can set them off as deductions against their individual income.

A uniform act (Uniform Limited Partnership Act and its 1993 revision) has also been drafted (and widely adopted) to govern limited partnerships. Like most uniform law, it is calculated also to fill in gaps, in this case, those in the partnership agreement. With few exceptions, the law provides default provisions that control issues and situations only in the absence of agreement to the contrary. A limited partnership must have at least one general partner (the individual with unlimited personal liability) and one limited partner, though it may have more partners of each type. Only the general partners can act in the name of the partnership, and they are responsible for its assets and debts. Limited partners must not engage in management, or they may lose their circumscribed status and be treated as a general partner (with attendant consequences to their liability). However, certain types of oversight are permitted to limited partners by statute. Finally, the withdrawal of a limited partner, her death, or her bankruptcy only affects her share, and does not dissolve the partnership.

Forms of Business Entities: Limited Liability Company

The limited partnership resembles closely the newly-sanctioned limited liability company (LLC). It provides a halfway house between the limited partnership form, and the full-blown corporation. Unlike limited partners, LLC members may engage in management. Moreover, no general partner, and therefore no individual with unlimited personal liability, is required to form an LLC. Unlike incorporation articles, the LLC agreement (which must be filed and contains pertinent financial information) need not be any more detailed than a partnership agreement. Nor must the complex forms of corporate governance be implemented when an LLC is created, but as a consequence, shares of the enterprise may not be publicly offered. Members of the LLC can organize both financial and managerial functions as they please. Taxation can be arranged in either the corporate or individual (like a sole proprietorship or partnership) form.

Forms of Business Entities: The Corporation

Given the options discussed above, it is likely that one or the other will suffice in forming your budding law practice. Nevertheless, for more elaborate business plans, the corporate form may be necessary. Corporations are distinct legal entities, and therefore have financial liability independent of their shareholders. Shareholders own shares of the corporation, stakes which represent ownership in the business entity, but they are not personally liable for its debts. Corporations own property and can sue and be sued in their own name and right. Corporate law is largely (though not exclusively) state law, though (as we shall see) many aspects of securities law are federal. The law of the state in which the entity is incorporated controls its governance, even though it may operate its business in other states. Because its law was "corporate friendly" early on, the small state of Delaware, though not without competitors, is the state in which many large corporations are incorporated. By consequence, its common and statute law is the most well-developed corporate law in the United States.

Were you to decide to incorporate your law practice, you would most likely create a closely-held corporation. In such a business entity, the shareholders are usually family members or business associates. Though it is not necessarily the case, the same individuals who own shares in the closely-held corporation will also usually be directors and managers of the business. A drawback to this option is that the creation of a corporation is complex: a full corporate governance structure must be established; directors appointed, shareholder meetings held; and compliance with other statutorily-created obligations to protect the interests of shareholders is required. In return for undertaking these burdens, limited liability is secured. However, with the advent of the LLC, almost all that is essential in terms of business aims can be achieved through its slimmed down requirements: corporate structure is probably unnecessary for your law practice and many other modest enterprises.

However, corporate structure is usually required for more ambitious manufacturing or commercial enterprises. It is difficult to imagine an entity like Microsoft operating other than as a full-blown corporation. But at formation as well, being able to limit liability is important to individuals when undertaking an enterprise in order to establish risk parameters. Consider the possible losses to owners of business entities in, for example, the asbestos industry, if their own personal wealth could also be reached by plaintiffs in addition to business assets. Evolving law has not fully insulated shareholders where fraud or deception can be demonstrated. It is the case, however, that lenders to new business entities often require personal guarantees for loans to establish fledgling corporations. Nevertheless, it is difficult to imagine our modern complex economic order without the legal recognition of the limited liability of corporations.

There are other advantages to the corporate form in addition to its limited liability. Although the management structure of the corporation may not be suitable for small businesses, governance by directors may in fact be an efficient means for running a business. Likewise, a corporation, unlike a partnership, can more easily survive its founders; shares in the corporation can be sold to others. Finally, the corporation is itself a taxable entity. Corporate earnings are taxable to the entity; and in addition, if dividends are paid to shareholders, they pay taxes on the amounts distributed. While this double taxation may seem disadvantageous, qualified dividends (particular type of dividend defined by tax law) in the United States are currently taxed at a lower rate than are earnings or interest on bonds or bank accounts. Moreover, closely held corporations may qualify for "S corporation" status, and have the corporate income taxed as individual income only when they are paid over to the shareholders.

Having parsed the advantages of the corporate form, we may consider its disadvantages. The primary disadvantage of corporations is the requirement that they observe the prescribed intricacies of corporate governance. To that, however, one must add complexity of formation: specific steps must be undertaken to establish a corporation. Articles of incorporation need to be filed in the state where the corporation resides, and a fee must be paid. A certificate of incorporation will be produced by the appropriate governmental office. This document includes the names and addresses of the incorporators, and the number of shares to be issued. While the articles may have some rules governing the corporation, such matters are more usually articulated in bylaws that must be drafted and adopted by the directors. Though the fees charged by the state are minimal, lawyers (and therefore their attendant billings) are generally required to set up a corporation. Moreover, while the dealings of the other entity forms are not public record, those of a corporation are. Privacy is therefore sacrificed when an incorporation occurs.

Apart from satisfying these creation formalities, the corporation is required to fashion an organizational structure with some complexity. Initially, when incorporation documents are filed, directors are appointed to manage the corporation until the first meeting of shareholders, at which time elections of directors by all the shareholders are held. Directors must meet at regular intervals and act collectively to create a business plan and to manage corporate affairs. Strategic policy issues are addressed at such meetings, officers appointed and removed, and dividends authorized. Directors owe a fiduciary duty to the corporation; they must act in an informed manner, in good faith, and in what they believe is in the best interests of the corporation. Another way of framing their obligation is to require them to act in the way in which a prudent person would deal with her own business affairs. Confidentiality must be maintained, and using information gained from their corporate position for personal gain is prohibited.

Breach of these duties may give rise to personal liability; the corporation and/or its shareholders may bring a cause of action against directors arising from misfeasance. The so-called "business judgment rule" provides a benchmark for determining whether the acts of directors may give rise to personal liability. When confronted with a claim by a shareholder that arises from a decision made by the directors, the court will not second guess the directors' decision and substitute its own judgment for that of the directors. If the decision was rational, and the course of action undertaken by them legal, the court will presume that the decision was taken in the best interests of the corporation, and will not sanction the directors for its failure, and for its consequential losses.

This fiduciary duty, in both directors and their selected officers, is owed to the shareholders, the individuals who in reality "own" the corporation. The rights of shareholders are governed by law, by a corporation's articles of incorporation, and through its bylaws. While in theory their rights are extensive, in practice, a shareholder's rights are like shareholder liability, limited. Shareholders elect directors at meetings that must be held at prescribed intervals, usually at least annually. If a shareholder cannot attend the meeting, she is entitled to vote by proxy: a contrivance to authorize another to exercise her voting rights. However, most shareholders do not have either the time or inclination to attend the general meeting, so they usually either vote by proxy (resolving issues placed before them by the directors in accordance with management's advice) or do not vote at all. Likewise, while the annual meeting also allows the directors the opportunity to bring matters to the attention of shareholders, and provide a forum for shareholder action, the meetings are usually sparsely attended. The Securities Exchange Act of 1934 (5 U.S.C. § 78a *et seq.*), New Deal legislation, and regulations promulgated pursuant thereto, have attempted to facilitate corporate democracy. However, for the most part, shareholders in large corporations are passive investors, individuals who have selected a particular corporation to invest in because they believe management has a profitable business plan in place. Very few are either willing, or able, to take an active interest in corporate affairs. One possible exception to shareholder quiescence is when fundamental changes to the corporation are proposed, such as a merger or an acquisition. At times, so-called activist investors may take significant positions in corporations in order to elect directors sympathetic to their view of the corporation's future and therefore effect change in management style. Activist investors are particularly interested in corporations which seem to be underperforming in their market sector.

Disgruntled shareholders may sue to enforce obligations that directors owe to the corporation. A useful tool to sanction managerial misconduct is the shareholder "derivative suit." A corporation may sue its directors for malfeasance, but it is unlikely to do so for the very simple reason that the directors are usually (but not always) the errant management. In a shareholder derivative suit, a single shareholder or group may sue the directors who have breached duties owed to the corporation. They are called "derivative suits" because the shareholders are bringing their action on behalf of the corporation; their right of action is derived from their share ownership, undertaken in theory because the corporation has not acted against its errant director or directors. Corporate law does not encourage such suits. Limitations are put in place to discourage such lawsuits against corporations by shareholders aiming to make certain that the right is not abused by the disgruntled. For example, to have standing to bring suit, the shareholder must have owned shares at the time that the directors' alleged breach of fiduciary duty occurred. Moreover, directors usually must be informed of the claim in advance of the action and be given the opportunity to take steps to remedy their alleged default, before the shareholder can have redress in court.

One exception to the rule of limited liability for corporations is so-called "corporate veil" theory of management. It is applied in situations in which acts by the directors and/or shareholders do not respect the corporate form of the business enterprise, and/or when they act as if the business was a partnership or sole proprietorship, rather than a corporation. The circumstances in which courts will so conclude vary by jurisdiction. Unlike most issues of corporate governance, where the law of the state of incorporation applies, it is the usually the law of the state in which the corporation operates that controls whether the act is questionable.

Let us begin to consider this doctrine with a straightforward scenario, not uncommon in closely-held corporations. Suppose, for example, the manager and primary shareholder of a closely-held corporation purchases building materials for her own home using a corporate purchase order. The corporation becomes insolvent, and the vendor is unable to have its claim for goods delivered satisfied out of the assets of the corporation. The vendor may proceed against the manager personally to collect the outstanding debt, thus "piercing the corporate veil." Having herself not respected the corporate form by co-mingling personal and corporate assets, the corporate actor cannot claim the benefits of limited liability. Another situation in addition to commingling in which the "corporate veil" is pierced is when the business entity does not observe the technical requirements of the corporate form: for example, if, after incorporation, the corporation fails to elect directors or hold shareholder meetings. In this case, the corporation will cease to be treated in law as a corporation, but rather as a partnership. Finally, individual shareholders of a woefully undercapitalized closely-held corporation may, in some jurisdictions, be held liable personally for debts, especially where the creditors are not banks or other financial institutions. Likewise, the courts may treat shareholders in such closely-held corporations liable for tort injuries for which the corporation may be liable.

Another particular circumstance in which the "corporate veil," may be pierced that also applies to public corporations may be offered. It is where a corporation is established by an existing corporation, and the parent corporation completely controls the business dealings of the other entity, the so-called "dummy" corporation; the parent corporation will be responsible for the liabilities of its progeny.

Corporate Equity and Debt

Thus far the issues addressing the various forms of business entities have been considered. Attention may now turn to some particular matters that concern corporations. The first is the distinction between debt and equity in a corporation. As we have seen, corporations are owned by their shareholders. Initial investors have paid money for a stake in the corporation. These are called "shares," and are of two types: common and preferred. Both are, in the case of public corporations, freely transferable (that is to say, they may change hands without the need for corporate approval) in the marketplace. Holders of common stock may vote for directors, and in such other matters that the directors place before shareholders. In addition, they also receive dividends declared by the directors, and they will receive a share of corporate assets upon dissolution of the corporation, both on a *pro rata* basis. Absent dissolution, the value of shares in a public corporation is controlled by the market, and share price is largely driven by calculations of future profits.

Preferred shares are also proportional ownership rights in the corporation. They are "preferred," however, because holders receive priority over common shareholders when dividends are calculated; declared dividends, some notional share of corporate profits, are paid first to preferred shareholders. Likewise, at liquidation, preferred shareholders receive the value of their shares before common stockholders. Their priority may result in some compensation being received by the preferred shareholders if a corporation enters bankruptcy, while common shareholders may walk away from an insolvency empty-handed.

In addition to the sale of initial shares in the corporation, working capital may be raised by issuing bonds. Bonds are similar to individual personal debt, unconditional promises to pay the principal sum borrowed on a given due date and are generally unsecured. Usually, the bondholder will receive periodic payments, though sometimes the interest payments are made at the end of the term. Bondholders own no part of the corporation, receive no dividends, and have no voting rights. The value of the bond may fluctuate in the market, when corporate interest rates move up or down during the term, or when estimates of the ability of the corporation to repay the debt are reconsidered by bond rating agencies.

Corporate Mergers and Other Acquisitions

Mergers are a way of life in the modern corporate world. In a merger, one corporation is devoured by another; all of the outstanding shares of the target corporation are obtained by the acquiring corporation, the "raider." If the directors favor the combination, they will call a special shareholder meeting, and put the merger to a vote. If the outcome is favorable, the merger proceeds, and the shareholders receive either shares in the acquiring corporation or secure a cash payment for their shares. All of the assets and liabilities of the target are assumed by the acquiring corporation.

While shareholder approval is required for a merger, the agreement of management is not necessary. The raider may merely purchase sufficient shares on the market to establish a controlling interest, or else it may make a tender offer directly to shareholders, asking them to sell their shares to it at a stipulated price—the so-called "hostile" takeover. Usually, the share price is set at a premium to the market price encouraging shareholders to part with their interest in the corporation. Some transparency in the process of an acquisition is required by law. When a market participant accumulates more than 5% of the stock of a publicly-traded corporation, that fact must be disclosed to the Securities and Exchange Commission (SEC), pursuant to the Williams Act of 1968 (Public Law 90–439) which amended sections of the aforementioned Securities Exchange Act of 1934. Likewise, a tender offer to purchase at least 5% requires a disclosure of the fact and purpose of the proposed offer—generally, but not always, as the prelude to a hostile takeover.

Management may be unwilling to recommend a merger for many reasons, not least of all, because the target corporation will probably not require two sets of managers; target corporation managers may lose their positions. Various strategies by directors have been developed to oppose mergers. Directors must, however, justify their defensive actions. They cannot simply act to save their jobs without regard for the best interests of the corporation, or shareholder profit. The first is to persuade the shareholders that a merger is not in their financial best interest by suggesting that the corporation and its shares are more valuable than the price set by the raider in its tender offer. Second, lawsuits can be initiated to challenge the raider's conduct, alleging a variety of issues. For example, that the merger may raise some antitrust concerns, or that the acquiring corporation did not follow the procedural niceties of acquisition established by Securities and Exchange Commission (SEC) rules. Further, more elaborate strategies, for example like finding a "white knight," a better suitor (at least in the minds of the directors), or taking a "poison pill", pursuing a strategy that devalues the target corporation, at least so far as the raider is concerned, may be undertaken. Finally, the directors of the target corporation can attempt to buy its own outstanding shares at a higher price than the tender offer, thereby disinclining shareholders to sell their own shares to the raider. Or the directors can come to some agreement with the raider by paying so-called "greenmail," purchases of the raider's own stock at an inflated price. Because some of these tactics are not in the shareholder's best interests, some machinations by the directors of the target corporation may give rise to questions of breaches of fiduciary duty by management and can engender shareholder suits against the directors for damages.

As discussed above, the directors of a target corporation have many tools at their disposal in order to defend the corporation from a take-over attempt. But directors are not free to wield completely unbridled power to defend the corporation. Because of their unique standing within the corporation, as employees and decision-makers, there are certain checks on their power, that must be adhered to, in order to protect the shareholders. Suppose, for instance, that the offer to take-over the company represents a significant premium over what the company is worth. For arguments sake, let us imagine an offer worth 4 times the value of the company. This would surely be advantageous for the shareholders and be in their best interests to accept. On the contrary, the directors may not find the offer in their interest; they may all be out of jobs should the merger occur. Thus, in order to justify the defensive measures taken by the directors, they must first satisfy a two-part test. First, while taking into account other constituencies, such as customers, workers, or the public, the directors must have reasonable grounds for believing that a threat to corporate policy or effectiveness exists. Second, the defensive measure taken must be reasonably proportional to that threat. *Unocal Corp. v. Mesa Petroleum Co.*, 493 A.2d 946 (Del. 1985).

Yet, our discussion does not end here, as even astute directors and herculean defensive measures may not be enough to stave off the take-over. At some point in the midst of this "battle," it may become inevitable that the target corporation will be taken-over. At that time, the duties owed by the directors to the corporation shift, from preservation of the company, to maximizing shareholder profits. *Revlon, Inc. v. MacAndrews & Forbes Holdings, Inc.*, 506 A.2d 173 (Del. 1986). The new focus becomes the price of the offer, and the quality of the assets offered to shareholders (cash rather than junk bonds, etc.). The directors can no longer take other constituencies into consideration and become akin to auctioneers seeking the highest value for the shareholders.

Not all combinations between business entities are mergers. Sometimes a corporation may purchase the assets of another but continue to operate the target corporation as a separate entity. This may be undertaken in order to acquire the target's assets or to take on the other corporation's particular product line, without also becoming responsible for all of the target's corporate liabilities. Likewise, part of a corporation may be "spun-off" into another separate corporation. Existing shareholders are given separate shares of the newly-formed entity. Finally, a corporation may decide (rarely in the case of public corporations though not so with closely-held corporations) to discontinue operations. Voluntary terminations are rare, and sometimes arise when the directors are deadlocked on a critical issue. Sometimes court intervention is necessary in such cases to protect the interests of the shareholders. Acquisitions, spin-offs, and terminations all require the assent of the shareholders.

Securities Regulation

Because so much of America's economy is driven by corporate entities, and vast amounts of personal wealth are held in the form of corporate securities, governmental regulation of the issuance and trading of corporate shares is essential to the nation's fiscal well-being. Securities law, both state and federal, can be summed up (if such recklessness is necessary) in a single word: "transparency." In order for investors to make informed decisions on whether, and with whom, to invest in the stock market, both individual and institutional financial players must have accurate information about a corporation's business affairs, and that information must be available to all participants on an equal basis. Thus, securities law seeks to make certain that corporations neither conceal "bad" news concerning their business prospects from the public, nor misstate their balance sheets. It also precludes individuals with access to sensitive information (news that might affect the value of the stock one way or the other) from dealing in shares on the basis of that data, so-called "insider trading."

American securities regulation law was promulgated in the aftermath of the devastating stock market crash of 1929, and the subsequent onset of the Great Depression. Two crucial statutes were enacted: first, the Securities Act of 1933 (15 U.S.C. § 77(a) *et seq.*) which sets requirements for the issuance of new securities; and second, the Securities Exchange Act of 1934 (5 U.S.C. § 78a *et seq.*), which governs securities already in the marketplace. Both laws require corporations to disclose relevant information in a formal fashion in order to avoid possible misapprehensions based upon statements made by other, possibly less-informed, sources. Another way of saying the same thing less delicately is merely to note that by requiring that information be released in a specific form directly from the corporation, corporate misrepresentation or "spin" may be minimized or entirely avoided.

Pursuant to the Securities Act of 1933 new issuances of securities, by *issuers, underwriters, and dealers* must be accompanied by a registration statement with a formal prospectus containing a variety of pertinent information, including the corporation's business operations, its financial circumstances, and the owners and distributors of the securities. These offerings are the way in which securities first come into the hands of investors. Ongoing trading in securities by the *general public* is exempt from the act, allowing the public to trade in securities without incurring liability under the act. Likewise, limited offerings to so-called "accredited investors," those exclusively directed to the more sophisticated institutional investors, are not considered public offerings, and are therefore exempt from the Securities Act. The Securities Exchange Act of 1934 governs the financial markets by regulating exchanges, brokers, and dealers, through the Securities and Exchange Commission (hereafter SEC). In addition, publicly-traded companies are required to disclose, in an ongoing fashion, pertinent information in order to permit investors to make informed investment decisions. On a quarterly basis, corporations are required to issue a report which discloses relevant information about their business dealings, including a detailed (and accurate) financial statement. Interim reports are required in certain circumstances, particularly when the company acquires or disposes of a significant quantity of their assets, or becomes insolvent. It also sets standards for corporate responsibility to its shareholders in communicating information with particular respect to issues upon which a vote is solicited. As noted above, proxies can be used by shareholders not present at a meeting to vote on a variety of questions placed before shareholders by management, and the law requires that "proxy statements" be filed with the SEC, and posted in advance to shareholders in order to inform them of the issues that will be placed before them by the directors at the shareholder meeting.

This summary treatment of securities law should highlight the important role of the SEC in monitoring the conduct of publicly-held corporations. The SEC is charged with both rule-making and law-enforcement authority. Its rule-making must be pursuant to the powers granted to it under federal law, and the rules issued by the SEC, subject to a notice and comment period, have the force of law.

Enforcement by the SEC works as follows. The five Commissioners of the SEC bring cases of non-compliance with securities law in the form of a complaint to an administrative law judge. Appeals from her decision may be taken to the Commission sitting as a tribunal, and then to the federal court of appeals for the circuit in which the complaint was lodged. Alternatively, the SEC may proceed as a plaintiff in the appropriate federal district court seeking an injunction, damages, or both.

No discussion of corporate securities law can be complete without mention of the ominous "Rule 10b–5," a regulation issued by the SEC to implement the 1934 Act. In substance it makes unlawful ". . . To use or employ, in connection with the purchase or sale of any security registered on a national securities exchange or any security not so registered, any manipulative or deceptive device or contrivance. . ." Rule 10b–5, then, is an anti-fraud provision, sanctioning those who make misrepresentations, and allowing recovery by those who have thereby suffered economic loss therefrom. Both the SEC and an injured investor can bring an action under Rule 10b–5, and its analogue dealing with proxy issues, Rule 14(a). In either case, the plaintiff must prove the elements of fraud at common law: a duty; a breach of duty; reliance; causation; and damages. Moreover, *scienter* must be shown: bad faith, rather than mere negligence, must be proved.

Considering each element of fraud separately, first, the duty: the fraudulent statement or omission (where a duty to disclose was breached) must be material. Somehow the representation or failure to inform must be regarded by investors as a reasonably significant piece of information used by them in reaching an investment decision. The alleged fraudulent statements may be of opinion, as well as fact, if the opinion refers to material facts. The interpretation of the term "material" is beyond doubt malleable, especially with respect to non-disclosure of information. Sometimes, confidentiality is required to manage a business efficiently, and business judgment employed to limit the disclosure of information is essential to efficient corporate operations. For example, at what point in time should a real estate development corporation publicly announce plans for a shopping center? Disclosure at an early stage might drive up land prices in the area, rendering the project more costly. If the directors decide to keep the project under wraps, and a shareholder determines to sell before the announcement at a lower price than she would have received after the announcement, can she sue under Rule 10b–5? Because of this, businesses commonly use what are called "forward-looking statements." These are statements of mere speculation; however, they can be misleading and be mistaken for factual representations. To protect itself, a business will make statements with terms such as, "believe," "expect," "predict," "plan," "anticipate," or a wide variety of other similar phrases that express the businesses intentions without expressing concrete facts.

It is not always a simple matter for plaintiffs to prevail under these rules. Reliance and causation are sometimes tricky to prove, given the standards that have evolved. The plaintiff must demonstrate that she would not have gone ahead with the purchase (or sale) of the securities in question, but for the false statement or omission. This requirement makes class action suits problematic (though they potentially may be brought leading to billion-dollar judgments, arguably deterring non-American companies from entering the American market) because each party must demonstrate her reliance. That the misrepresentation was merely a contributing factor to the purchase or sale of the security may be insufficient. Likewise, the misrepresentation alleged must be the source of the loss, so that if the corporation misstated (or perhaps less likely omitted stating a relevant fact/s) some element of its business, and upon its revelation the stock thereafter "tanked," plaintiff could recover. However, if the loss was occasioned because the market in general declined, or some other collateral event occurred (such as the market downturn due to the COVID-19 pandemic) affecting share price, causation would not be proved.

Another area of Rule 10b–5 securities law is its penalties for insider trading. These cases arise when a corporate director (or indeed any officer, lawyer, or other individual privy to confidential corporate information, such as the proverbial printer, *Chiarella v. United States*, 445 U.S. 222 (1980), who generates the entity's financial statements) trades on the basis of information to which the public does not have access at a given time. Access to confidential information creates a duty in corporate officers not to trade their stock in the corporation (or even in others with which their corporation are involved in deals) at certain times without disclosure. And full disclosure is not always possible for directors: the officer may be barred from disclosing the inside information by state law, except at particular times and in a specified fashion. Thus, Rule 10b–5 seems to give rise to an obligation by corporate directors and others who have been "tipped" (received the non-public information) not to trade, and one which may be breached. The person who knows of the information and shares it (the "tipper") is liable if he shared information with another, (the "tippee") in situations where tipper received a *quid pro quo* or the tipper furnished the information gratuitously with the intent to benefit the tippee. The tippee, on the other hand, is only liable if she knew the communication passed was "inside information."

But to whom is the duty owed; who can bring the cause of action—who has lost because of the "inside trade"? Arguably, the purchaser of stock from the insider, but given the nature of the stock market, how can an individual prove that she was the one who actually purchased from a person with inside information, the individual who was under a duty not to trade? Perhaps even more difficult to sustain, is for a seller to demonstrate they sold to someone with inside information, or that they were damaged by a sale through an offer which they extended to any willing buyer. For this reason, insider trading cases are generally brought by the government, rather than by individual investors, though class actions are not uncommon.

Further complicating the issue is determining exactly who is liable, and when liability attaches. First, we start with the "tipper," the individual with the insider information. Next, is the "tippee," the individual receiving the insider information from the tipper. As discussed above, the tipper, with access to confidential information, has a duty to not trade on that information. But what happens when that individual does not trade on the information, but instead, shares it with someone else? It is generally accepted that a tipper breaches his duty when he discloses confidential information for his own personal benefit. This personal benefit can be direct or indirect and can be found even in the reputational benefit he might gain by sharing the information. But what of the tippee? Are they free to trade on this information, with liability only attaching to the tipper? Not necessarily. A tippee "inherits" the duty to not trade on confidential information, and would be held liable if they did so, when they knew (or should have known) that the tipper breached his duty by disclosing the information.

Thus, American securities law attempts to create a level playing field for investors, as well as to encourage the free flow of information, transparency, in corporate affairs. Supporting the policy is the notion, naïve or otherwise, that the informed investor is more likely to make the correct decision, taking into account her individual financial circumstances. With the internationalization of financial markets, securities regulation has become a global, rather than a national matter, and will require transnational cooperation to provide market participants with sufficient protection.

Antitrust Law

All business entities, foreign or domestic, operating in the United States are subject to American antitrust laws. Indeed, antitrust enforcement is an area of business law which has seen some degree of transnational cooperation, if not significant co-ordination. The antitrust authorities of the two largest western economies, the Federal Trade Commission (hereafter FTC) in the United States and the European Union's Directorate General for Competition, often find themselves investigating the same mergers—though not always with the same results (as General Electric and Honeywell discovered in 2001)—and similar business practices, as Google is fast learning.

But not always. In April 2012, the Commission cleared, with conditions, the proposed acquisition of Synthes Inc. by Johnson & Johnson, both US companies active in the area of orthopedic medical devices. The Commission's investigation confirmed that, subject to the divestment of Johnson & Johnson's trauma business, the merged entity would continue to face competition from a number of other strong competitors and that customers would still have sufficient alternative suppliers in all of the markets concerned. The FTC concurred.

In the modern global-business world, the reach of antitrust law is thus inherently extraterritorial; it draws attention to business practices contrived and/or undertaken, either within or outside national borders, ones that they reckon may have deleterious effects upon national economies.

The debate on the goals that American antitrust law should seek to accomplish is heavily influenced by various schools of economic thought. But enforcement is largely a creature of politics. Although private individuals may bring actions under antitrust law, most actions (given their inherent complexity) are commenced by the federal government. So the way in which the philosophical wind is blowing in the White House is crucial to the application of antitrust law. During the free-market heyday of the Reagan Administration, the antitrust views of the more conservative, neo-classical economists were in the ascendancy. Their watchword was "efficiency." The goal of competition between business entities, they held, should be limited to the efficient production of goods and the provision of services for consumers. With a wide range of products and service providers available to choose from, the consumer should be free to select amongst the lot, taking into account her needs and her individual and personal estimations of quality and price. In response to consumer choice, the market then would operate to "correct" supply: there are winners and losers in the arduous race to produce and sell products and services to the public! Thus, consumer preference dictates production for the marketplace. The role of government should be as an umpire; it is limited to ensuring that competitors play fair.

The liberal economic thought employed by the Clinton Administration imagined a more far-reaching aspiration for antitrust law and policy. According to its view, there is some greater societal objective to antitrust law. Government should be proactive, as well as reactive. The market power of large competitors should be monitored, and if need be, regulated; entry barriers to the market removed; and active promotion of consumer choice undertaken. With the second Bush Administration, the pendulum swung back toward the *laissez faire* "Reaganomics" mode.

In his campaign for president in 2008, Candidate Obama chided the Bush Administration for its causal attitude towards antitrust, vowing more rigorous enforcement. Yet the numbers suggest continuity rather than change. The Obama administration started off its antitrust enforcement only mildly more aggressively. In 2009, the Antitrust Division of the Justice Department (hereafter DOJ) pursued 74 antitrust investigations, about 10% more than the previous year. As a percentage of merger filings, merger investigations increased to approximately 10% in 2009, from less than 5% in 2008. His second term saw more mergers thwarted, but the fact is that more were proposed. As a proportion of denials to proposals, the Clinton Administration was probably tougher than the Obama regime. Perhaps this is because the Obama era antitrust enforcement was largely driven by perceived consumer protection concerns.

Not surprisingly, the Trump Administration is more friendly to mergers as the recent approval of the T-Mobile-Sprint merger suggests. The Court of

Appeals for the District of Columbia Circuit upheld the district court's decision against the AT&T/Time Warner transaction, finding that the DOJ did not meet its burden of proof in challenging the deal. The FTC itself approved two vertical transactions with Democratic Commissioners arguing that the remedies did not adequately address the anti-competitive aspects of the transactions. These cases point to divergence among the FTC Commissioners on the proper approach to vertical merger enforcement further complicating the vertical merger landscape under the Trump Administration. However, there is some hope that merging parties will receive some clarification on vertical merger enforcement because Justice Department is working with the FTC to update its guidelines.

By way of contrast, in the first quarter of 2019, the European Commission was more interventionist. It cleared six mergers in control proceedings in which remedies were required, including acquisition by global players such as BASF and Spirit. The Commission also prohibited two mergers, which is highly unusual, stating that the proposed remedies were not sufficient or too complex to address its competition concerns. One was particularly controversial: the Siemens-Alstom railway products transaction. Although the German and French governments placed political pressure on the Commission to approve it, the transaction was blocked reaffirming that industrial policy objectives (European joint action to prevent Chinese dominance in an industry) have no role to play when it comes to applying EU merger control rules.

Back to this side of the pond, it is interesting to note that the raw material with which each shade of the political spectrum, Republican or Democratic, has to work is similar—the now 13 decades old (though with some more modern accretions) Sherman Act of 1890 15 U.S.C. §§ 1–38, as well as the Clayton Act of 1914 15 U.S.C. §§ 12–27, 29 U.S.C. §§ 52–53, and the Federal Trade Commission (FTC) Act of 1914 15 U.S.C. §§ 21–58. The Sherman Act has two sections: the first prohibits joint action by economic actors "in restraint of trade;" and the second, regulates the conduct of monopolies. The Clayton Act more directly addresses mergers, as well as other specific business practices that may be anti-competitive, such as price discrimination, price-fixing, and tying. The FTC Act sets up a regulatory commission, one with a mandate to seek out potential instances of unfair competition.

Let us begin the study of American antitrust law by considering the first section of the Sherman Act. The threshold issue that a party must prove to prevail in an enforcement action, be it the government or a private plaintiff, is an agreement (or a tacit understanding) between separate business entities. If the requisite concord can be proved, the court must then determine whether the joint action contemplated is "per se" unlawful, or whether it should be analyzed within the so-called "rule of reason." The determination is crucial for the parties; the "per se" rule does not allow the parties to explain and defend their agreement; it is deemed unlawful. However, those agreements scrutinized under the "rule of reason" permit the actors to use the circumstances surrounding the agreement to argue that its anti-competitive aspect is a reasonable one (or that the agreement has pro-competitive effects that outweigh the anti-competitive ones producing overall advantages to the consumer), and therefore the agreement does not violate the Act. Under which track (per se/rule of reason) an agreement will be analyzed depends upon what the businesses have agreed. Likewise, the allocation of types of agreements to each track may change. Recently, the application of the rule of reason in the Supreme Court has been in the ascendency as more types of agreements have been subjected to the rule of reason. In a recent case, retail price maintenance (manufacturer mandates to its distributors not to sell below a fixed minimum price), hitherto considered a per se violation was subjected to the rule of reason. Justice Kennedy set out a complex economic test to guide business entities and courts as to which factors should be considered in determining whether retail price maintenance should be permitted. *Leegin Creative Leather Prod., Inc. v. PSKS, Inc.*, 551 U.S. 877 (2007).

Horizontal agreements, those between entities at the same level of the production and distribution chain (for example, between or amongst manufacturers, or between and amongst distributors, or between or amongst retailers), are more likely to be considered "per se" violations of Section 1 of the Sherman Act than are vertical ones (those between business entities at different levels of the production and distribution ladder). This is particularly the case with agreements to divide markets geographically or by product line, and/or exclude parties from dealings with non-parties to the agreement (boycotts). Yet, examples of such conduct can be cited in which courts have permitted "rule of reason" analysis, allowing a discussion of justification for the allegedly anti-competitive agreement. For example, with respect to price-fixing, the court has permitted associations of authors, composers, and publishers of music to charge a fixed "performance royalty." The court found that the alternative would be unauthorized copying, and that "efficiencies" produced in collection and monitoring benefited the consumer; under the system in place, artists would more likely agree to have their work marketed than would be the case if there was no fixed royalty assessment and collection scheme. *United States v. Am. Soc. of Composers, Authors, Publishers*, 627 F.3d 64 (2d Cir. 2010). Television broadcast of intercollegiate athletics provides an example of "rule of reason" analysis in a boycott situation. The National Collegiate Athletic Association (NCAA) is an organization comprised of most American universities, and it negotiates television contracts with broadcasters for the television transmission of intercollegiate sports. When some member universities threatened to deal directly (and therefore separately) with broadcasters to televise their games, the NCCA threatened to exclude their teams from NCAA play. The court conceded that the NCAA's boycott might be reasonable, but when it weighed pro-competitive and anti-competitive effects, it found that the boycott violated the Sherman Act: the freedom to compete by allowing separate deals would provide more games on television, and therefore more choice for the consumer, and that ultimately college sports would not be greatly harmed by their action. *Nat'l Collegiate Athletic Ass'n v. Bd. of Regents of Univ. of Oklahoma*, 468 U.S. 85 (1984). Falling under the "rule of reason" rather than the "per se" analysis does not always result in a judgment in favor of an agreement, horizontal or vertical. Rather, it merely allows the defendants their day in court to raise economic justifications for their conduct.

As previously stated, vertical agreements are those between business entities at different levels of the production and distribution ladder. Frequently, a manufacturer of a product decides that the more efficient way of marketing a product or service to the consumer is to use independent distributors and retailers rather than to create their own sales network. These distribution agreements may fall afoul of Section 1 of the Sherman Act. After all, they are agreements, and they restrain trade: those distributors and retailers not selected will be unable to sell the particular product or service. Courts have been willing to uphold these vertical agreements, because in their view (and that of most economists), they provide the manufacturer with an efficient distribution system for its product, and the scheme may also benefit the consumer by creating a network of informed distributors and/or retailers. So long as there is sufficient inter-brand competition, these agreements, though they limit the number of competing distributors or retailers, should not cause an increase in prices.

Thus, certain provisions within vertical agreements are permitted if reasonable. For example, as noted above, the Supreme Court in *Leegin,* allowed retail price maintenance by the manufacturer if the practice provides a benefit to the consumer. Agreements bestowing territorial exclusivity are also subject to a "rule of reason" test. Manufacturers frequently like to carve out distribution regions, and would prefer to avoid cross-boundary competition between individual members of their network in separate regions. For example, prestige car manufacturers often designate a single distributor-dealer in a metropolitan area. Manufacturer refuses to allow other dealers to sell their marque. At first, such territorial restrictions were held to be "per se" violations of the Sherman Act. But the court has now been persuaded that the manufacturer ought to be able to assert the pro-competitive argument, and they are now analyzed under the "rule of reason." Why? The consumer benefits from a high service distributor who can make investments in marketing the car and provide after-sale service if the dealer does not have intra-brand competition from another outlet. While a manufacturer will agree that the dealer will have no other competitor in his district, absolute territorial exclusivity is not permitted. Passive sales to customers outside the region cannot be permitted. Assume Tesla has dealers in New Orleans and Houston, each with territorial exclusivity in their distribution agreements. So, living in New Orleans and desirous of a Tesla, I can call a dealer in Houston and buy a car from Tesla of Houston. What the

Houston dealer cannot do is to actively solicit sales in the New Orleans market.

Finally, vertical agreements frequently include exclusive dealing and tying provisions. Exclusive dealing agreements are those in which a distributor or retailer agrees not to sell the competing products of other manufacturers. These provisions in distribution agreements are analyzed under the "rule of reason" test. So long as other sellers are not foreclosed from a market, that is if competitors are able to secure other dealers to distribute their own products, an exclusive dealing agreement may be reasonable. Inter-brand competition compensates from the loss of intra-brand competition.

Tying is another matter. Such agreements are generally regarded as "per se" unreasonable. In "tying," a dealer is required to buy other products from the manufacturer or distributor in order to have access to the product it wishes to handle. Suppose desirous to distribute Vitamin K, a profitable tablet and one in which the manufacturer has a near-monopoly over production, the manufacturer agrees to supply Vitamin K to me on condition that I also order the same quantity of Vitamin C, easy to obtain from other manufacturers, and at a more competitive price. Tying, it is believed, almost invariably leads to market foreclosure, and may be an example of abuse of market power on the part of the supplier. After all, it is able to require purchase of both products, even though the distributor or dealer wants only one.

The second section of the Sherman Act is calculated to protect against the market power of monopolies. Arguably, monopolies are not efficient, because, in the absence of serious competitors, monopolists can set product production numbers to suit their own interests, and charge the consumer such prices as they please. Yet, it has been suggested by some economists that monopolies are efficient; after all, corporations generally get to be monopolies largely because they produce products that the consumer wants to purchase at prices that they are willing and able to pay. Why punish, as the analogy goes, the winner of the race? So long as others can come into the market, if entry barriers are not erected by the individual monopoly, the consumer is protected from high prices and shoddy products.

This argument has yet to prevail, at least in American antitrust jurisprudence. If a business entity has market power, it may be regarded as a monopoly. In order to determine market power, the relevant market for an individual product must be calculated; and how the market is defined may determine whether a particular product has sufficient market power. Should, for example, the relevant market for Coca-Cola be cola drinks, or all soft drinks; Coke would prefer the latter because its market share is higher in the former than it is in the latter. Thus, it may have a monopoly in cola drinks, but not in the market for all soft drinks.

The relevant market for an individual product may be defined in a variety of ways. One way is through modeling "cross-elasticity of demand": if the price of one product rises, and the consumer substitutes the cheaper for the dearer, that is the consumer is prepared to switch brands, it can be surmised that both products occupy the same product market. Another way of determining the market is from the "supply-side." If a producer raises prices, would other business entities then consider entering the market to compete by offering the same or similar product at a lower price? In addition to these hypothetical measures, market definition also includes some geographical component. For some products, the relevant product market may be national; for others it is local. Once the market for a product is determined, the court must consider precisely what share of the market the business entity actually controls. If it holds over 90% of the market, the business entity is deemed to have monopoly power. As a rule of thumb, the range of market share that might trigger "market power," depending on the type of product, is at least over 50% but less than 90% of the relevant market. However, other factors to determine whether market share equals market power may be taken into account, in particular, the individual business's profitability.

Having demonstrated that a business is a monopoly, the courts usually require the business to undertake a monopolistic act before it can be held to have violated the Sherman Act. Some earlier cases did adopt the position that a monopoly will inevitably engage in anti-competitive behavior, and they sanctioned the entity without requiring proof of a monopolistic act. More recent cases look carefully at the monopoly's conduct, and seem willing to search for efficiencies that might justify their actions. The effects upon consumers of the acts of these large players in the market are carefully gauged. Such litigation is necessarily very complex and fact-driven.

Finally, American antitrust law is concerned with mergers. The purpose of regulating mergers is, in part, to ensure that no business entity is able to attain monopoly status in a given market by gobbling up its competitors. The financial crisis of 2008 led to a consolidation in the banking industry when the value of bank shares plummeted. When oil prices decline, larger oil companies frequently prefer to buy competitors because it is cheaper to purchase their reserves than it is to engage in further exploration. The decline in the price of oil during the COVID-19 pandemic should have led to consolidation amongst oil companies. Oddly it has not.

Congress amended the Clayton Act of 1914 in 1950, in order to bolster the protection provided by the Sherman Act, to further prohibit concentrations, horizontal (between competitors) and vertical (by parties on different levels of the distribution chain) if the effects of such a merger "substantially . . . lessen competition." There is a political cast, as noted above, to gauging the impact of mergers. Congress required notification of the intent to undertake a merger by major corporate entities, and the disclosure by them of vast quantities of information in order to enable the Justice Department to make an informed determination as to whether it should take steps to prevent the merger. Initially, the courts read Congress's mandate broadly, but the court backtracked. Then, in 1982, the Reagan DOJ's own Guidelines took a more benign view of mergers, and its policy focused almost exclusively on the "supply-side:" it considered only whether a merged entity had the ability to raise its prices, and if it had undertaken this action, whether or not competitors were attracted to the marketplace. In addition, the requisite market share that triggered market power (and an inquiry) was set at the higher range of the scale outlined above (50 to 90%). Though subsequently amended by a more liberal-leaning Clinton Administration, business entities were still permitted to demonstrate the pro-competitive effects of their proposed merger. The Bush Administration's approach is more similar to the Reagan paradigm embodied in the 1982 guidelines. Although it is not always clear which economic theory is in play, antitrust enforcement policy has been articulated in the language of economics, as much as through that of the law. The Obama Administration took a more aggressive stand on mergers, particularly when consumer interests were believed to be at stake. The Trump Administration has returned to a lenient stance towards combinations.

Conclusion

Our odyssey through the extensive realm of American business law illustrates that, despite the free-market rhetoric that often characterizes the American political dialogue, most aspects of businesses are subject to significant regulation by federal or state government. This is particularly the case for publicly-owned corporations whose practices come under heavy scrutiny to protect investors. Though a large number of Americans own shares in publicly-traded corporations, shareholder democracy is the exception rather than the rule. The thrust of securities regulation is to ensure that investors get what they have bargained for, that the corporations whose shares or debt that they have purchased have fully and honestly disclosed their financial positions. Recent events suggest that this particular mission has not been fully accomplished.

Regulation is present in the variety of other areas of business law that we have explored. Antitrust law regulates the conduct of businesses to make certain that large players do not control consumer access to goods and services. Scrutiny of horizontal and vertical agreements, as well as of mergers, is calculated to make certain that no single entity can control the flow of goods and services, and therefore dictate their price. Current American anti-trust law resembles European Union competition law, but the recent trend here is towards leniency, or at least allowing business entities their day in court to demonstrate that their agreements have sufficient pro-competitive effects to outweigh any anti-competitive impacts.

CHAPTER 10

AMERICAN LABOR LAW: LAISSEZ-FAIRE—FREEDOM TO CONTRACT; LIMITATIONS REGARDING DISCRIMINATION

Introduction

Most business entities employ workers, and therefore, managers and their lawyers require a basic knowledge of labor and employment law to run their enterprises. Compared to many other advanced economies, American labor markets are "flexible," and employment law seems decidedly *laissez-faire* in its approach to the regulation of the employment relationship. In the absence of expressed contractual provisions, employment is generally considered to be "at will," which means that either side of the employment relationship can terminate it without cause. Like much of American law, "efficiency" rationales are offered to support this regime of scant regulation; it leaves both sides, if dissatisfied, with the current employer-employee relationship free to look elsewhere. If the current connection does not suit either side's requirements, the employee can seek a more satisfactory job, and the employer can look for worker who better suits the enterprise's needs. To the extent it is required, the market, exponents of the system argue, will offer any necessary protections to workers (since they have been more vulnerable historically). "Bad" employers will lose their best workers to "good" employers; and to avoid their loss which would not bode well for the enterprise, "bad" employers will mend their ways in order to keep "good" employees. Moreover, where market forces do not achieve equilibrium between the two, unions will spring up and prosper in order to protect vulnerable workers. This sketch of the theoretical economics of labor markets has a quality reminiscent of Peter Pan's "Never-Never Land."

Indeed, it bears only a slim relationship to the contemporary labor scene. The idealized paradigm set out above, the *laissez-faire* approach to the employment relationship, has been modified in the course of the twentieth century, but it must be conceded that variation has occurred only around the edges. Change began in the nineteenth and early twentieth centuries with the notion that some categories of potential workers required protection, the obvious example being the concerns that arose over the proliferation of children in the workplace. But, there was also a movement over time for legislation that more generally limited hours of employment, established worker's compensation schemes, prescribed a minimum wage, and set occupational safety standards. More recently, anti-discrimination measures have been adopted to prevent employers from taking account of race, religion, gender, age and disability (and now more recently on account of sexual orientation and gender identity) in the hiring, advancement, and dismissal of workers, and there is now even a right in America for workers to demand family leave, though, unlike many other industrialized societies, it is unpaid. Again, state law is a player here. For example, workers and employers in some states now contribute to an insurance scheme that provides for payments for those whose circumstances make family leave necessary.

These measures may seem at first blush to derogate from the market-driven ideology of American labor law, but its justification fits within its theoretical bounds: regulation is necessary to compensate for market failure. Labor markets are not perfect ones. There are disconnects, and government regulation should step in to help correct these market deficiencies. But regulation creates costs, and there are tradeoffs; at the very least, it can be said that regulation adds transaction costs to products and services, money which might better be spent on wages and benefits, or to keep down the prices of goods and services to the consumer. Three areas of law will be covered in this section: the law governing employment; employment discrimination law; and that of unions and collective bargaining.

Employment Law

Employment law is complex and is a mélange of both state and federal statutes and common law. As noted in the introduction to this section, in employment law, the *laissez-faire* principle obtains: absent agreement to the contrary, employment is at will. Thus, employees may be "fired" by their employers, and they may leave their jobs: and both sides may act without notice to the other. That said, few American workers actually turn up for work on Monday and are immediately given their walking papers. Once again, this harsh regime is a default rule: contractual agreement can and frequently does alter it, and notice periods for termination on both sides are frequently written into the employment relationship. In the diminishing number of industries which remain unionized in the United States—in 2019 there were 14.6 million union members, down from 17.7 million in 1983—the percentage of workers belonging to a union in the United States (or total labor union "density") was 10.3%, compared to 20.1% in 1983—unions negotiate complex terms of employment with management for their members. These collective bargaining agreements may include specific dismissal priorities (the seniority principle that creates an order in which employees are terminated based upon years of service) and lay-off procedures. Likewise, some non-unionized workers have "tenured" positions (university professors, for example), and can only be terminated for cause or if teaching requirements or the economic conditions facing the university become dire. Public employees, federal, state, and local, may not be dismissed without a hearing in which some misconduct or incompetence must be alleged, and more importantly, proved. Moreover, in order to attract high-quality employees, many employers voluntarily commit themselves to discharge processes. The tech industry is a good example. A dearth of high-quality workers in the Silicon Valley allows those employed there (and in their industries) to have terms of employment that even academics might envy. Finally, "wrongful termination" has been recognized as a tort in some states; employers who terminate employees for a variety of reasons regarded as improper, or violations of that nebulous concept "public policy" (for example, refusal to follow instructions by the employer that may be illegal, or "whistle-blowing," informing the authorities if the employer acts unlawfully) may be sued for damages or reinstatement. Privacy laws, both state and federal, have been adopted also to prevent employers from gathering information on employees through an array of surveillance techniques.

Employee benefits are likewise a matter for individual negotiation. The labor market is competitive, as well as flexible. While there is no legal obligation for employers to do so, they generally provide a wide array of benefits, from health care to pensions and life insurance for their employees. Tax laws are configured to provide incentives to encourage employers to offer these programs, and employees are frequently required to contribute to them. Social Security law requires employers (and workers) to contribute to a fund that provides payments for those over the retirement age (and their spouses) and for the disabled. Family leave provisions have been adopted by Congress, though at present there is no requirement that employers do anything more than allow time off, but without pay. Some states mandate payment. Employers also contribute to a state insurance program for those who become involuntarily unemployed: unemployment insurance. These payments allow workers a breathing period (generally 26-weeks) to seek alternative employment, but they are not ongoing payments. However, in times of high unemployment, the benefit period is usually extended.

Both state and federal law govern health and safety standards in the workplace. The Department of Labor is empowered under the Occupational and Safety Act of 1970 (29 U.S.C. ch. 15 § 651 *et seq.*) to set safety standards in the workplace, and to enforce them through inspection. Workers are protected by state-administered schemes allowing them compensation for workplace injuries, without having to prove either employer negligence or their own exercise of due care. These workers' compensation statutes provide an alternative to civil lawsuits for workplace injuries; the compensation is received in lieu of the right to sue and may be less than the worker could have received from a jury. That said, the scheme is not without benefit to the employee: the costs of litigation, and its inherent risk, is avoided.

Employment Discrimination Law

The law of employment discrimination is a very vibrant area of American labor law. Title VII of the Civil Rights Act of 1964 (Pub. L 88–352) bolstered by the Civil Rights Act of 1991 (Pub. L. 102–166) covers all employers with 15 or more employees, and prohibits discrimination based on race, color, religion, and gender, and most recently the Supreme Court (in *Bostock v. Clayton Cty., Georgia*, 140 S. Ct. 1731 (2020)) added bias on the grounds of sexual orientation. Age-based discrimination is prohibited by the Age Discrimination in Employment Act of 1967 (29 U.S.C. § 621 *et seq.*), and the Americans with Disabilities Act of 1990 (42 U.S.C. § 12101 *et seq.*) prevents employers from discriminating against otherwise qualified workers based upon "physical or mental impairments." Each act sets its own particular standards and its own enforcement proceedings. The logic underpinning anti-discrimination legislation is once again "efficiency:" excluding otherwise qualified workers on economically "irrational" grounds (that is to say, based on some prejudice) limits the pool of available labor, and therefore, raises the costs of providing goods and services to the consumer. Moreover, discrimination in the past has created an economically dependent underclass that required the government to create expensive economic assistance programs for those thereby disadvantaged. Anti-discrimination laws, particularly those dealing with employment, help to ameliorate both sets of ills. Both intentional discrimination and neutral practices that create a "disparate impact" on the protected class can give rise to an action under Title VII of the Civil Rights Act of 1964 as amended (42 U.S.C. § 1981). Discriminatory intent may be proved either by direct evidence (statements made by management of a policy of bias) or by circumstantial evidence of prejudice (patterns of advancement of employees that suggest preferences and biases). Disparate impact may be proved by hiring and promotion practices that set standards which make it more difficult for protected groups to find positions and advance in the organization. For example, height and weight requirements set by both police and firefighters tend to discriminate against women, who are typically of shorter stature. Yet, under certain circumstances, employers may use gender or race as an employment

qualification in limited circumstances where there is
a "bona fide occupational qualification": an example
is the requirement that wait-staff be of a certain
national origin at a particular ethnic restaurant.
Those who claim that they have been subject to
discrimination in violation of Title VII generally
must exhaust their administrative remedies before
bringing an action in court, except where the
discrimination alleged is intentional. Both federal
and state tribunals have been created to investigate
claims, and if a case submitted to the various
Commissions is found to be meritorious, the
Commission can proceed on behalf of the claimant by
filing suit in either state or federal court. Back-pay,
reinstatement, and prospective pay may be awarded
in order to compensate the claimant for her losses
due to the discriminatory treatment. Title VII also
bans sexual harassment in the workplace: both
unwanted sexual overtures and the creation of a
hostile environment for disadvantaged groups are
prohibited.

Unlike many other industrialized counties,
mandatory retirement ages (with few narrow
exceptions—state employees or airline pilots) and
discrimination in hiring, promotion, and dismissal
based upon age are prohibited. Back-pay and
reinstatement can be ordered in civil actions brought
by employees who have been dismissed in violation of
the terms of the Act. Employers may provide
monetary incentives to encourage older workers to
retire voluntarily. To prevent over-reaching on the
part of employers anxious to rid themselves of older,
better-paid employees, Congress has established a

framework for assuring that such packages are accepted by the employee only with full knowledge of her rights under the law.

The Americans with Disabilities Act of 1990 (42 U.S.C. § 12101 as amended in 2008) goes further than most anti-discrimination employment laws by requiring affirmative steps by employers with 15 or more employees to provide "reasonable accommodation" for workers with physical or mental impairments. While the term "reasonable" suggests that the obligation under the law is not without limits, employers have been required to reconfigure existing physical facilities (to provide access for the physically disabled and purchase equipment to facilitate their continued employment) and to restructure jobs (including work schedules) to accommodate those workers with actual impairments. Like actions under Title VII, employees need show either intentional or disparate-impact discrimination. The disabled person must be provided equal benefits; and employer-sponsored employee benefit plans may not exclude the disabled employee on the grounds that premiums may rise because their inclusion increases exposure to risk. The Act provides allowances and exemptions for employers if compliance would cause undue hardship.

American Unions

Finally, we consider the law governing unions and collective bargaining. Unions in the United States are not nearly as strong as their counterparts in most other industrialized nations, and current union membership here is a scant 10% of the work force. Much discussion has mooted the reasons for the decline of union membership, and whether it has been a positive or negative force in the current economic climate and the overall complexion of industrial relations in the United States. Suffice it to say that American employers have long been wary of unions, and the movement of industry from the northeast and the mid-west of the United States to the southern states after World War II was partly engineered to weaken union control over labor. Likewise, foreign industrial transplant factories, for example German or Japanese car assembly plants in America, are most often found in the more "union-skeptic" regions of the country, like the American south. The decline in union membership suggests to some that workers must believe that there are better ways to secure jobs and improve working conditions than through conventional labor unions. Yet, some vibrant unions continue to survive and are able to negotiate significant benefits for their members.

The law governing labor unions is largely federal law, such as the National Labor Relations Act of 1935 (29 U.S.C. § 151 *et seq.*) adopted during the Great Depression, though some states regulate industries exempt from the Act and from other federal law. The American labor relations system it has generated has some distinctive aspects that differ from those of many other industrialized countries. The first is that unions have no intrinsic right to represent workers; thus, the right of unions to represent workers in a particular firm is determined by an election supervised by the National Labor Relations Board (hereafter NLRB) in which management participates. Recently, Volkswagen workers voted against unionization of their factory in Tennessee, even though the corporation was said to support it. Secondly, much union representation of workers is local and piecemeal: a union's bargaining authority is created and exercised on a factory-by-factory basis, or even trade-by-trade within a factory. But, these "local" unions generally are connected to national unions (like the American Federation of Labor and the Congress of Industrial Organizations—the AFL-CIO) that represent competing firms within the industry. American unions are closely monitored by a variety of law enforcement agencies to ensure that union democracy is upheld, that union funds are not misappropriated, and that the rights of workers to decline to join the prevailing union are protected. Finally, American law prohibits the so-called "closed shop," where workers must be union members in order to be employed. However, "union shops" are permitted in most states; an employee need not join the union. but must pay dues in amounts that help defray the costs of collective bargaining.

Once a union has been certified as the elected representative of the employees by the NLRB, it is the bargaining agent for the workforce. Both union and management are under a legal obligation to negotiate in good faith over contracts stipulating wages, hours, and working conditions. But there is no obligation to negotiate over a variety of crucial issues including, for example, plant closures or capital investment in a factory, though in practice both sides (union and management) are prepared to engage in talks over these so-called "permissive" subjects. If the parties reach an impasse in the negotiation process, the union can give notice of an intent to strike, and the employer can likewise give notice that it will either implement its offer to the union or "lock-out" its employees (not permit them into the factory to work). A cooling-off period is required before such action can be taken, and the Federal Mediation and Conciliation Service will attempt to find a solution to their differences. In the event of a strike, usually called after a vote of the union's members, workers withholding their labor may not be terminated, though management may hire replacement labor unless the strike has been called over unfair labor practices. The president can intervene and seek to enjoin the strike if it presents a threat to national health or safety. When the strike has ended, usually by a vote of the membership, striking workers have priority to return to their jobs, but the replacements may continue to be employed.

Disputes that arise under existing collective bargaining agreements are usually dealt with through an agreed process of arbitration. Some conflicts may be sufficiently serious to be considered an unfair labor practice. If so, the NLRB will investigate. If the charges are considered meritorious, a complaint is brought before an administrative tribunal. Both evidence and testimony are considered, and the administrative law judge makes findings of facts and conclusions of law. In the absence of an appeal, the judge's decision stands. Appeals are heard first by the NLRB and are subject to judicial review by the appropriate United States Court of Appeals.

Conclusion

In the United States, labor is contracted freely, and without much government intervention. That said, aspects of terms of employment are controlled by federal law, ensuring workers' access to employment without reference to race, gender, religion, disability, age, and now sexual orientation and gender identity. In this area, American law reaches farther than in most other industrialized nations. Finally, access to unions and the right of unions to collective bargaining is preserved in what might be called "post-union America," allowing those workers, who wish to join, the right to do so.

CHAPTER 11

CRIMINAL LAW: (MUCH) CRIME AND (SEVERE) PUNISHMENT IN MODERN AMERICA

Introduction

In contemporary America, crime is nothing short of a national obsession. While statistics may demonstrate a decline in the number of many recorded criminal offences in most parts of the country, levels of criminality remain an area of public concern. Consequently, an ongoing debate concerning both the purpose of the criminal law and its effectiveness rages. All facets of the issue are mooted, from its origins—the root social and economic causes of lawlessness, namely, racial disparities in enforcement—to its ultimate penalty—the grisly process of human beings putting other human beings to death.[1]

And art imitates life. Crime drama is a staple of American television, cinema, theatre, and fiction, though standard fare is increasingly questioned by some who reckon that it portrays crime-fighters as heroes in a ceaseless struggle against cunning and vicious criminals. Recent instances of police misconduct and brutality indicates a more multi-faceted dimension to the struggle between "cops and robbers:" the police and those they try to apprehend. Another venue for the drama that is criminal justice

---

[1]   As this chapter was being revised, in July of 2020, the federal government executed three men after a seventeen-year hiatus.

in the United States is the courtroom, as portrayed both fictionally and factually in American media. The broadcast of both live trials and taped excerpts abound, as do the dramatized versions based loosely on actual cases. Both provide a veritable immersion course in police crime-detection practices. Aspiring lawyers can receive more than a mere introduction to both the criminal law and trial practice on the airwaves.

Fear and fascination with crime therefore go hand-in-hand in the contemporary American imagination. There is reason to believe that both are overplayed. The trends suggest a substantial decline in criminality. The two most commonly cited sources of crime statistics in the U.S. both show substantial decreases in the violent crime rate since it peaked in the early 1990s. The Federal Bureau of Investigation (hereafter FBI) complies an annual report of serious crimes reported to police in more than 18,500 jurisdictions. Those statistics indicate that violent crime fell 51% between 1993 and 2018. Another national survey, this one conducted by the Bureau of Justice Statistics (hereafter BJS), interviewed people who might have been victims of unreported crime. It polled approximately 160,000 Americans ages 12 and older, asking whether they were victims of crime regardless of whether they reported the offense to the police. Using the BJS data, the crime rate fell by 71% during the same twenty-five-year time span. That said, the truth is usually stranger than fiction: what Americans think is the situation on the ground is more important than its reality.

Criminal law is a branch of American law, as well as American culture, and many of the themes developed in other chapters, in areas of private law, also obtain for the criminal law. In particular, both state and federal government inhabit the same space in crime's kingdom, as they do in other areas of the substantive and procedural law. Though criminal acts are more frequently prosecuted in state courts under state law than in the federal system, there is numerous errant conduct that constitute both state and federal crimes, and there are also a number of discrete federal crimes, particularly the so-called "white collar crimes." Each state has its own criminal law embodied in a criminal code, though the substantive variation amongst the jurisdictions is relatively modest. Indeed, many states have adopted in whole or in part the Model Penal Code (hereinafter, the MPC) promulgated by the American Law Institute in 1962. Other states have enacted provisions in their own codes consistent with many of its tenets.

Likewise, though the substantive law of crime in both the federal system and in most states is statutory rather than "judge-made," there is reasonable play in the language creating offences, justifications, and excuses (indeed, in some states and in the federal system, the latter two are common-law developed in the cases) to allow judges ample latitude to make law by way of statutory interpretation.

In addition, the jury plays a significant role in the criminal justice system, as it does in civil proceedings, usually by determining guilt or innocence (some criminal cases, for example those involving a defendant who waived his right to a jury trial in exchange for a plea deal, are heard by judges without a jury), and sometimes by mulling over proportional penalties. By finding a defendant not guilty, the jury may be playing fast and loose with its application of the law, or mitigate its harshness in a particular case (known as "jury nullification," a time-honored concept in Anglo-American jurisprudence).

Finally, the technicality of the criminal law is apparent, perhaps more so in criminal procedure, where constitutional protections place limitations on the conduct of police investigation, than in the discussion of substantive criminal law that follows.

Basic Principles of the Substantive Criminal Law

Criminal liability attaches to particular acts (or, more infrequently, omissions) when accompanied by a culpable state of mind. For criminal liability to attach, the law requires a wrongful act (*actus reus*) be committed with a prescribed state of mind (*mens rea*). The requisite act must be voluntary, so conduct otherwise deemed criminal that is committed while asleep or unconscious cannot give rise to criminal liability. Omissions are rarely punished as criminal. Only where there is a duty to act is the failure to do so tantamount to a criminal act. The classic example is that of an individual who watches another drown when she could have easily saved the hapless swimmer without endangering her own life. Criminal liability does not attach to her failure to act unless there was some recognized legal relationship that would give rise to a duty to act, for example, the parent-child bond, or that of guardian and ward (or perhaps based on contractual obligations, if she were a lazy lifeguard employed to rescue those who are in need of assistance).

The requisite *mens rea* for criminal liability to attach is more complicated. Wrongful conduct undertaken intentionally is clearly culpable. But what about acts that are reckless or negligent? If, for example, I stroll down the street brandishing a revolver without intending to discharge it, but the gun goes off and kills a person, does criminal liability attach? My act, though not intentional, is either reckless (undertaken with the knowledge that the conduct creates a risk of harm to others) or negligent (conduct that a reasonably prudent person would realize created risk of harm to others). Most negligent conduct is not criminalized, with the major exception of negligent homicide.

The criminal law also contains a modest number of offenses in which strict liability obtains. One is felony murder: a homicide which occurs during the commission of a predicate felony. An example: Smith intends to commit a robbery, uses a gun to further his design, and the weapon is unintentionally fired during the course of his act killing his victim. Similarly, some minor traffic offences, or sale of liquor or cigarettes to minors, are examples of offenses in which *mens rea* (the intent to reach a particular speed which is over the limit, or to sell smokes to minors) need not be proved. One major offence in which *mens rea* need not be proved is statutory rape, where the offender had sexual intercourse with a minor regardless of whether the offender knew the victim was underage. Offenses that involve possession of a prohibited substance or goods may not always require that the actor had a culpable state of mind accompanying his or her conduct.

In limited circumstances, one may be criminally liable for the acts of others. Vicarious liability sometimes attaches to an employer when, for example, the conduct of an employee is proscribed, and, as in situations in which a corporate entity violates the law, to the corporate officers.

Finally, criminal law requires that the wrongful act causes the harm proscribed. Causation must both be actual ("but-for" the accused conduct, the harm to the victim would not have occurred), and proximate (no supervening act broke the chain of causation). Resorting to my gun play on a public street, the bullet from the weapon in my hand has to cause the injury when I squeeze the trigger. If another person grabs the gun from my hand and fires a shot killing a bystander, her conduct is an intervening cause, and the proximate cause of the death is not my act, unless her conduct was a foreseeable consequence of my own. The requisite causation will still lie if the intervening act was either responsive and not abnormal, or coincidental, and foreseeable. So, if the injury caused by the bullet is not fatal, but the wounded person is taken to hospital where a surgeon incompetently operates to extract the slug and the botched procedure causes the victim's death, then the shooter may still be guilty of homicide because the doctor's actions were responsive and his incompetence not necessarily abnormal. Or if after being non-fatally wounded by my shot, the victim runs into the street, and is fatally injured by a car, the shot may still be regarded as the legal cause of death. While the arrival of the car was coincidental, the victim's conduct, running into the street, was foreseeable.

Particular Offences: Murder

The common law created a distinction between felonies and misdemeanors. Felonies were punishable by death, and misdemeanors usually resulted in some form of corporal punishment. Most American jurisdictions retain the division, but the classification differs; felonies are generally defined as more serious crimes punishable by imprisonment for one year or more, with misdemeanors regarded as acts of lesser moment that carry a lesser penalty (less than one year in jail). Murder, a homicide, committed with "malice aforethought" is a felony; shoplifting a bottle of bourbon is likely to be charged as a misdemeanor.

Although the modern criminal law has created a vast array of offences, a few can be singled out as examples of the general pattern of criminal liability in America. The most serious of crimes is homicide, the killing of a person. The legal classification of the act, and consequently, the severity of punishment for it, is directed by the *mens rea* that accompanied the act. If it was committed with "malice aforethought," the homicide is categorized as murder. This quaint term attempts to isolate particularly evil acts that are the most culpable and is defined in various ways. The MPC regards other homicides as murders when the underlying circumstances that surround the killing "manifest an extreme indifference to the value of human life." Model Penal Code § 210.2(a) (AM. L. INST., 1962). In short, when they were committed "knowingly" or "purposefully."

Courts have used a variety of more imaginative turns of phrase but, in general, murder requires evidence of intention to kill or to do serious bodily harm to the victim. Likewise, a death occasioned through extreme recklessness—a state of mind supported by evidence demonstrating conscious disregarded of the fact that her conduct created a high risk of death, or that she nevertheless proceeded with "an abandoned and malignant heart"—also likely will result in a murder conviction. *See Commonwealth v. Malone*, 47 A.2d 445 (Pa. 1946).

Many states also subdivide murders into degrees, with first-degree murder reserved for particularly heinous killings, which under certain circumstances and in some states, allow the jury to impose the death penalty. Most states (though not the MPC) also consider felony murder (a homicide which occurs during the commission of a predicate felony, for example a death that happens during a burglary, even though the perpetrator has no specific intent to kill) first-degree murder.

Manslaughter

Homicides in which either there was no intent to kill, or if the killing occurred in the "heat of passion," are deemed to be manslaughter. Some states (though not the MPC) break the category into two parts: voluntary and involuntary. To reduce an intentional killing from murder to voluntary manslaughter, the provocation endured by the perpetrator must be such that would arouse a "reasonable" person (a law-abiding or ordinary individual) to kill, and the retaliation that results in death must be immediate, before passion cools and more sober judgment takes over.

The "traditional" example of voluntary manslaughter is that of a spouse who returns home to find his or her partner in the arms of another, and who immediately proceeds to kill the spouse and/or lover. If, however, the wronged spouse takes an hour or so to ponder the appropriate course of action for the betrayal, and then kills either, the charge should be murder. In states that draw the distinction between voluntary and involuntary manslaughter, the latter is most frequently charged when a death results from a negligent act: the driver who proceeds to operate an automobile without due care and attention, and consequently runs down a pedestrian in a crosswalk with his car.

Rape

Another crime against the person is rape. The original crime was reserved for cases of the forcible penetration of a woman by a man against her will and without her consent, and required her to "resist to the utmost." Because marriage implied consent to sexual intercourse, a husband was deemed incapable of raping his wife. However, since the 1970s, when various groups pressed for the modernization of the law to fit circumstances such as "date rape," the law has undergone change. For example, spousal immunity has been abrogated in most jurisdictions, though the MPC retains it, and the crime of rape has been extended and subdivided to include other forms of unwanted sexual conduct, regardless of the sex of the perpetrator or the victim. Another "modernization" of the rape law "shields" the victim; if she testifies for the prosecution, her identity can be protected and much of her prior sexual conduct is not admissible to prove consent. This alteration in practice was intended to provide a greater incentive for victims to come forward and assist in the prosecution of their assailants.

Crimes Against Property

Crimes against property were traditionally divided into burglary and larceny. The former dealt with theft or entry (originally limited to that of a dwelling in the nighttime) in order to commit a felony on the premises, while the latter concerned other dishonest appropriations of property. For burglary to be proved in the past, it was necessary for the prosecutor to show both a "breaking" and an "entering." Climbing through an open window would not suffice for the former; remaining in a public premise after they have closed for the night might not suffice for the latter. Some, though not all, modern statutes have abrogated the need for a forcible breaking and have defined an entry broadly. Likewise, it is no longer necessary to enter the premises at night, or for the premises to be a dwelling for an unlawful entry to be charged as a burglary.

Theft offenses have proliferated in recent years. The most common is larceny: the appropriation of property of another with the intent to deprive its owner or possessor of the property permanently. Even if a person comes into the possession of another's property without dishonesty (for example, it is found or handed over by another in the mistaken belief that it is her property), one may be guilty of theft by not seeking to deliver it to the owner. Coming into property by false pretenses and embezzlement are also larceny. Blackmail, bribery, and money laundering have also been added to the list of traditional theft offenses.

Racketeer Influenced and Corrupt Organizations Act: Innovating Crime

The legislature has been active in creating new crimes. An example is the Racketeer Influenced and Corrupt Organizations Act (RICO) enacted by Congress in 1970. RICO creates a cause of action against those who participate in an enterprise that engages in "a pattern of racketeering activity," loosely defined as committing more than a single criminal act (out of a comprehensive list of state and federal crimes) that are related and ongoing. It is also a violation of RICO to acquire an interest in, or even to make an investment in, an enterprise that engages in a pattern of racketeering activity, as well as to enter into a conspiracy to violate RICO.

RICO was calculated initially to target organized crime "families" in an effort to convict crime bosses participating primarily in legitimate businesses, and therefore protected from prosecution because their own activities were legitimate (for example, where an organized crime figure owns a bank, but one that engages in money laundering). However, creative lawyering has expanded the intended scope of RICO to encompass and prosecute white collar offenses such as wire fraud, and sex trafficking conspiracies,[2] among other offenses. A legitimate enterprise, like a law firm that intentionally and consistently over-bills its clients, might similarly be guilty of "racketeering" under RICO. Penalties for RICO violations are severe, and include both lengthy prison terms, as well as the forfeiture of property and proceeds derived from, or to facilitate, the illegal enterprise.

Defenses to Criminal Liability

The individual charged with a criminal offence may, of course, deny having committed the act as charged. The burden to prove both the requisite *actus reus* and *mens rea* of a criminal offense is on the government's prosecutor. The prosecutor's burden of proof is high: proof beyond a reasonable doubt. Unless and until the prosecutor satisfies this burden,

---

[2]   *See United States v. Raniere,* 384 F. Supp. 3d 282 (E.D.N.Y. 2019). (using RICO to prosecute the leader of a hierarchical sex cult known as NXIVM).

the defendant is afforded a presumption of innocence; if the burden is never met, the defendant is acquitted.

In addition, the criminal law recognizes a number of affirmative defenses to criminal liability. By raising an affirmative defense, the defendant essentially concedes that she committed the act as charged, but she contends that additional facts exonerate her. The burden of proof is upon the defendant to prove the facts and the elements of the affirmative defense alleged.

Self-Defense

The classic affirmative defense is self-defense: the defendant concedes that she has intentionally committed the homicide (or other criminal act, like an assault) as charged, but puts forward additional facts that justify her use of deadly force. The ability to assert that a violent act was committed in self-defense is limited. The law permits an individual to use reasonable and proportional force to deter an attack that threatens to inflict upon her imminent death or serious bodily harm. Under certain circumstances, force may also be used to defend others, to apprehend criminals, and to defend property. Again, the force used in these situations must be measured, proportionate; in other words, deadly force is generally not available to an individual as a defense unless imminent deadly force is being marshaled against her. With respect to property, deadly force is rarely permitted, generally only to defend one's home against a violent attack.

Insanity

Another affirmative defense is that of insanity, a defense available not to justify the killing but only to excuse it. The test initially formulated was the *M'Naghten* rule: owing to a mental disease, the individual did not know the "nature and the quality of the act" she had committed (she didn't realize that she was doing it), or if she did, she did not know that the act was wrong. *Queen v. M'Naghten*, 8 Eng. Rep. 718 (1843). This "right-wrong" test focused on the nature of the mental disease alleged, and whether the criminal act was a consequence or result of the disease.

Other, more lenient, formulations have been offered. For example, many states have adopted the MPC which permits persons to use the defense if they lack "substantial capacity" to understand that their conduct is wrongful, or they similarly lack the "substantial ability" to conform their conduct to the requirements of the law. Other states have used the "product rule," allowing the insanity defense where the defendant's mental disease was connected to the criminal conduct. The insanity defense has long been the subject of controversy and reform. Some states have augmented it with the "extreme emotional disturbance defense." New York's version (paraphrased) is as follows: where the perpetrator accused of murder acted under the influence of extreme emotional disturbance for which there was, in the view of a similarly situated person, a reasonable explanation or excuse for the profound loss of self-control. The defense transposes the offense from murder to manslaughter.

But not all jurisdictions have moved toward more lenient treatment of those mentally troubled. After the would-be assassin of President Ronald Reagan was found not guilty by reason of insanity, Congress amended federal law to mirror the earlier (and stricter) *M'Naghten* formulation of insanity, and some states followed suit. It was perhaps not an inappropriate reversal, since the rule was initially formulated to deal with an earlier attempt on the life of a political leader. Some states have also responded to a general discomfort with the notion that a killer may be sent to a psychiatric hospital and freed when doctors decide that the perpetrator is no longer dangerous or mentally ill by creating a new verdict: guilty, but mentally ill. In such circumstances, the defendant is sent to prison for a term, but is ordered to receive psychiatric treatment while incarcerated.

Other Affirmative Defenses

Another affirmative defense is that of duress. Here, the defendant also admits to having committed the crime, but only because of a real and imminent threat of harm to herself or to others. So, a person who is coerced into participating in a crime may be exonerated. An example is the bank president who receives a call from one of a group of bank robbers telling her that her family members are in their custody and will be killed if she does not open the vault.

An analogous defense is necessity, where the illegal action is justified if it is the "lesser of two evils." This defense is also of limited application. While moralists may debate whether the hungry may steal food, the law is fairly well aligned against this option. Nor should the "terrible temptation" of a shipwrecked crew permit it to eat one of its own, or to throw passengers overboard to lighten the load. *See Regina v. Dudley and Stevens* (1884) QB 273 (DC). After all, it is a moral, and at times a legal, duty to sacrifice oneself so to save another. And the conduct of John Q. of Hollywood fame, the father who barricaded himself in a hospital until his son received a life-saving heart transplant, would likewise not be excused. The MPC has fashioned a so-called "balance-of-evils" test, but it remains vague in application. One wonders whether this benchmark is any more useful than the existing ones that try to apply duress and necessity standards to the variety of human conduct. The MPC holds that the defendant's conduct is excused if she believed that the evil which she sought to avoid by undertaking an illegal act was greater than the evil "sought to be prevented by the law defining the offense charged." Model Penal Code § 3.02(1)(a) (AM. L. INST., 1962).

Finally, entrapment is an affirmative defense, but one that is infrequently successful. In order to apprehend criminals, police often use undercover agents who solicit the crime for which the participating individual is subsequently charged. A simple example is the narcotics officer who cruises the streets in areas of known drug use, sees someone loitering on the corner who may be a drug dealer, but not known to him as such, and asks to buy some illegal drug, and then charges the person with the sale of drugs. Far more intricate undercover work can also be undertaken, even to the extent of setting up illegal businesses to attract customers in order to arrest them subsequently for illegal dealing. Questions can also arise in the current "war on terror" in which police may make contact with individuals who may not be inclined to act, but ultimately instigate plots, and are arrested before their culmination.

To argue entrapment, the defendant must admit that she committed the offense, but go on to demonstrate that the sole inspiration for the criminal act came from law enforcement officers. The main issue for the jury to ponder is how willing the defendant was to join in the criminal enterprise. Under the "subjective test," the jury can consider whether the defendant was predisposed to commit the criminal acts anyway, and therefore was essentially waiting for the opportunity to commit the criminal act charged; when the trap was baited, the defendant readily joined. If so, her defense of entrapment fails. Under the subjective formulation, the defendant's prior conduct can be introduced to show the requisite propensity, perhaps leading the jury to convict her for the alleged bad conduct, and not merely the particular crime under consideration. Under the objective test, on the other hand, the jury does not consider the defendant's character, but merely determines whether, under the circumstances, the average innocent person would be induced to participate in the criminal act as charged; if so, the entrapment defense is available.

Crime and Punishment

For centuries, the purpose of criminal penalties has been debated. Is the purpose of criminal sanctions retribution or rehabilitation? Or rather, is it simply deterrence? Though some efforts are made to return American prisoners to society, after their terms have been served, better able to function as law-abiding citizens, many argue that prisons are at best merely warehouses of individuals waiting to be released to continue in a life of crime, or at worst, "trade schools" in which criminal skills can be further honed. The prison doors, it is said, are revolving ones, with an endless process of the same persons entering and exiting. As for prison life, it can only be described as brutal, with some scenarios seeming downright inhumane. Even in the more quiescent federal prisons for non-violent offenders, life is unattractive; in most prisons, it is unbearable.

America has a staggering number of individuals incarcerated in the state and federal prisons that dot the countryside. Penalties for a variety of crimes are decidedly severe, even when the crimes charged are not violent. In a recent corporate fraud case, the 63-year old founder of Worldcom received a 25-year sentence. For all intents and purposes, his is a life sentence; under federal parole law, he must serve at least 21 years, thus emerging no earlier than the middle of his ninth decade. Likewise, the septuagenarian Ponzi-scheme fraudster, Bernie

Madoff, received a 150-year sentence, by imposing the maximum sentences for each of the eleven counts against him. Press Release, The Federal Bureau of Investigation New York Field Office, Bernard Madoff Sentenced to 150 Years in Prison (June 29, 2009). By so doing, it is arguable that the sentencing judge enforced the legislature's goals of retribution (punishment proportional to blameworthiness) and deterrence (a nod to like-minded offenders: you will be caught and punished to the fullest extent of the law) while providing solace to victims during their healing process. Whether such severe sentences prevent others from following his path is unclear. Scholars argue that the requisite deterrence function would be better served by more convictions, rather by than draconian penalties for the few successfully prosecuted.

For state crimes, the penalties vary by offense and by jurisdiction. Most states have indeterminate sentences, with a specified minimum and maximum time: 25 to life is, for example, a common sentence for murder; for armed robbery, the range is generally from three to ten years. Some discretion is accorded to judges to fix the sentence within the prescribed bounds established by the criminal code. But the actual release date of an individual prisoner is usually set by the state parole board, a group comprised of individuals selected by the state's governor, charged with the task of considering the prisoner's petition for release after his minimum sentence has been served. The parole board usually interviews the individual, considers the convict's behavior in prison, and may also hear testimony from the victim(s) or the prosecuting attorney.

There is a certain random quality to the parole process. Opponents of these indeterminate sentences argue that offenders who commit similar crimes may be treated differently; proponents of the system regard this flexibility as desirable, allowing the parole board to review carefully each individual case and tailor sentences accordingly. Some states have opted for mandatory sentences, and require that a minimum sentence be served before a prisoner can be released. As a practical matter, the parole board is still actively involved in determining the exact release date after the minimum has been served.

In the federal system, more precise sentencing guidelines were promulgated by United States Sentencing Commission, established by an act of Congress, to allow the judge to consider both the offense committed, and whether there were aggravating or mitigating factors when setting a sentence within the bounds specified. Congress also allowed the courts to take into account the defendant's criminal background. A recent Supreme Court case decided that the guidelines violated the Sixth Amendment's right to a trial by jury if the judge took into account factors that the jury may not have found to be true beyond a reasonable doubt (like whether or not the defendant used a weapon) in reaching their verdict when determining a sentence. *See United States v. Booker*, 543 U.S. 220 (2005). Yet, in an opinion that seemed to some contradictory, the Supreme Court held that trial judges could continue to consider the guidelines as advisory—that is, trial judges could consult them but were not bound by them, and appellate judges could review lower court sentencing for "reasonableness." Suffice it to say that many appeals will now be lodged by federal prisoners challenging the "reasonableness" of their term. Recently, there have been efforts to gain bipartisan support in Congress for a framework for releasing prisoners with lengthy sentences for nonviolent drug-related crimes. The First Step Act (P. L. 115–391) was enacted in 2018 to reduce the size of the federal prison population by reconsidering sentences.

America remains one of the few modern industrialized countries (along with Japan, though their use of capital punishment is far more infrequent) to retain the death penalty. Perhaps no interpretation of the Constitution seems so outmoded to non-Americans than the current view on what constitutes "cruel and unusual punishment." Half of the states maintain the death penalty for murder, and many are indeed sentenced to death, but few executions are actually carried out. Some state supreme courts have cast doubt upon the constitutionality of their death penalty statutes as written, or as applied in particular cases. Other states, like Illinois, are concerned with whether some on death row are actually innocent. Its governor commuted all death sentences to life imprisonment before he left office. Likewise, the Supreme Court banned the execution of those who are mentally disabled, and those sentenced to capital punishment for crimes committed as minors, on grounds that the imposition of the death penalty in such cases would violate the Eighth Amendment's protection against "cruel and unusual punishments." *Roper v. Simmons,* 543 U.S. 551 (2005); *see also Atkins v. Virginia,* 536 U.S. 304 (2002). The tide may be turning against the death penalty, though in one state, Texas, prisoners are executed with grisly, though declining regularity (40 in 2000; 3 in 2020).

Conclusion

By the standards of most industrialized nations, America is a violent society. The COVID-19 pandemic coupled with recent killings of black men at the hands of police (by no means limited to America as recent international protests have illuminated) have demonstrated that, when the system of law enforcement is strained, civil society totters on the verge of collapse. Precisely why America diverges from the international norm with respect to criminality is unclear. Whether it can be attributed to the lack of an effective welfare safety net or its stark individualist bent, Americans must eventually come to realize that the national approach to the issue of crime has failed, and that crime is a problem that demands attention. The response thus far, and a largely unsuccessful one, has been to increase the number and types of criminal offences and to meet violence with harsh penalties, such as mandatory minimums oft for low-level drug offenses; this practice, to some extent, places America outside the mainstream of current thoughts on controlling levels of aberrant behavior.

Yet in large measure, the substantive American criminal law probably resembles the criminal law of other societies. Perhaps with the exception of the recent focus on "white-collar crime," those acts singled out for punishment in America are probably also crimes elsewhere. It is with respect to the more severe penalties and the draconian treatment of prisoners that America criminal law has gone its own way. Another realm where practice diverges is in the area American law labels, "criminal procedure," that is, the way in which the accused are apprehended by the police and tried in the courts, the subject of the next chapter.

CHAPTER 12

CRIMINAL PROCEDURE: THE "LONG AND WINDING ROAD" FROM APPREHENSION OF CRIMINALS TO THEIR RELEASE

Introduction

This chapter outlines criminal procedure in American courts. It charts the "long and winding road" mapped out by the criminal justice system for each criminal act allegedly committed, from the initial criminal investigation undertaken by the police through to post-conviction relief. Apprehension of a suspect, the filing of the criminal complaint by the prosecutor, the pre-trial aspects of the criminal case, the criminal trial, and the post-conviction phase, including sentencing, appeals, probation, and parole are visited along the way.

As with the criminal law, criminal procedure varies slightly amongst the jurisdictions. To this mix the complications of "our federalism" are added. Congress passes federal criminal laws. Those laws are enforced by over twenty federal law enforcement agencies, the most prominent being the Federal Bureau of Investigation (hereafter FBI) and the Drug Enforcement Administration (hereafter DEA). Then exists the particularized mandate of the Secret Service: to afford the President protection and investigate the counterfeiting and forgery of banknotes. The United States Attorney's Office (one individual office for each of the 94 judicial districts) and lawyers for the Department of Justice prosecute individuals charged with federal criminal offenses in federal court. Those convicted are sentenced by federal judges; a sentence to prison is to a federal facility; probation is processed through federal probation officers; release is monitored by federal parole boards.

In a parallel system, state legislatures enact their own criminal statutes (often supplemented by local, county, or municipal government laws); policing occurs at the state and municipal level;[1] prosecution of these offenses is in the hands of county district attorneys, usually elected, who appoint assistants to try cases in specially constituted criminal courts. While awaiting trial, since he or she is presumed innocent, a defendant may be bailed, an age-old English derivative that is the subject of much reform.[2] Those convicted are sentenced to state prison or allowed state-regulated probation; state prisoners are released when their sentences are completed, or when the state parole board

---

[1] At the time of the writing of this edition, much police reform at the federal, state, and municipal level is under consideration in response to the deaths of African-Americans at the hands of law enforcement.

[2] For example, the New Jersey Criminal Justice Reform Act was enacted in January 2017 and affords all defendants, other than those facing life imprisonment, a presumption of release. N.J.S.A. § 2A:162–20. Specifically, defendants can be held only if release would impose an unacceptable flight risk or pose a danger to the community. *Id.* Many states now similarly allow those who do not pose a risk to the community to be released without bail. *See About the Public Safety Assessment*, ADVANCING PRETRIAL JUSTICE (2020), advancingpretrial.org/psa/psa-sites/. Needless to say, these reforms are not without their critics.

determines that they should be discharged. *See About the Public Safety Assessment, supra* note 2.

What makes the process complicated (and perhaps uniquely American) is the United States Constitution. The Fourth, Fifth, and Sixth Amendments directly address criminal procedure. The Fourth Amendment boldly proclaims:

> The right of the people to be secure in their persons, houses, papers, and effects, against unreasonable searches and seizures, shall not be violated, and no Warrants shall issue, but upon probable cause, supported by Oath or affirmation, and particularly describing the place to be searched, and the persons or things to be seized.

Perhaps no passage of the Constitution has given rise to as much complex jurisprudence and academic discussion as has this "run-on sentence." It is peppered with legal terms of art: what are "searches" and "seizures;" and what circumstances render them "unreasonable"; what constitutes "probable cause" to issue a warrant; and what is the status of evidence seized without one?

Moreover, a prohibition against self-incrimination is embodied in the subsequent Fifth Amendment (a person may not "be compelled . . . to be a witness against himself."). A criminal defendant is entitled to decide against testifying at his own trial. But this "right to remain silent" also extends to police interrogation; once in police custody, a suspect must be informed that he need not answer police questions, and that he may have a lawyer present during any questioning.

Finally, the Sixth Amendment requires a speedy trial by jury, and a fair one. In the course of her trial, the defendant may present witnesses in her defense, confront witnesses summoned against her, and be represented by counsel.

These points should serve as a background. A sketch of the criminal justice structure in the United States, and a more detailed discourse on the influence of its Constitution, follows.

The Criminal Justice Process: From Arrest to Appearance

The police are usually the first to be involved officially in investigating a crime and apprehending a suspect. Police may arrest an individual if they observe a crime being committed, or if the reports of witnesses or physical evidence lead them to conclude that there is "probable cause" to believe that an individual has committed a crime. What is the definition of that illusive term? More than a hunch or reasonable suspicion is required to arrest for probable cause; rather, the arresting officer must have enough *facts* to support a reasonable basis for making the arrest. That said, an officer may also rely on her own experience in law enforcement and information that she has obtained from reliable informants. Most arrests in a public place occur without a warrant; those in homes generally require an arrest or search warrant (after all, a person's home is their castle!). When the police arrest without a warrant the officer/s must promptly bring the accused before a judge for a determination of probable cause. Here, "promptly" means without unreasonable delay *e.g.* within 48 hours. Should the police dally longer, and the holding of arrestee exceeds 48-hour mandate, they must show that extraordinary circumstances existed to justify such delay. This is often a prudent course, because if the apprehended individual contests the warrantless arrest (arguing the police did not have probable cause and the police did not conform to the 48-hour mandate above) and prevails, any evidence acquired as a result of the arrest (for example, a search of her person turns up the murder weapon) will be excluded from being entered into evidence at trial.

After arrest, the prosecutor reviews the evidence gathered by the police and makes a determination of whether or not to charge the suspect. Prosecutors have wide discretion to determine whom they wish to prosecute and need not justify their decision. Indeed, prosecutorial discretion is absolute; even if there is an ironclad case against an individual, the prosecutor may decide not to proceed. Such a decision is generally not reviewable in the courts.

If the prosecution decides to go forward with a case, an information—a piece of paper formally notifying the accused of the exact charge or charges—is filed with the court. Absent exceptional circumstances, as soon as practicable and within 48 hours, the accused must be brought before a judge or magistrate for a determination of probable cause and to address the issue of pre-trial release. At this

314 CRIMINAL PROCEDURE CH. 12

hearing, the prosecution must provide the court with a sworn statement, usually by a police officer in the form of an affidavit, establishing probable cause to believe that the accused has committed a crime. The accused may appear with counsel either retained privately if the defendant has sufficient means, appointed by the court if circumstances warrant, or assigned by the public defender's office in jurisdictions in which the state or local government employs attorneys to defend those lacking the means to hire private counsel.

If the crime is a minor one, a misdemeanor, the defendant will usually be released on his own recognizance; the defendant is allowed to remain in the community in return for a promise to appear when summoned for further proceedings. If the charge is more serious, jurisdictions now differ on whether the defendant should be required to post bail. In the past it was generally the case that a judge would require the defendant to post bail—a cash sum held by the court to be forfeited should the defendant not return to court when duly summoned to appear for further proceedings in the case. The amount of bail depended on the nature of the offense charged, the strength of the evidence thus far discovered against the accused and presented to the judge, and the financial position of the defendant. The court could also consider the extent to which the defendant might be a so-called "flight risk," whether the accused might leave the jurisdiction to avoid trial, and a possible conviction and sentence.

As an example of a flight risk, in July 2020, Ghislaine Noelle Maxwell, a British socialite, and daughter of the deceased British newspaper publisher Robert Maxwell, infamous for her association with financier and convicted sex offender Jeffrey Epstein, was charged with the crimes of enticement of minors and sex trafficking of children. A New York federal judge denied Ms. Maxwell bail after determining that her flight risk was "simply too great." Why? Her net worth is estimated to be well over $20 million dollars.

Today, as noted above, many jurisdictions tend to reserve bail for cases in which the defendant is a flight risk or a threat to public safety. In the most serious offenses, jurisdictions provide for the defendant to be held without bail for a specified period of time within which the prosecution must bring the case to trial.

The Criminal Justice Process: Pre-Trial Phase

If the accused is charged with a felony, he will be entitled to a preliminary hearing before a judge or magistrate unless the prosecutor obtains an indictment from a grand jury. The purpose of both is similar: to determine whether there is sufficient evidence to bring the accused to trial. While the evidence compiled must still lead to a conclusion of probable cause that a crime was committed, the level of scrutiny thereof is higher than at the appearance stage.

Should the prosecution opt for or be required to obtain a grand jury indictment, a panel of twelve to twenty-three ordinary citizens is assembled. The prosecution presents its case to the grand jury behind closed doors. The defendant (or her counsel) is neither present nor able to present evidence. In other cases, the prosecutor may opt for a preliminary hearing. At a preliminary hearing, the defendant is present and may be represented by counsel, so the defense has the opportunity to hear the extent of the prosecutor's case against it and assess its strengths and weaknesses. The defense may also cross-examine prosecution witnesses and present its own witnesses.

Shortly after the indictment is returned by the grand jury or the information is filed by the prosecutor, the defendant is formally arraigned, or charged with the offense. At this point, the defendant must enter a plea of guilty or not guilty. The Constitution requires the prosecutor to disclose any exculpatory evidence that the prosecutor or police have uncovered—that is, evidence that would be useful in preparing a defense. The prosecution is usually required to disclose much of the evidence it intends to produce at trial, including the accused's statements, physical evidence, and forensic evidence. Because at this point in the drama, the defendant's counsel now has a clearer indication of the prosecutor's evidence, the defense may now file motions to exclude evidence obtained in violation of the aforementioned variety of Constitutional provisions (further discussed below).

At many phases of the process, but especially after arraignment, the prosecutor may present the defendant with a plea bargain: the prosecutor may offer to charge him with a lesser offense if the defendant will cooperate with the prosecution by revealing useful information relating to additional crimes carried out by others (this is particularly the case in organized and white-collar prosecutions). Alternatively, the prosecutor may agree to recommend a less severe sentence in exchange for valuable information on the criminal acts of others. As a practical matter, many defendants decide not to run the risk of conviction on a greater charge, accept the plea-bargain deal, and plead guilty to a lesser charge. So long as the agreed plea is voluntary, and the defendant understands its consequences—in particular, that the right of trial by jury is thereby waived—then the plea agreement will stand and be accepted by the judge and implemented by the court. Thus, the plea bargain serves as a weapon in the prosecutor's arsenal to develop a case to charge and convict those whom she believes are more culpable, but perhaps more difficult to prosecute successfully than the defendant. Offering the criminal defendant a reasonable plea bargain saves the prosecutor the effort, and the government the expense and resources, of a jury trial, while still exacting some degree of punishment from the offender.

The Criminal Justice Process: Trial

Though relatively few in number, most arrests having resulted in the charges being dropped or pleaded out, criminal trials provide perhaps the most dramatic moments in American law. Who can forget the words of one of America's premier trial lawyers, the now-late Johnnie Cochran, O. J. Simpson's brilliant defense counsel, who, blood-stained glove in hand, uttered the now-famous rhyme, "If it doesn't fit, you must acquit." High profile or not, the criminal trial is the American adversarial system at its most dramatic, where freedom or imprisonment are at stake, and where a life itself may be on the line. Of course, most criminal trials are decidedly more mundane affairs, not all defendants are prominent athletes with lawyers given to poetry, and progress without much excitement. Nevertheless, the potential for high drama is always present when prosecutor locks horns with defense counsel in criminal court.

The Constitution requires a "speedy" trial, and both state and federal law place limits on the amount of time that may transpire between the charge and trial. The defendant may, however, seek a delay and request additional time to prepare a defense, particularly if free from pretrial detainment. After all, the prosecution has had a head-start; the case against the defendant was necessarily constructed, at least to some extent, prior to indictment or information. Indeed, the prosecutor may have only recently disclosed exculpatory evidence to the defense. Moreover, the defense may use the delay to find witnesses who may bolster its case. Alternatively, the defendant may hope that a delay might cause the prosecution's witnesses to lose interest in the case, or for their memories of events to dim.

The defendant has the constitutional right to a trial by jury. That right, however, may usually be waived (as we also saw with the plea bargain process), and the defendant may instead elect a bench trial before a judge, though many jurisdictions now allow the prosecutor in effect to veto a waiver in certain instances. Defense counsel's choice between the two, a bench or a jury trial, is not always a straightforward one. Much of her calculus may depend upon the crime committed, and the strength of the prosecution's case against her defendant. A judge is likely to be more dispassionate, and decide the case based on the facts before her; therefore, defense counsel might prefer to try a weaker case before a judge than a jury. On the other hand, juries are more driven by emotion; thus, a jury might be more likely than a judge to strain the law and ignore salient facts in order to acquit a sympathetic defendant, even in cases in which the facts, taken together, point towards a guilty verdict.

Criminal juries are comprised of twelve individuals summoned to the courthouse (randomly called from voter lists and driver's license records) for jury duty. Jurors must be disinterested, and unfamiliar with the case. In most states, the prosecutor and defense counsel question potential jurors (in a process quaintly called *voir dire*) to ferret out, at least in theory, any bias. In the federal system, the judge, rather than counsel, conducts the interviews with the pool of potential jurors. Jury selection has become a science; each side creates a profile of the hypothetical juror that might be more favorably disposed to its client (the "People" or the defendant) and its case and attempts to exclude others whose predispositions may be otherwise.

Lawyers on either side may request that any potential juror be excluded from serving for cause (usually knowledge or bias), and have a limited number of peremptory challenges, that is, the ability to exclude any potential juror without cause, provided the opposing side does not contend that the exclusion was discriminatory on the basis of race, ethnicity, or sex. *See Batson v. Kentucky*, 476 U.S. 79 (1986).

The American criminal trial is adversarial. Each side prepares its case independently. Because the defendant is presumed to be innocent, the prosecution presents its case-in-chief first and must prove each element of the crime charged beyond a reasonable doubt. If, at the end of its presentation, the prosecution has failed to make a *prima facia* case (that is, the prosecution has failed to show that the jury could convict beyond a reasonable doubt on the case presented), then the defendant can move to dismiss the charge. If the judge denies the motion, the defense proceeds with its case. The prosecutor may then present a rebuttal case, limited to countering the defense's evidence. Each side presents its closing argument, summarizing its respective case and, usually, disparaging (or at least debunking) the one put forward by the other side. Thereafter, the judge instructs the jury on the law, and the jury retires to reach its verdict behind closed doors. The jury's verdict must be unanimous. *Ramos v. Louisiana*, 140 S. Ct. 1390 (2020) (requiring state criminal verdicts to be unanimous). If the jury is unable to reach a verdict, it is said to be "hung," resulting in a possible retrial if the prosecution is so inclined. If the defendant is acquitted by the jury, the Fifth Amendment protects her from being be tried again for the same offense, quaintly known as "double jeopardy."

Witnesses are crucial participants in the criminal trial. Both lay and expert witnesses may be called by the lawyers for each side, and reluctant witnesses may be subpoenaed. Each side may cross-examine witnesses produced by the other. Rules of evidence have been devised to exclude unreliable or prejudicial evidence from the jury. The most frequently invoked evidence rule is that which excludes "hearsay," (statements uttered by others reported by a witness and therefore not subject to cross-examination offered to prove the truth of the matter asserted). The defendant has the option of testifying: if she does not, the jury may not draw an inference of guilt; but once she does, the right against self-incrimination (also contained in the Fifth Amendment to the United States Constitution) is waived, and the prosecution may cross-examine. The prosecution's cross-examination of the accused can be wide-ranging and hostile, and the defendant may be compelled to answer all relevant questions posed by the prosecutor, even those that probe previous criminal conduct. Thus, the decision of the accused to testify is a difficult one, and not one entered into lightly.

The Criminal Justice Process: Post-Conviction

Upon conviction, the judge hands down a sentence, consistent with guidelines. Federal crimes have guidelines established by the United States

Sentencing Commission; state court judges determine sentences according to their own guidelines. Both the prosecutor and defense counsel have an opportunity to make sentence recommendations within the established bounds. Inquiry will be made into the defendant's background, and in particular, any previous convictions. Because the vast majority of cases involve minor offenses, a term of probation, rather than incarceration, is the sentence most frequently meted out by judges; a fine and court costs may also, or alternatively, be assessed. That said, the prison system is choked with those convicted of drug offenses (46.2% of federal inmates—contrast that with 5.6% inmates for white-collar offenses such as fraud and extortion, and 0.2% for banking and insurance offenses, counterfeit, and embezzlement). Offenses, Statistics, Federal Bureau of Prisons (Aug. 8, 2020), bop.gov/about/statistics/statistics_inmate_offenses.jsp.

Much of this disproportionality has to do with mandatory minimums sentences imposed for what often are low-level drug offenses. Where probation is the sentence imposed, the probationer must follow the terms and conditions (often very detailed and restrictive) established by the judge, and have her conduct monitored by a probation officer. A violation of the terms of probation, namely, a failure to adhere to the requirements and restrictions mandated by the court, may result in its revocation and usually lands the probationer in prison. In addition to the determined sentence, be it probation or incarceration, a forfeiture of property illegally acquired and/or used in the crime may be ordered.

Convicted defendants have the right to appeal, and as a practical matter most exercise it, sometimes even when they plead guilty. Others, like President Trump's briefly serving National Security Advisor, Michael Flynn, even attempt to withdraw a guilty plea. In some states, a special tribunal hears criminal appeals, while in other states (and in the federal system), criminal appeals are heard by an intermediate appellate court of general jurisdiction. If the conviction is affirmed, the defendant may seek review in the state supreme court (usually discretionary); if there is a claim under the United States Constitution, a writ of *certiorari* in the United States Supreme Court may be granted (also discretionary). To set aside a conviction, the appeal must allege that a significant error made at trial resulted in prejudice to the defendant, or that the verdict was inconsistent with the evidence.

In addition to an appeal, a person convicted, sentenced, and incarcerated may also bring a writ of *habeas corpus* in federal district court against the prison's warden, seeking release on the grounds that the imprisonment violates the United States Constitution or other federal law. In bringing the writ, the petitioner does not appeal the conviction or claim innocence, but rather she launches a collateral attack, arguing that some aspect of the trial was legally flawed such that they "may be imprisoned without sufficient cause." *Ex parte Watkins*, 28 U.S. 193 (1830). Disquiet has been registered for some time over the use of *habeas corpus* petitions by prisoners. The Supreme Court has curtailed its use, by limiting it to cases in which the state court denied a fair hearing on the issues raised, and by refusing to allow a claim that the defendant's lawyer did not raise the now-alleged constitutional issue on appeal in state court.[3] Likewise, Congress has adopted a statute requiring, among other things, that *habeas corpus* petitions be filed within a year after all state court proceedings have been exhausted. In cases in which the death penalty has been imposed, the appeals process described is much more protracted, rendering it likely that a condemned person will spend a decade or two languishing on death row awaiting, should all appeals and collateral attacks be unsuccessful, execution.

Parole

Although life sentences without the possibility of parole are not uncommon, as are terms of years that extend beyond the likely lifetime of the person, most prisoners are returned to the community and release usually occurs before the completion of their sentence. Indeed, only about one-half of the prison time meted out by judges is actually served behind

---

[3] In a 2008 decision, the Supreme Court also held that the privilege of the writ of *habeas corpus* generally extends to noncitizens, including enemy combatants, detained by U.S. officials. *Boumediene v. Bush*, 583 F. Supp. 2d 133 (D.D.C. 2008). For fans of constitutional law, the Court's holding is said to be supported by the language of the Fifth Amendment's Due Process Clause, which proclaims that, "No *person* . . . shall . . . be deprived of life, liberty, or property, without due process of law". U.S. CONST. amend V (emphasis added).

bars. Some state penal laws allow "time off" of a sentence if the prisoner does not violate prison rules during incarceration. The Congress enacted, in 2018, the First Step Act of 2018 (Pub. L. 115–391) which was calculated to reduce the federal prison population, particularly by releasing those who are serving long sentences for drug-related crimes.

Likewise, after serving the minimum term or a percentage of a sentence, an inmate may apply for parole. The parole board reviews the prisoner's crime and prison record, and also interviews the inmate to consider whether a release should be ordered. Parolees are, like probationers, required to abide by a set of individualized rules and restrictions; if a parolee fails to observe them, and the offending conduct is discovered by a parole officer or law enforcement, the recalcitrant individual is returned to prison to serve some or all of the remaining sentence.

Finally, state governors and the president have the power to commute sentences or pardon prisoners under their jurisdiction. Some governors have used the power to commute death sentences to life imprisonment in cases in which there is some question as to guilt, and more rarely when the inmate has reformed. The wholesale commutation of those on Illinois' death row by the state's governor, on the grounds that some evidence used to achieve the penalty was questionable, is an exceptional example of the process.

In addition to the usual parole process, some efforts have been made to free other inmates; older prisoners serving life sentences, or a "virtual" life sentence, are often considered as candidates for release. Similarly, inmates who are unlikely to be repeat offenders often benefit from such initiatives, allowing them to spend their last years in society and with dignity, rather than languishing in prison at great cost to the government often for crimes long-since forgotten. It must be said that victims' families may not have put the trauma out of their mind quite so quickly and may oppose pardon. The presidential power to pardon (or grant executive clemency) to federal prisoners has recently come under scrutiny.[4] But other presidents have been charged with using the power under questionable circumstances. Prior to leaving office, President Clinton commuted sentences of a number of individuals, some of whom were alleged to have been linked closely to his earlier campaigns and to the senatorial campaign of Hillary Rodham Clinton.

Constitutional Criminal Procedure: "The Criminal Goes Free Because the Constable Has Blundered"

The above proposition (articulated by Judge, later Supreme Court Justice, Benjamin Cardozo in *People v. Defore*, 150 N.E. 585, at 587 (1926) nearly a century ago) may well summarize the constitutional conundrum presented to police, prosecutors, and the courts. It is known in the trade as the "exclusionary

---

[4] As this edition was being revised, President Trump, and not without controversy, commuted the sentence of Roger Stone, who had been convicted of seven crimes for which he was sentenced to prison for forty months.

rule." Should evidence collected prior to or at the time of arrest which is gained from an "unreasonable search and seizure" (one that violates the Fourth Amendment) be nevertheless admissible in a criminal proceeding against the defendant? Or should a confession or other incriminating statement obtained from a suspect who was not informed of the Fifth Amendment right to remain silent be excluded from evidence at trial? And what about evidence discovered pursuant to an unlawful arrest or an involuntary confession? The conundrum: in or out of evidence at trial?

While at first blush, there is logic to excluding evidence obtained "unconstitutionally," it is not axiomatic that the exclusion must necessarily follow to observe the constitutional mandate. While surely society ought not to encourage police misconduct, other options are available to dampen errant police behavior. Our blundering constable might be fined, or dismissed from the force for misconduct, or the accused might bring a civil action for monetary damages against the constable or the police force. However, these penalties have been largely ineffective. Consequently, the "exclusionary rule," jurisprudence that has developed over the course of nearly a century, remains a controversial, though a central, feature of American criminal procedure.

A few points by way of introduction. The first is that the Fourth, Fifth, and Sixth Amendments protect only against the conduct of government and its agents (initially those of the federal government, but subsequently, in the 1960s, made applicable to actions taken by state authorities through the Fourteenth Amendment). So when Detective Briscoe or Capt. Olivia Benson of "Law and Order" (a long-running American arrest through trial television drama) fame, two of "New York City's finest" (police detectives—at least on television), burst into a suspect's house without a warrant in hand, or "stops and frisks" a person because he or she sees (or would like to see) a supposed bulge in said person's pocket, or forgets to "Mirandize" a suspect in the precinct's interrogation room before questioning, the resultant evidence may be excluded from the prosecution's case-in-chief on defense motion. The jury will not be informed of it, and they therefore cannot consider it. In such a case, the jury must render their verdict without a piece of relevant, indeed possibly pivotal evidence, in establishing guilt or innocence. On the other hand, if each of the above acts is undertaken by a private citizen, there is no constitutional violation, because there is no state action. Thus, if a private detective hired by the victim or her family searches the house of another believed to be connected to the crime, and turns the evidence over to Capt. Benson, then it may be admitted so long as there was no police complicity in arranging the private operation.

Second, the application of the exclusionary rule is remarkably arcane. There are numerous nuances, glosses, and exceptions to the exclusionary rule that have developed over time. And necessarily so: after all, the facts of each individual case, the context in which searches transpire, can vary greatly. One size cannot fit all. Arguably the exceptions have swallowed the rule. But not quite. Nevertheless, at times, whether the envelope containing the illicit drugs seized was in the glove compartment, the trunk, or on the dashboard of the automobile searched might actually determine whether it is admissible, and not infrequently, whether the state has a viable case against a particular defendant.

Unconstitutional Searches

When the police undertake a search, they are usually searching property (the suspect's house, her car or even a public place that she may frequent) to uncover evidence of a crime. Certain areas are protected from police investigation without a warrant issued by a judge upon a showing of probable cause. If Detective Briscoe gets a warrant to search the house of a murder suspect and finds nothing, but upon leaving the house, notices a garbage bag out in front of the house which contains the same rat poison that killed the victim, was the search of the bag constitutionally permissible?

Probably. The Fourth Amendment is said to protect people, not places, and only areas in which the suspect had an "expectation of privacy" are exempt from search without being specified in the warrant. It is unlikely that such an expectation exists with a garbage bag placed outside a house. Thus, the warrant to search the house probably allows the search of garbage inside and on the stoop, and also one on the street. Beware of what you toss away!

The notion that a warrant is necessary to intrude upon areas in which the suspect had an expectation of privacy is particularly strained when technology is involved. When the police overhear conversations through an electronic listening device, even one fixed to a public phone booth, it is a search. But a tape recording that results when a police informant, who is wired, meets the suspect in a bar and engages her in a discourse about a crime, is admissible because one may not reasonably expect another, even a friend, to withhold incriminating information from the police. Aerial surveillance and photography over a home may not be a search, but "thermal imaging" of property is. In a recent case, the police scanned a house in which they believed marijuana was being illicitly grown under high-intensity lamps with a heat-seeking device; it was held that the use of such imaging technology was a search. On the other hand, the drug-sniffing dog does not "search" when he meanders around your luggage at the airport, trained to distinguish between dirty clothes and dirty bombs. Similarly, the Supreme Court has also held that attaching GPS tracking to a car so as to monitor the its movement constitutes a search within the meaning of Fourth Amendment because such tracking physically occupies private property for the purpose of obtaining location information in violation of one's "reasonable expectation of privacy." *United States v. Jones*, 565 U.S. 400 (2012).

Unreasonable Searches

Having come to terms with the slippery concept of what constitutes a "search" under the Fourth Amendment, attention may now turn to whether the one undertaken was reasonable. For it to so qualify, there must be probable cause, reasonable grounds to believe that evidence will be uncovered in a particular, specified place. Although the Constitution requires probable cause for a search warrant to be issued by judicial officers (a document that describes with particularity the place to be searched, the evidence to be seized, and alleges the circumstances that constitute the police's conclusion that a search will turn up stipulated evidence), it has not been read to require search warrants in every case. Certain exceptions have been recognized: those in which the police may undertake the so-called "warrantless search."

But, with or without a warrant, the police must have probable cause in order to search premises. Warrantless searches are permitted in exigent circumstances. For example, when Capt. Benson knocks on the door of a house to interview a person regarding a crime, and hears a scream, she may enter the premises; if she sees white powder that may resemble heroin and a needle, she may seize it, and if found to be the illegal drug, it may be introduced as evidence in a case against the occupant for possession of a controlled substance. The foregoing is an example of both the "exigent circumstances" exception, and the "plain view" doctrine: if the police officer has a legal right to be somewhere (and here she does), and observes incriminating evidence, it is admissible even if the officer had no warrant to search for it.

Another exception to the search warrant requirement pertains to automobiles. If the police stop a car because they suspect criminal activity, they may search the car and occupants if they have probable cause that some illicit activity is occurring or had occurred. Whether this exception, and a rather broad one given the attachment of Americans to their buggies, is based upon the "exigent circumstances" doctrine is unclear—the fact that a car is mobile and can be driven out of the jurisdiction suggests so, as such an exit may ensue if police are precluded from searching the car without a warrant. It trumps the conflicting "reasonable expectation of privacy" argument that the occupants believe they might have within their automobile. The police may even move the car to a crime lab to undertake a more extensive search than would be possible on the streets.

Another exception to the warrant requirement is searches incident to arrest. If there is reasonable suspicion that a person has engaged in or is engaging in criminal activities, a police officer may search the person placed under arrest (and the area immediately surrounding her) to protect herself from a concealed weapon, or to prevent the destruction of evidence. If the police find evidence to charge the accused with a separate crime during this search, for example, a search of the person arrested for robbery turns up illicit drugs, the latter may be admitted as evidence of the additional offense.

Moreover, the Supreme Court has permitted police to "stop and frisk" individuals on lesser grounds than probable cause. If an officer has "reasonable suspicion" that an individual is armed and dangerous, perhaps by observing the individual's particular conduct, then the officer may stop that person and temporarily detain him for the amount of time reasonably necessary to confirm or dispel such suspicion. *Arizona v. Johnson*, 555 U.S. 323 (2009). The officer may also "frisk" the detainee (pat down outer clothing) for weapons. *Id*. This "stop and frisk" standard is applicable to individuals encountered by police during a traffic stop or as a pedestrian. *Id*. If weapons or contraband are found, they are admissible as evidence. While an anonymous tip alone may not be sufficient to constitute the requisite threshold suspicion, running from police in a high crime area may be adequate.

Confessions

The Fifth Amendment does not preclude an individual from confessing to having committed a crime. Rather, a person cannot be "compelled" to be a witness against herself. Involuntary confessions are therefore inadmissible; those which are voluntary may be entered into evidence. Voluntary, however, is a relative term. Few would regard a confession extracted by torture as freely given. Less brutal treatment, like isolating the suspect and subjecting her to hours of continuous interrogation, is generally unacceptable. But police deception to rouse a confession is permitted; Capt. Benson can offer a promise of leniency ("We'll ask the District Attorney to go lightly on you if you tell us where you hid the body") or overstate (or even lie about) the physical evidence obtained against the suspect to entice a confession ("We've got your DNA on the murder weapon so you might as well come clean").

The circumstances under which the police question suspects are also regulated by the *Miranda* rule. Statements obtained during a custodial interrogation are inadmissible, unless the suspect has been informed of her rights and voluntarily waives them. Even casual fans of police drama on television can recite the precise words of the warning given by an officer upon the apprehension of a suspect:

> You have the right to remain silent. If you give up the right to remain silent, anything you say can and will be used against you in a court of law. You have the right to the presence of an attorney. If you desire but cannot afford one, an attorney will be appointed for you before questioning.[5]

Once the suspect requests a lawyer or indicates that she wishes to remain silent, interrogation must end, or the statements elicited by the police or the prosecutor are inadmissible at trial unless the suspect reinitiates the conversation.

Like other constitutional safeguards, *Miranda* is not without its exceptions. In the first place, both rights—the rights to remain silent and to have a lawyer present during questioning—can be waived in whole or in part. A criminal defendant's Sixth Amendment right to counsel attaches upon all critical stages of the proceedings, including interrogation, and its waiver is clear only in cases in

---

[5] The actual words as articulated in *Miranda* are not required so long as notice of the right is reasonably conveyed to and understood by the suspect. *Florida v. Powell*, 559 US 50 (2010).

which the defendant does so voluntarily, knowingly, and intelligently. Once cautioned, the validity of implied rather than expressed waivers, and evidence obtained thereafter, remains uncertain. *Montejo v. Louisiana*, 556 U.S. 778 (2009). In addition, *Miranda* warnings are only required prior to custodial interrogation (defined as a point in the arrest spectrum when the accused's liberty is significantly curtailed) in a manner similar to an arrest, even though no formal arrest has occurred. Thus, police questioning in a suspect's house or during a routine traffic stop does not require the officer to issue a warning.

Some other exceptions to *Miranda* are permitted. A police undercover agent need not caution. If a suspect is being booked and freely reveals information merely by stating his identity or an interrogation occurs to abate a dangerous situation, the evidence taken may be used against the accused even though *Miranda* warnings have not been read.

Not only is the physical evidence or statements of the accused inadmissible if obtained in violation of the Fourth or Fifth Amendment, but any evidence or statements which result from them is also inadmissible under the eloquently phrased "fruit of the poisonous tree" rule. Thus, if the warrantless and illegal search led to a confession that independently reflects upon guilt, it may be inadmissible. Likewise, if the warrantless search of the suspect's house for stolen goods turns up a vault key, and stolen goods are found in the suspect's safety deposit box, the evidence cannot be admitted: it is a product (or the fruit of) an illegal search.

Exclusionary Rule Exceptions

While the current Supreme Court has narrowed the exceptions to the exclusionary rule, it is still a robust principle of American constitutional law. If, for example, the police act in good faith, an arrest may be valid even though the warrant issued was defective. Recent cases have upheld arrests in which a flawed warrant was issued due to a computer glitch. Likewise, the exclusionary rule did not kick in to suppress evidence of a firearm obtained during a traffic stop when police conducted the search in "objectively reasonable reliance" on binding judicial precedent and with a good faith belief that their conduct was lawful. *See Davis v. United States*, 564 U.S. 229 (2011). Specifically, the exclusionary rule seeks not to deter such conduct but was created only to discourage deliberate or reckless disregard for Fourth Amendment rights. *Id*.

In addition, the evidence otherwise excluded from the prosecutor's case-in-chief may be offered to impeach the defendant's testimony under certain circumstances. If, for example, the accused takes the stand and proclaims her innocence, an otherwise inadmissible confession (for example one obtained in the absence of *Miranda* warnings) may be used to impeach the witness's credibility. The Constitution, it is said, does not condone perjury. Finally, the extent to which evidence is the poisonous tree's fruit has been to some degree circumscribed. If the discovery of incriminating evidence by the police in an illegal search was otherwise inevitable, the evidence can be admitted, even though it was initially discovered in the course of an illegal search.

Conclusion

Some commentators believe that it was the Supreme Court that committed the blunder in fashioning the exclusionary rule. After all, the government against which these protections were cast was the "oppressive" British colonial regime, and not one "of the people, by the people, and for the people." Moreover, the crimes committed by the colonists were largely political in nature. What grounds are there to extend the protection against tyranny to common criminals? Yet the ultimate logic is simply that the government must play 'fair" with its citizens.

Contrary to popular belief, it is in practice rare for evidence to be excluded and convictions overturned because constitutional safeguards have been violated. Police are trained to conduct inquiries consistent with constitutional requirements. Likewise, judges generally believe police versions of their actions, and are reluctant to exclude probative evidence when offered in court. Nevertheless, the exclusionary rule remains a central feature of the criminal justice system.

No doubt the establishment and enforcement of the exclusionary rule hampers police in apprehending criminals. By the same token, the protections offered the defendant in criminal trials also make the prosecutor's job more difficult. Yet these provisions provide a measure of protection for ordinary citizens against an intrusive government. The duel between the government and its less than upstanding citizens continues and must be played according to rules; and while they are part of an ongoing dialogue, the state is bound to follow them.

CHAPTER 13

A BILL OF RIGHTS FOR ALL SEASONS

Introduction

The earlier chapter on the allocation of governmental authority stressed that a major concern of the framers of the Constitution was to limit the powers of the federal government. In the minds of the newly-minted Americans, the Revolution and independence was essential because of the oppression of British colonial rule. Thus, an objective of the Framers was to ensure that government, even the limited and democratically-elected one carefully conceived and fashioned in Philadelphia in 1787, would not be able to infringe upon individual liberties. In 1791, the Bill of Rights, the first ten amendments to the Constitution, was adopted to achieve that goal: to protect the people against the possibility of governmental tyranny.

That was then; and over two centuries have since passed. No document drafted in the last years of the eighteenth century can easily address current concerns regarding civil liberties that obtain amongst twenty-first century Americans. But the Bill of Rights, though it has fewer guarantees than more modern charters of liberty (for example, the European Convention on Human Rights or many European constitutions like the Italian and German ones drafted in response to fascism), preserves religious liberty, provides for free expression of ideas, tempers criminal law enforcement, and protects both personal privacy and private property.

Because the Constitution establishes a process for amending its provisions, albeit a tortuous one, other safeguards have been added. In particular, the post-Civil War Amendments (Thirteenth through Fifteenth) abolished slavery, guaranteed citizens of the United States the "equal protection of the laws," and provided the right to vote to all American citizens regardless of race, with the vote, however, limited to males.

But it has arguably been judicial interpretation rather than emendation of the text that has modernized the limited litany of rights catalogued in the Bill of Rights. Having been granted the power to resolve disputes arising under the Constitution and laws of the United States (and having asserted the power of judicial review of legislative and executive acts in *Marbury v. Madison,* 5 U.S. (1 Cranch) 137 (1803)), the judiciary (state and federal) has been frequently called upon to determine whether a particular governmental act infringed upon the liberties granted to citizens in the Constitution, and if it did so, pronounce that act void. The process of measuring governmental actions against vaguely worded constitutional mandates has given American courts the power to expand upon the scope and extent, and embellish upon the nature, of the liberties specifically guaranteed in the Bill of Rights.

Whether judges should do so is the subject of much debate. In the minds of some, the Bill of Rights and other constitutional protections are organic; broadly articulated protections against governmental overreach that may be applied in modern contexts to address issues that probably never occurred to the Framers, the most controversial of which (at least currently) is the right to privacy, and in particular, reproductive rights. Through this process, it is argued, the Bill of Rights may remain today as it was intended in the past, a vigilant protector of individual liberty. To others, only those rights originally (hence the term "originalism" has been coined as shorthand for their theory of constitutional interpretation) and expressly elaborated by the Framers should be protected; if changing times, shifting mores and beliefs, require additional protections, resort should be to the amendment process. This discourse is politically charged, and the ultimate outcome is uncertain. With its leading exponent, Justice Antonin Scalia no longer on the bench, it is uncertain the extent to which the theory will continue have the same weight as it did while he was the leading conservative voice on the Supreme Court. On the other hand, it would be premature, given the current composition of the Court to believe that the bell has tolled on the premise.

The process of applying constitutional provisions has already been visited in our earlier discussion of criminal procedure. The implications of the Fourth, Fifth, and Sixth Amendments on the conduct of police investigations, and the rights of criminal defendants have been explored.[1] We also observed 'takings'

---

[1] *See above*, Chapter 12.

jurisprudence in the chapter on property.[2] This chapter focuses on a variety of rights that promote the free expression embodied in the First Amendment, and considers the meaning of the Fourteenth Amendment's rather vague mandate requiring that all citizens to be granted the "equal protection of the laws." It then addresses the controversial issue of the extent of the right to privacy embodied in the Ninth Amendment. Finally, it considers that most American of constitutional protections: the right to bear arms embodied in the Second Amendment.

First Amendment: Religious Expression and Tolerance

A number of American colonies were established as refuges for persecuted religious minorities. Contrary to British practice, the Framers sought to create a state without a formally-recognized religion. The First Amendment ("Congress shall make no law respecting the establishment of religion. . .") was designed, so it has been said, to build a wall between church and state. Both freedom of religion—the right to worship without government interference—and freedom from religion—that government (which has been read to apply to all levels of American government, federal, state, and municipal) should not be used to advance particular religious beliefs are embodied within First Amendment protection.[3]

---

[2] *See above*, Chapter 8.

[3] To some that separation seems arguable; whenever one spends a buck, it has "In God We Trust" emblazoned on it.

Easier said than done. The essence of the protection of free exercise, what one might call the "benchmark principle" creates a conundrum. To be sure the Constitution must allow *religious* groups the ability to practice their *religious* beliefs free from governmental interference. It is said that for government to interfere with the exercise of religious practice, it must usually be demonstrated that there is a compelling need to do so. Yet at times a less rigorous standard is applied: the Supreme Court seems to retreat and only require government to show that it does not intend to interfere with a religious practice. An example of the conundrum: in the era of COVID-19, can state governments ban religious services on the grounds that gathering in an edifice may violate social-distancing protocols?

Which position the Supreme Court will take on "free exercise" cases is not always easy to discern; the Supreme Court's record is mixed, though recent cases have strongly protected the "free exercise" right. Three 2020 cases of the Roberts Court seem to have expanded its protection." First, the Supreme Court held that employers may refuse to provide birth control pills as part of their health care coverage if it violates their religious or moral beliefs. *Little Sisters of the Poor Saints Peter & Paul Home v. Pennsylvania*, 140 S. Ct. 2367 (2020). Another case, allowed Montana to indirectly provide state funded scholarships to religious school students. *Espinoza v.*

Students pledge allegiance to "one nation under God." The explanation may be that religion is accommodated, but a particular religion is not. That generic religion is, of course, the Judeo-Christian tradition. There is no escaping the disconnect.

Montana Dep't of Revenue, 140 S. Ct. 2246 (2020). Finally, employees at Catholic schools were excluded from federal employment discrimination law. *Our Lady of Guadalupe Sch. v. Morrissey-Berru*, 140 S. Ct. 2049 (2020). In each of these cases, at least arguably, "free exercise" trumped separation of church and state.

Earlier cases may seem to exhibit an element of contradiction. On the one hand, the enforcement of criminal penalties for polygamy, a tenet of the Mormon faith, was permitted, and more recently, the Supreme Court allowed state government to sanction an employee who was using an illegal drug, though its use was claimed to be part of a Native American religious ceremony. But the Court, on the other hand, has also protected Old Order Amish religious scruples by exempting their children from public education. Likewise, it has struck down a provision banning ritual animal slaughter citing "free exercise" principles.

The First Amendment guarantee also prevents government from becoming excessively entangled in religion. Government should not in general further a particular faith or religion. The current benchmark rule considers three factors: whether the government's action, arguably supporting religion, is secular in purpose; does not unduly advance religion; and does not result in excessive entanglement in religion. Thus, sanctioning a particular prayer or allowing a reading from the Bible (usually the New or Old Testament) in public school violates the establishment clause. But government may "accommodate" religion, by, for example, allowing religious displays on public property (though not at the government's expense) or by providing free transportation or educational services for students in religious schools where the same services are offered to those in public schools. Likewise, religious student groups must be permitted to use school property on the same basis as other student organizations. Consistent doctrine?

Because religion is an integral part of American life, it has not been easy to fix the perimeter of the wall that separates it from government. Perhaps a single case best illustrates the dilemma. A parent objected to his child pledging allegiance to the American flag, a routine daily exercise in public schools. When a student rises in the classroom and pledges allegiance to the United States, must she pronounce (as the words confirm) that ours is a nation "under God?" Is there religious significance to the rote affirmation? And if there is, whose God is the nation under? And what about the sensibilities of those who may believe that that there is no God, or if there is, that this meager daily recognition of God is insufficient to satisfy our nation's indebtedness to divine providence? In its judgment, the Supreme Court did not address the constitutional issue, because the challenger lacked standing. Chief Justice Rehnquist's concurring opinion indicated that the pledge was a secular act reaffirming our national heritage. Justice Thomas did not find the pledge to be coercive, and therefore did not constitute the establishment of a religion. *Elk Grove Unified School District v. Newdow*, 542 U.S. 1 (2004).

First Amendment: Free Expression

The First Amendment also precludes Congress from "abridging freedom of speech or of the press." Once again reference to the colonial experience explains the Framers' insistence that government not impede the free flow of political ideas and opinions. British colonial governments, consistent with practice in the mother country, had attempted to quell dissent by forbidding both its public, or even private, expression.

But the logic of free speech transcends time and geography. Other legal orders, with very different histories and traditions, value free expression. It seems axiomatic that informed choice in a democracy can only be undertaken when a variety of political positions are fully aired. Likewise, expression is an essential aspect of the human personality; limiting it impedes personal intellectual and emotional development.

Early American free speech cases narrowly read free expression rights. In the same decade that the Bill of Rights was adopted, Congress passed a group of four statutes collectively known to historians as the "Alien and Sedition Acts," which among other things, made criminal the publication of "any false, scandalous, and malicious writing." Opposition newspaper editors and other anti-governmental political activists were arrested and fined, though with the election of Thomas Jefferson, they were pardoned, and the fines repaid. Subsequent decades saw further curbs on political expression: opposition to the Civil War was silenced; those sympathetic to the Russian Revolution were jailed in the early twentieth century; John Scopes was prosecuted for teaching evolution in violation of a 1935 Tennessee statute; and public libraries banned certain volumes from appearing in their collection due to their content.

In the 1920s, a line of cases began to develop a test for determining the circumstances under which government can curb free speech. A number of considerations are to be weighed in deciding whether or not the government can silence a speaker. In the first place, the government ought not to be able to regulate speech merely because it disagrees with the message. All content-based regulation is therefore suspect. Thus, an ordinance banning hate-speech was held invalid, because it was premised on an objection to the speaker's message. Whether the current climate of tolerance for hate speech should continue may be rethought. Hate speech is abusive expression exhibiting racist, anti-Semitic, Islamaphobic or homophobic prejudice. Other democracies seem to be more willing to curtail it, but the American exceptionalists amongst us seem to believe that the Constitution must protect it. Last year, I was sent a button from my undergrad university which read 'Hate has no place at UMass;' if it doesn't (which it should not) it is difficult to see why *hate speech* has a place. Former President Obama has a different view. In a speech before the United Nations General Assembly in 2012, he argued: "The strongest weapon against hateful speech is not repression; it is more speech—the voices of tolerance that rally against bigotry."[4] Both of us have been wrong before!

On the other hand, what is classified as content-neutral regulation of expression may be permitted. For example, an ordinance requiring a permit for a parade or other political demonstration is constitutional. Free speech rights are currently in focus with widespread and ongoing protest over the death of George Floyd in May of 2020, and in support of racial justice and equality. To what extent can a curfew be enforced that limits political speech; can the press be targeted or interfered with by the police while reporting on such activities? In short, can free speech be curtailed if the government explicitly or implicitly proclaims a state of emergency due to national health concerns? The 2020 pandemic presents a contemporary lens through which to view the Bill of Rights under stress.

Second, the line between the permissible and impermissible regulation of expression is not easy to draw. It is not correct to say that content-based speech is always protected. For example, can pornography be banned? Surely a law so doing is content-based. Must cable television providers be required to transmit signals from broadcast television stations? After all, the express intent of the regulation was to bring their content to the eyes of the public.

---

[4]   https://obamawhitehouse.archives.gov/the-press-office/2012/ 09/25/remarks-president-un-general-assembly#:~:text=We %20do%20so%20because%20given,of%20understanding%20and% 20mutual%20respect.

The importance of free speech in a democratic society allows government to intervene only when it is protecting a compelling societal interest. And the Supreme Court has been generally reluctant to find instances in which speech can be curtailed. Thus, convictions for flag-burning as a symbol of protest (and other symbolic speech) have been overturned, because the government was unable to demonstrate a sufficient public interest to ban the conduct. Nor was a conviction under an anti-obscenity law sustained when a protestor displayed "Fuck the Draft" on his jacket. Members of the American Nazi party have been permitted to march through a Jewish neighborhood near Chicago. Protecting the tender sensibilities of citizens is not, in the Supreme Court's view, a sufficiently compelling interest to silence these speakers. The rise of social media has cast a new dimension to the debate. It raises a myriad of issues that the computer-illiterate Framers did not consider. Should social media companies be able to block/ban certain groups from access to their platforms? What about allowing bogus political ads to be displayed? Should 'lies' posted online be regarded as protected speech? And does non-intervention by the platforms promote interference in American elections similar to the alleged Russian meddling in the 2016 presidential election? Tough work lies ahead for the Supreme Court.

Third, for government to silence speech, the harm that occurs in permitting the speaker to be heard must constitute a "clear and present danger" to an individual or to society in general. Justice Holmes said that a person did not have the right to shout fire in a crowded theater, because the pandemonium that would result would be immediately harmful to those in attendance. *Schenck v. United States*, 249 U.S. 47 (1919). Thus, racist speech, threats to the president, and warnings of violence cannot be curbed where the speaker does not have the potential to carry out the violent conduct expounded. But when "fighting words" are expressed directly to an individual, and the potential to carry out a plausible threat exists, convictions have been sustained. In the latter case, and not the former examples, the danger is imminent: it is "clear and present."

Fourthly, free speech may be restricted only when the government has no other means of protecting its compelling interest. If, for example, a city is concerned with litter on the streets, may it ban the handing out of leaflets? Surely, more litter is produced in incidental commerce than in leafletting, and McDonald's continues to be able to market their burgers wrapped in paper and foil (though thankfully no longer in foam). There are other means to deal with the litter problem raised by leafleting that is less restrictive to free speech than an outright ban on their distribution: a few extra recycling bins on the street will absorb the additional trash.

A more recent example of the sometimes-overbroad nature of regulation of free speech comes from the area of child protection. May Congress ban sexually-explicit phone solicitation because children might hear the messages left? A complete prohibition was considered to have gone too far in curbing speech in order to protect the young from obscene conversation.

Sable Commc'ns of California, Inc. v. F.C.C., 492 U.S. 115 (1989).

Precisely what expression the Framers considered to be "speech" (and therefore subject to First Amendment protection) is not clear (though arguably political ideas were paramount in their own thinking). The discussion thus far illustrates that the First Amendment protects more than political speech. While the Court has protected symbolic speech, and artistic performance, it regards some forms of discourse to be outside First Amendment protection. The best example is that of child pornography and obscene expression with no redeeming social value. Commercial speech also receives considerable protection, though not quite as much as political discourse. A number of cases have held that municipal ordinances that ban advertising signposts violate freedom of expression. Sometimes commercial speech may be less than truthful. In such situations, usually advertising cases, it may be curbed. But even if it is accurate, the government need only show a substantial interest in regulation (rather than a compelling one), and the regulation must directly advance the asserted governmental interest (not that it is the least restrictive alternative).

Finally, some mention must be made directly of the freedom of the press. The Supreme Court has generally held that both press, and free speech rights are coterminous, and expression rights granted to newspapers have been extended to other media, though access to the broadcast media can be regulated due to the inherent quantitative limits of the airwaves. With the advent of cable, satellite, and the internet, however, these scarcity concerns have been largely ameliorated. An issue that confronts the media particularly is that of "prior restraints:" must permission be sought from government before publication of a news item or other information? The Supreme Court in the famous case involving the release of the secret so-called "Pentagon Papers" during the Vietnam conflict held that even where criminal charges could be brought against individuals for revealing secret information, the government could not enjoin its publication. More recent examples are attempts to curtail the publication of classified material by Edward Snowden of material he obtained as a Central Intelligence Agency employee and the copious classified information released by WikiLeaks founder Julian Assange.

First Amendment: Assembly and the Right to Petition

The Framers considered the right to collective action as linked closely to political speech. And the Supreme Court has tended to see demonstrations (exercise of the right to assemble) largely as raising free speech issues. The right to collective action embodied in the assembly clause has given rise to an ancillary right to "association." Thus, the Supreme Court has prevented the government from requiring "unpopular" groups to provide it with their membership lists. Political association is particularly protected. The most controversial recent associational issue deals with campaign financing limitations, because they impact the ability of political parties or interest groups (all associations) to have their message heard. While limitations on campaign contributions by individuals has been allowed, the Supreme Court held in 2010 that the Free Speech Clause of the First Amendment prohibits the government from restricting independent expenditures for political communications by corporations, including nonprofit corporations, labor unions, and other associations. *Citizens United v. Federal Election Commission*, 558 U.S. 310 (2010).

The Second Bill of Rights: Equal Treatment Before the Law

We now skip forward in time, and move from individual conscience to equality under the law. Before the Civil War, the liberties discussed above did not apply to a large proportion of the population of the United States: the millions of African-Americans who were enslaved. With the Union's victory over the Confederacy in 1865, Congress moved to extend a variety of rights to the newly-freed slaves.

In form, Congressional action was swift and impressive. In a scant five years, the Thirteenth Amendment banned slavery; the Fourteenth Amendment mandated equal treatment for all people;[5] and the Fifteenth Amendment extended the right to vote to all citizens, and specifically, to former slaves. While the Thirteenth Amendment was enforced according to its terms, the right to vote was largely withheld from the descendants of slaves until rigorous enforcement by the Federal Government was achieved through the Voting Rights Act of 1965. A recent Supreme Court case, however, has limited its application, in part by no longer requiring pre-clearance of voting regulation changes in some states. *Shelby County v. Holder*, 570 U.S. 529 (2013).[6] However, it is the "equal protection" and "due process" clauses of the Fourteenth Amendment that have fulfilled, at least in some measure, the promise of equality to all Americans regardless of race.

The Due Process Clause

Over time, the interpretation of the Fourteenth Amendment's words "nor shall any state deprive any person of life, liberty or property without due process of law" has varied. Does it simply mean that individuals have procedural rights when the government acts against their perceived personal or property interest? Stated another way—does it simply mandate that states must adopt a fair judicial or administrative process when interfering with Fifth Amendment rights of the accused or of property holders? Alternatively, does the recitation accord

---

[5] While the Equal Protection Clause and Due Process Clause of the Fourteenth Amendment apply to all people, the Privileges and Immunities Clause only applies to U.S. citizens.

[6] This year (2020) four cases were decided that likewise limited access to the polls by minority groups.

some substantive rights? If it is the latter, does the due process clause mandate that government may not intrude into areas of personal autonomy, particularly where economic freedom is at stake? Does government regulation of working conditions, wages and hours, even where they are protective, violate the clause, because such a limitation might infringe upon one's own ability to negotiate individual terms of employment? While the content of procedural due process has varied only slightly over time (though modern notions of procedural fairness have been enhanced before both criminal and administrative tribunals), the notion that substantive rights emanate from the Fourteenth Amendment has historically been a source of controversy.

One aspect of the substantive impact of the Fourteenth Amendment is clear: the Due Process Clause extends virtually all of the individual protections of the Bill of Rights to actions by state government. The text thereof specifically refers to actions by Congress and the federal government; protection against state excesses could be found only in state constitutions. The Due Process Clause of the Fourteenth Amendment now "incorporates" the enumerated limitations on all levels of government, and states and their emanations must also observe and apply them.

In the early twentieth century, however, a number of cases seemed to indicate that further substantive rights were implied in the Due Process Clause. Accordingly, it was held that individuals had the right to be free from economic regulation that might impede upon their ability to contract for their own labor. Such an approach was consistent with *laissez-faire* views of economic regulation that held sway in early twentieth-century America. The most significant case was perhaps *Lochner v. New York* in which the Supreme Court struck down a statute that limited the hours that a baker could work to 60 hours per week or 10 hours per day on the grounds that such regulation curtailed one's ability to freely contract for labor. *Lochner v. New York,* 198 U.S. 45 (1905).

The onset of the Great Depression made inroads into the notion that government ought not to regulate business practices, and shortly after the end of the Second World War, the Supreme Court repudiated *Lochner* and substantially abrogated the economic component to substantive due process. Thereafter, the Due Process Clause took on a different guise. At the same time economic rights were quashed, the Supreme Court began to shift the substantive guarantees of the clause from the economic to the personal. More recent cases dealing with privacy and associational rights now draw on the Due Process Clause as a source of substantive rights. An example is *Lawrence v. Texas* in which the Supreme Court used the Due Process Clause to prevent the state from prosecuting same-sex consensual sexual relations. *Lawrence v. Texas,* 539 U.S. 558 (2003).

The Equal Protection Clause

Just as the Thirteenth Amendment's promise of suffrage for former slaves was broken, the path towards equality under the law was likewise not fashioned until nearly a century after the adoption of the Fourteenth Amendment. Two landmark cases stand out as shameful symbols of America's betrayal of Black Americans: the *Civil Rights Cases*; and *Plessy v. Ferguson*. A brief description of both is necessary to place modern doctrine in perspective.

In 1875, Congress, concerned with state laws enacted after the Civil War which regulated the conduct of former slaves, the so-called "Black Codes," passed the Civil Rights Act (18 Stat. 335–37). The Civil Rights Act guaranteed equal treatment in a variety of public accommodations (though privately-owned and managed), such as inns and theaters, as well as in transport. Congress premised its legislative authority on the Fourteenth Amendment's Equal Protection Clause, and its power to enforce "by appropriate legislation" its terms. The Supreme Court struck down the legislation in the *Civil Rights Cases*, holding that Congress had the power to regulate state conduct, but not that of private actors. *Civil Rights Cases*, 109 U.S. 3 (1883). A decade later, the Supreme Court in *Plessy* upheld a Louisiana law that required separate accommodations for the races on the railroads. *Plessy v. Ferguson*, 163 U.S. 537 (1896). When a man of mixed race sat in the whites-only accommodation, he was arrested, and the constitutionality of the act was tested. *Plessy's* counsel argued that both the Thirteenth and

Fourteenth Amendment precluded separate accommodation: first, the Thirteenth, that separation of the races was a remnant of slavery (which it had abolished); and second, that his privileges and immunities as an American citizen were abridged by unequal treatment—that he was denied the equal protection of the law under the Fourteenth Amendment. The Supreme Court rejected both arguments, ratifying the contentions of southern states, that "separate but equal" accommodation was consistent with the Fourteenth Amendment's equal protection guarantee.

It was not until the movement for civil rights, after the Second World War, that this mantra was reversed. In *Brown v. Board of Education*, the Supreme Court simply held that separate public education for Blacks and Whites was inherently unequal. *Brown v. Board of Education*, 347 U.S. 483 (1954). The following year, the Court ordered states with segregated school systems to comply with the judgment with "all deliberate speed."

Whatever was meant by the enigmatic phrase aside, integration of public schools did not occur immediately. In fact, desegregating schools presented considerable practical difficulties, even when undertaken in good faith (which it frequently was not). Education in the United States is largely a municipal concern. In large cities, school attendance was assigned by neighborhood; where neighborhoods were segregated, schools remained segregated. A number of federal courts ordered the busing of students from place to place to foster racial balance in the classroom, a process that was largely unpopular with the parents of students. Another problem with the decision was that the judiciary was never quite sure exactly how much integration was required by *Brown*. Moreover, in some places, Whites abandoned cities, moving to suburbs without significant Black populations, rendering urban schools as segregated after *Brown* as they were previous thereto. Other parents sent children to private schools (that were largely White) which were untouched by *Brown*. While the public-school systems of contemporary America are far more integrated today than they were in the 1950s, particularly in the once-segregated southern states, most Black children do not receive an education on par with that obtained in the best schools in primarily White neighborhoods. There are many reasons for the disparities. Money is one. School funding is often tied, at least in part, to municipal property taxes, and therefore schools in underserved communities receive less funding and consequently, can provide only a poorer quality education. Unequal access to quality education is one factor that has led some to charge that modern America is plagued by so-called "systemic racism."

Other areas of racial discrimination have been addressed in the years since *Brown*. Laws forbidding interracial marriages, loss of the custody of a child due to an interracial second marriage, licensing laws that use race-based criteria, and jury challenges based upon race have also been held to violate the Equal Protection Clause. Likewise, the results of the *Civil Rights Cases* have been partially undone by more flexibly in determining what constitutes prohibited "state action" in race-based discrimination. Thus, covenants promising not to sell residential real estate to Black purchasers, though between private parties, were held invalid because such provisions could only be enforced by state action in the courts. *Shelley v. Kraemer*, 334 U.S. 1 (1948). Similarly, a private restaurant in a public building was subject to non-discrimination laws. *Burton v. Wilmington Parking Auth.*, 365 U.S. 715 (1961).

It is probably true that there is a consensus in America that race discrimination is immoral, as well as illegal. Support for the "Black Lives Matter" movement is widespread amongst Americans of all races. Yet how far to act to reverse centuries of discrimination remains a subject of debate. There is a controversy in contemporary America concerning so-called "reverse discrimination." In order to assist members of racial minorities to overcome the past burden of discrimination, some government programs are dedicated to "affirmative action," giving preferences to individuals who are members of historically disadvantaged groups. Higher education has been in the forefront of the battle over affirmative action, with questions as to whether race may be taken into account in selecting individuals for admission to public universities. While the Supreme Court recently reaffirmed its earlier opinion that race may be taken into account in the admissions process of public universities, it made clear that it should not be the dispositive factor. The Court decided that a particular system in Michigan that assigned additional "points" to each candidate who was a member of a racial minority was invalid. *Gratz v. Bollinger*, 539 U.S. 244 (2003). A more recent case, brought by a white woman who was rejected from the University of Texas, argued that the school's two-part admissions system, which takes race into consideration, is unconstitutional. The University's admissions policy was as follows: it first admits roughly the top 10 percent of students in every in-state graduating high school class, a policy known as the Top Ten Percent Plan, and then reviews several factors, including race, to fill the remaining spots. The Court held that the University's policy met the standard of strict scrutiny, and that a school should be given reasonable leeway in its review process if it has considered other ways to create diversity. *Fisher v. University of Texas*, 136 S. Ct. 2198 (2016).

Because much of American higher education is private, admissions policies at such universities and colleges is not a manifestation of state action and are subject to different standards. Recently, Yale University conceded that it discriminated against Asian-American students, limiting their acceptance because a substantial number of applicants exceeded their admission standards. The entering class would be, without subjecting them to higher academic standards than others, disproportionately Asia-American. Yale's policy is reminiscent of the one implemented before and after World War II to limit the number of Jewish-Americans in many undergraduate and professional schools, and to say the least is controversial.

In employment as well, affirmative action continues to be used to attempt to reverse the impact of years of discriminatory practices in hiring, but not without controversy. Universities, public and private, as well as other employers, frequently advertise positions, and seek out members of minority groups to add diversity to their workforce. Federal, as well as many state and local governments, have policies that make certain that minority-operated businesses have an equal opportunity to share in public contracts, though strict set-asides have been invalidated. However, federal contractors are required to have an affirmative action program for hiring minority workers.

Finally, the Equal Protection Clause has been extended to protect classifications other than race. The Civil Rights Act of 1964 (42 U.S.C. § 21) outlawed discrimination on the grounds of national origin. Immigration policy is a matter of fierce national debate; current law bars discrimination based on alien status. The Immigration and Nationality Act (8 U.S.C. § 1324B) prohibits employers from discriminating against individuals based on their citizenship or immigration status, or their national origin, during the hiring, firing, or recruiting processes.

Gender discrimination has been examined to a lesser degree, because the Supreme Court has not characterized women as constituting a "discrete and insular minority" without the usual protections offered by the political process, and it has relegated cases arguing gender discrimination to only intermediate scrutiny. Regardless, gender-based discrimination in state and federal law has been struck down in a series of decisions. An example is *United States v. Virginia,* a landmark case, in which the Supreme Court struck down the long-standing male-only admission policy of the state-run Virginia Military Institute. *United States v. Virginia,* 518 U.S. 515 (1996). Gender-based affirmative action is permitted when necessary to remedy past discrimination.[7] The inherent gender bias in dealing with pregnancy issues has led to a complex series of cases that on the one hand, do not regard pregnancy health benefits as discriminatory, but on the other hand, has struck down mandatory leave for pregnant teachers. *Cleveland Board of Education v. LaFleur,* 414 U.S. 632 (1974).

Privacy Rights

The discussion of the Due Process and Equal Protection Clauses herein illustrates the creative nature of constitutional interpretation by the Supreme Court. Though a half-dozen decades separate *Plessy* and *Brown,* and deeply-held beliefs about the nature of a just society and social mores may explain the Court's reversal in course, the plain truth is that the same words were read differently in the two cases by two different sets of justices. These two cases illustrate the point made earlier, that the Constitution can be regarded as an organic document, and it bolsters the argument of some

---

[7] For a summary of the cases, *see* https://openscholarship. wustl.edu/cgi/viewcontent.cgi?article=1080&context=law_ urbanlaw.

commentators and judges that particular provisions therein must be interpreted consistent with the historical moment. Of course, there is a danger here: the words in the Constitution by consequence would mean what a scant handful of unelected judges at any time decide that they mean.

This dilemma also surrounds the Ninth and Tenth Amendments to the Constitution. While recent Supreme Court opinions have found a right to privacy therein, the word is never specifically mentioned in the document. Yet the Ninth Amendment implies that there are other rights held by the people than those enumerated, and that the failure of the previous provisions to mention them does not mean that they do not exist. What else must the following passage mean: "The enumeration in the Constitution, of certain rights, shall not be construed to deny or disparage others retained by the people"? The Tenth Amendment, which restates the principle of a limited federal government by reserving all governmental authority not delegated "to the States respectively, or to the people," may be regarded as even more enigmatic, though its virtue is that it has rarely been invoked.

There is certainly some historical authority to the notion that the Framers were aiming for a government that meddled in the lives of the citizens only to the extent necessary. At the time of the Revolution, British colonial government was, at least to the eyes of colonial Americans, regarded as needlessly intrusive. So, the notion of a "penumbra" of privacy is not historically implausible or unwarranted. The difficulty, perhaps, is that it remained undiscovered until the 1960s. In *Griswold v. Connecticut*, the Supreme Court exhumed it to strike down a state law banning the use of contraceptives by married persons. *Griswold v. Connecticut*, 381 U.S. 479 (1965). The decision was extended in the next decade to include any ban on sale of such items.

The link between the Ninth Amendment and reproductive privacy, though of recent vintage, was sufficiently strong to lead the Supreme Court in *Roe v. Wade*, 410 U.S. 113 (1973) to conclude that a woman's right to terminate her pregnancy was within its ambit. Subsequent decisions have narrowed that right, but they have also reaffirmed the basic principle of a woman's right to choose. The decision is sufficiently controversial to provide the primary discussion point when new justices are appointed to the Supreme Court.

The most recent Supreme Court case on the issue suggests that even a more conservative court may continue to respect a woman's right to choose to abort a fetus within the current parameters. In *June Med. Servs. L.L.C. v. Russo*, 140 S. Ct. 2103 (2020), the Court was faced with a Louisiana statute which required doctors who performed abortions to have admitting rights in hospitals within 30 miles of their clinic. The statute was, for all intents and purposes, identical to a Texas statute struck down in 2016. The case, the first abortion challenge heard by the Supreme Court since the addition of President Trump's two appointees, was closely watched by activists on both side of the abortion debate, partly because of its close similarities to the Texas case. The decision was 5 to 4. Justice Stephen Breyer, writing for the majority, viewed the issue as one of abortion rights: the Louisiana law would make it virtually impossible for many women to obtain a safe, legal abortion in the state and imposed substantial obstacles on those who could. But the cause was saved by Chief Justice Roberts, no friend to abortion rights, who concurred in the result on the grounds that he was bound by the precedent the Court had set just four years ago when it rejected a similar law in Texas.

Two recent cases since the opinion in *Lawrence v. Texas* suggest that the current Supreme Court still believes that the government's intrusion in private life should be limited. The first is *Obergefell v. Hodges* which required all states to issue marriage licenses to same-sex couples and to recognize same-sex marriages validly performed in other jurisdictions. *Obergefell v. Hodges*, 576 U.S. 644 (2015). This established same-sex marriage throughout the United States and its territories. In a majority opinion authored by Justice Anthony Kennedy, the Court examined the nature of fundamental rights guaranteed to all by the Constitution, the harm done to individuals by delaying the implementation of such rights while the democratic process in legalizing them plays out, and the evolving understanding of discrimination and inequality that has developed.

The second case dealt with gender equality. *Bostock v. Clayton Cty., Georgia,* 140 S. Ct. 1731 (2020). Prior to the decision it was legal in more than half of the states to fire workers for being gay, bisexual or transgender. The decision denying employers the ability to discriminate extended workplace protections to millions of people across America. The majority opinion was written by Justice Gorsuch, a President Trump appointee. The Court found that gender equality was contemplated as within the Civil Rights Act of 1964, which prohibits discrimination in the workplace on the basis of (amongst other classifications) gender and sexual orientation.

The Second Amendment

No words in the Constitution have been the subject of more debate, well maybe, than the enigmatic language of the Second Amendment: "A well-regulated Militia, being necessary to the security of a free State, the right of the people to keep and bear Arms, shall not be infringed." An originalist might argue that those words were calculated to make certain that the federal government would not hold a monopoly over the military in the newly-formed United States. Indeed, the victorious Continental Army was an amalgam of state militias—the American equivalent of the British so-called "trained bands." The Founders, always skeptical of too much power at the federal level, probably intended the military to be as much a set of state institutions as they did a federal force. Clearly, they did not imagine the American military enmeshed in a war in

Afghanistan for 20 years. Well, it did not turn out that way. State militias do continue to exist, as the National Guard, but the American military as we understand it today is largely a federal enterprise.

All that said, what about an individual's right to own a gun? While government in the time of the Framers did not prevent individuals from having guns, the individual right is not specifically enshrined in the words of the Second Amendment. Or is it? In 2008, the Supreme Court ruled that "[t]he Second Amendment protects an individual right to possess a firearm unconnected with service in a militia, and to use that arm for traditionally lawful purposes, such as self-defense within the home." *District of Columbia v. Heller*, 554 U.S. 570 (2008). Those words came from a textualist justice, who was unwilling to so freely interpret constitutional language in privacy cases. That said, the decision about the extent of gun rights, what can be prohibited rather than what cannot, is a highly charged, political one. The epidemic of gun violence that plagues America, from mass shootings to sporadic duels on the city streets, has taken a dreadful toll. But the response has been uneven: some more liberal states have moved towards rendering gun ownership more difficult, and created limitations on certain types of weapons; in other, more conservative states, legislation to broaden gun rights has been adopted.

Conclusion

The protection of individual rights in American Constitutional law is a vast and fascinating subject that can only be glossed in a handful of pages. The mind may boggle at the simple fact that a handful of passages added to the Constitution in 1791, and only very modestly supplemented in the intervening years, provides a framework for human rights in twenty-first century American society. To justify the current situation by saying (as many Americans do) that these provisions have served us well is to ignore the very lengthy history of racial discrimination that marked, and marred, the first two hundred plus years of the American experiment in government.

The more immediate question is not the past, but the future: whether the safeguards and the process of elaborating them are sufficient for present-day American society; and whether judgments over the extent of individual liberties ought to be in the hands of unelected judges with life tenure who interpret rather vague notions like "the equal protection of the laws." The rub is to find an alternative that might better serve the American people. It would not be an easy matter to re-write the Constitution. It would require America to forge a consensus on the place of government in the lives of its citizens. Until that daunting task is undertaken, human rights law in the United States is governed by the present prevailing notion of an eighteenth century understanding of the extent to which government ought to keep its now very large nose out of the daily life of Americans.

CHAPTER 14

ADMINISTRATIVE AGENCIES AND THEIR LAW: THE FOURTH BRANCH OF AMERICAN LAW

Introduction

A generation ago, an introduction to American law could safely skirt administrative law, that part of law's kingdom that concerns the variety of rulemaking powers and decision-making processes undertaken by an array of administrative agencies of both federal and state government. But the structure of the American legal system has changed significantly in the course of the twentieth century. More is demanded of government, and administrative agencies (defined for purposes of this chapter as an extension of the legislative and executive branches, operating apart from each as a governmental authority empowered to make and enforce rules and adjudicate disputes) have been established to oversee a wide variety of governmental functions. Both the number of administrative agencies and their significance in ordering American life and the law has expanded, requiring a student with aspirations to expertise in American law to acquire a basic understanding of the mélange of legislative, executive, and judicial rules that are bundled under the rubric "Admin law."

As noted earlier, separation of powers, a division of labor amongst the branches of government—a legislature that makes the laws, an executive that enforces the laws, and a judiciary that interprets

them when disputes between parties arise—
characterizes the American legal system. In large
measure, the administrative agency, be it regulatory
(like the Securities and Exchange Commission or the
Environmental Protection Agency), or one
responsible for social welfare (like the Social Security
Administration or the Federal Emergency
Management Agency) may appear to be a
compendium of all three "branches." Most
administrative agencies appear to legislate because
they make binding rules pursuant to congressional
delegations of authority (or, for state agencies,
pursuant to the state legislature's delegations). But
they also enforce federal (or state) laws and their own
rules, and set federal (or state) governmental policy.
Finally, they adjudicate disputes that arise in their
discrete areas of competence.

Thus, administrative agencies may seem to some
as many-headed governmental monsters, even if it is
grudgingly conceded that modern government could
not function without them. Because regulatory
agencies restrict rights of individuals and business
entities, more attention initially focused on them
than upon welfare agencies that bestow government
largess. However, with the growth of government-
sponsored welfare programs in the last half of the
twentieth century onwards, there are vast numbers
of individuals whose lives and well-being depend on
the policies of administrative agencies, and their
implementation. The operation of welfare agencies is
now of equal concern to lawyers.

Many explanations can be offered to understand the reasons for the rise of what has been called the "administrative state." Like much of American law, efficiency considerations probably underlie many of them. There are practical limitations upon the ability of the legislature to articulate comprehensive norms with requisite specificity; policy goals can more easily be set by statute, while leaving to specialist agencies the authority to fill in the precise, and oft-times technical nuances and detail of regulatory or social welfare programs. Moreover, the administrative agency is generally delegated its powers in a specific field; its officials should therefore be able to develop the particular expertise required to undertake their prescribed role. Indeed, bestowing upon a single unit the panoply of public functions may minimize the duplication inherent in complex modern multi-level governments, federal and state. Ideally, administrative agencies are also non-political.

Although federal agency heads are often appointed by the president (and therefore may have political or ideological allegiance) and are usually part of the executive branch (some are fully independent and their heads cannot be removed by the president), administrative agencies, both state and federal, comprise a civil-service bureaucracy that manages day-to-day affairs in areas under its mandate. It therefore may be hoped that administrative agencies are largely free of partisan politics, though it is questionable that this obtains in any administration, let alone the one of the current White House occupant. Some continuity and consistency can therefore be afforded in discrete governmental programs, even when political shifts occur within elected branches of government. Of course, this sword is doubled-edged. Without political accountability and sufficient safeguards—and, no doubt, administrative law aspires to provide them— there is the danger that an all-powerful bureaucracy may lose sight of broader public interest concerns and run rampant over individual rights.

Bearing in mind the justification for the administrative state offered above, a sketch of federal administrative practice follows to determine whether the balance between efficiency and public need is satisfied. Though state administrative law may differ in detail, the discourse provided herein describes patterns broadly applicable to agencies of the states.

Functions of Agencies

Agencies make law, or perhaps better stated, agencies make regulations that advance enacted law: they issue binding norms of general applicability, and then they interpret them. But they do so within bounds. Agencies are creatures of the Congress and the president. The Constitution (Article II, Section 2) authorizes Congress to establish "officers" of government and provides that the president appoint them either with or without Senate confirmation, as Congress so directs. The agency's rulemaking authority is set by statute, and the extent to which Congress can delegate lawmaking authority to administrative agencies is not unfettered. Congress must offer the agency an "intelligible principle," that is to say, provide reasonable guidance to the agency when authorizing it to make rules to implement a federal program or policy embodied in a statute. Congress's ability to delegate is not unfettered. In *Gundy v. United States*, the Supreme Court considered the delegation powers of Congress. *Gundy v. United States*, 139 S. Ct. 2116 (2019). Congress used the Sex Offender Registration/ Notification Act (SORNA) to delegate authority to the attorney general to prescribe rules for registering sex-offenders and allowed the attorney general to apply such registration requirements retroactively. A plurality of the court queried whether the legislation set out an "intelligible principle" to guide the rule-maker.

The process of rulemaking is controlled by the Administrative Procedure Act (hereafter APA) which provides guidelines for adopting legislative rules (rules promulgated by agencies that create legal obligations related to enacted federal law) unless Congress has specified another process. With respect to legislative rules, the APA requires an agency to make public in the Federal Register (a daily government publication) its proposed rule, and provide a "notice and comment" period (unless there is good cause to omit it) for interested parties (and the general public) to offer reactions to its proposed rule. While the agency need not abandon, or even revise, its rule in light of comment, it is required to engage in "reasoned decision-making." 5 U.S.C.S. § 553 (LEXIS through Pub. L. 116–155). Specifically, the agency is required to review and respond to all comments, significant and germane, so long as the comment is relevant to the proposed rule. This process, however, provides parties averse to the proposed rule an opportunity to slow, or even halt, the rulemaking process; those seeking to do so may simply submit extensive documents for comment, forcing the agency to sift through thousands of pages of material and to provide responses thereto. If an agency does not respond to all relevant comments, they will often find themselves embroiled in litigation. The final rule is published in the Code of Federal Regulations and becomes effective upon the date mandated.

This process of rulemaking is decidedly casual in comparison to congressional lawmaking, but formal in terms of other actions taken by administrative agencies; consistent with its form, it is often referred to outright as "notice-and-comment rulemaking." *See, e.g., United States v. Mead Corp.*, 533 U.S. 218 (2001). For example, no formal hearings are required. Congress may, in its legislation, require an agency to engage in a more elaborate process to allow a greater degree of transparency in reaching a result, though it does so infrequently.

Agencies act through other means. Interpretive rules, those issued to address the implications of administrative rules in a particular context, require even less formal promulgation. The form of interpretive rules may vary. Some of these interpretive rules seem themselves to have a rule-like quality to them. They may not set additional burdens; if they do, then they are legislative rules. Others are in more informal guise, for example they appear as responses to "Frequently Asked

Questions." Though an official notice-and-comment period is not generally observed when promulgating interpretive rules, thus thwarting their ability to carry "the force of law," interested parties are able to challenge the agency's interpretation. In addition to these interpretive rules, agencies also may issue policy statements—pronouncements that are calculated to give interested parties guidance on the agency's application and interpretation of its rules and the federal law with which it is charged, future rulemaking, and the agency's potential enforcement plans. The agency may also respond to public inquiries, usually on issues of individual compliance with mandated rules, though the advice given is often non-binding.

In addition to making rules, agencies adjudicate disputes arising over the application of rules to individuals. Certain acts by an agency against an individual or business entity require a formal adjudication affording the private party some rights, consistent with the Constitution's Fifth Amendment protection against deprivations of "life, liberty, or property, without due process of law." This due process right has been broadly construed to attach to most governmental action that allocates entitlements. Though a complex area of constitutional law, the due process standard that is required depends upon the nature of the right infringed. The court will balance the character and importance of the individual interest that is at stake with the government's not inconsequential need to act efficiently and expeditiously.

Adjudications in the wide array of administrative law tribunals usually occur when an adverse decision has been made against a party by the agency involved. If, for example, a person has applied for disability payments through the Social Security Administration, and the application was denied, she has a right to demand an evidentiary hearing (though the rules of evidence do not generally apply) that roughly approximates a trial to present her case. The hearing is conducted by an administrative law judge. At a minimum, the following due process rights are generally observed: notice of the particulars under review is required; the right of the petitioner to present evidence is permitted, and the right to rebut evidence offered by the agency through cross-examination is allowed; the right to counsel is preserved; a record of the proceedings must be made; and a written decision explaining its legal and factual basis offered. Depending upon the particular agency's practice, the ruling is either in the form of a recommendation to the agency head, or it is phrased as a final determination of the disputed claim. The agency may have its own appeals process, which may in turn be subject to judicial review, as discussed below.

While a formal adjudication is often available to individuals, most decisions as a practical matter are made (and accepted) without such a hearing. Given the sheer numbers of potential complainants, it would be impractical for the system to work otherwise.

Judicial Review of Administrative Acts

Most administrative acts, both the rulemaking and the adjudicative, are subject to judicial review. Indeed, most federal statutes creating administrative agencies explicitly so provide. But where the statute is silent, the courts will consider whether the power of judicial review is implied in the enabling legislation passed by Congress. Even in cases in which the legislation creating the agency mandates that an agency decision is "final," the courts have been reluctant to determine that review by the courts is precluded, particularly where personal liberties or property rights protected by the United States Constitution are at stake. At the very least, the courts will intervene to ensure that procedural due process rights have been respected by the agency's tribunal: that the party had the opportunity to present its case, and the review process was fair.

Judicial review of an administrative determination resembles an appellate proceeding, though appeal may not necessarily lie with a circuit court of appeals. The appeal must be timely (within the period stipulated), and the appellant must have standing; she must be personally affected by the determination of the administrative tribunal. Review is on the administrative record produced in the hearing. Even newly-discovered and wrongly-excluded evidence may not be considered on appeal. Deference is given to findings of the administrative agency or judge: after all, the agency is "specialized" in the matter at issue.[1] Unless the administrative decision is unreasonable, "arbitrary or capricious," and not made in good faith or based upon substantial evidence, it will likely be affirmed by the reviewing court. Because statutes generally allow agencies considerable discretion in fulfilling their delegated tasks, overturning a decision of an administrative tribunal is frequently difficult. With respect to state administrative agencies, some states have broadened the power of judicial review, and made the procedure by which it operates more flexible, particularly in cases that raise individual rights.

Legislative and Executive Control of Agencies

The power of administrative agencies is not unfettered. Because Congress and the president create each agency, and fashion its mandate through legislation, the legislature and the executive may also terminate or limit its powers by the same means. Of course, such action is rarely taken. Influence, however, can be brought to bear in less direct ways.

---

[1] Notably, deference to an administrative agency by the reviewing court is dependent upon whether the issue concerns agency rule or policy. *See Mead*, 533 U.S. at 234. Agency rules promulgated pursuant to notice-and-comment rulemaking are said to carry the "force of law." *Id.* at 230–31. Contrarily, agency policy or interpretive rules generally do not carry the force of law because their issuance was without such formal rulemaking procedures. *Id.* Accordingly, an agency decision is shown great deference, known as *Chevron* deference, when the issue concerns a more formal rule carrying the force of law. *See Chevron, U.S.A., Inc. v. NRDC, Inc.*, 467 U.S. 837 (1984). An agency receives less deference, or *Skidmore* deference, when the issue concerns non-binding policy or interpretive rules. *See Skidmore v. Swift & Co.*, 323 U.S. 134 (1944).

Because the president appoints the heads of most administrative agencies, the tenor for agency conduct can be set by the chief executive. Moreover, the president can seek to remove the head of an errant agency, though the process varies depending upon the agency and is not straightforward. While the impeachment process set out in the Constitution is recognized as available to oust the heads of administrative agencies, it is implicit rather than explicit, and it is cumbersome, and rarely invoked. Whether the president can simply remove an agency head by executive fiat depends upon whether the agency is an independent one, and whether the agency is one exercising executive authority. At a minimum, the president always maintains the power to remove any executive official—independent or otherwise—for good cause. If an agency is independent, the term of the head is generally fixed, and political influence, the will of the president, is not sufficient to cause removal. For example, the United States Office of Special Counsel is an agency from which independence from the president is desired for obvious reasons; it may produce evidence that would lead to the president's impeachment.

But if it is not independent, and the agency performs executive functions, the president should have the power to remove the head. Because Article II, Section 3 of the United States Constitution charges the president with the obligation to see that the laws are "faithfully executed," the chief executive may remove the head (or more likely force a resignation) if he is dissatisfied with the agency's performance. The heads of those agencies that perform merely administrative functions are another matter. Employees of these agencies are federal workers who may not be dismissed, except for cause.

Congress, too, has significant power to control administrative agencies. Like all governmental expenditure, Congress appropriates the funds necessary to run each agency. The "power of the purse" is a very real one, and can be an effective way of disciplining errant agencies. Moreover, specialist Congressional committees often scrutinize agency activities to make certain that they faithfully perform their duties consistent with the powers delegated to them by law. Congressional oversight can often provide a counterbalance to executive influence, particularly when the president and the majority of Congress are of different political parties or diverse ideological bents. Congress has also established independent "watchdog" agencies such as the General Accounting Office and the Congressional Budget Office to evaluate the performance of agencies, and to ensure that their funds are properly expended. Ultimately, Congress controls the actions of agencies because it can overturn decisions made by them with which it disagrees by enacting statutes which mandate different policies or their implementation. Of course, that process requires majority votes of both houses and a presidential signature.

Conclusion

Administrative law is a vast and complex subject, as diverse as the agencies themselves. It raises a variety of issues that may only be glossed in an introduction to American law. Agencies have been created to regulate the conduct of business and the individual, and to dispense government welfare. Some are independent of, while others are creatures of, the executive branch. Almost no American is beyond the reach, directly or indirectly, of this very powerful "fourth" branch of government.

The administrative agency is an anomaly in the American legal system. Because it may make a rule, and then implement that rule, and finally adjudicate a claim arising under that rule, the administrative agency may seem at first blush tyrannical in a democratic society, seemingly "unchecked" and "unbalanced" in a legal order that is structured to limit governmental authority through the concepts of separation of powers and federalism. Even the brake on agency conduct through congressional and executive oversight seems less than robust. Likewise, judicial review of administrative actions seems unduly deferential to the administrative agency's judgment.

Yet without a system of administrative agencies, neither the federal nor the state government would be able to accomplish the peoples' business. The administrative state is probably a necessary evil, and the question for administrative lawyers is how to fashion a law and a procedure that protects individuals from the heavy-handedness that may be intrinsic to the operation of a cluster of powerful bureaucracies.

CHAPTER 15

INTERNATIONAL LAW IN THE AMERICAN LEGAL SYSTEM: IS IT REALLY THERE?

Introduction

Recent events may have cast some doubts on the extent to which America respects its responsibilities under international law. Certainly, in the area of international affairs, the United States under the current Trump Administration has acted in ways that exhibit consternation with the "old world order." An example is his threat to withdraw from the World Health Organization, his disquiet with some members of the North Atlantic Treaty Organization, so-called trade wars with both friend (the European Union) and foe (China) alike, and his withdrawal of the United States from the Paris Agreement setting an agenda to combat climate change.

America's allies and adversaries probably believe that the current president has strayed from the traditional paths of American foreign policy. But the same might have been said for former President George W. Bush, who went to war in Iraq without the support of key allies, and refused to adhere to the Kyoto Accords which the Clinton Administration actively supported. But it is one matter to act in accordance with a colorable interpretation of responsibilities under international law, and quite another to flout it. Refusing to sign on, ultimately, to the Kyoto Agreement, or to join the International Criminal Court may have been unpopular with other nations but the United States (or for that matter any other sovereign state) has no binding legal obligation to join a treaty on global warming or subject its nationals to international criminal jurisdiction. Likewise, the failure to seek further authorization from the Security Council for engaging in armed conflict in Iraq may have been imprudent, but it was arguably justified given the vague wording of earlier resolutions. Moreover, the Trump Administration is not the first to object to NATO countries' flagrant violation of defense spending commitments. President Obama likewise chided America's partners. And President Trump did ultimately support a reconfiguration of the North American Free Trade Agreement (NAFTA), which he derided as the worst trade deal in history. America is not the only nation that acts unilaterally to protect perceived national economic interests. Witness France's recent unilateral attempt to tax internet companies like Google, or Britain's departure from the European Union, an organization that it had been a member of for over 40 years.

But foreign policy aside, others perceive more troubling examples of America's lack of due regard for international law in her domestic tribunals. An instance of the questionable application of international law in domestic jurisprudence is the Supreme Court's refusal to block the execution of an alien convicted of murder who had not been accorded rights under the Vienna Convention on Consular Relations. *LaGrand (Germany v. United States)*, Judgment, I.C.J. Reports 2001, p. 466; *see also Medellin v. Dretke*, 544 U.S. 660 (2005). Perhaps it is the conjunction of America's current unpopular foreign policy, its rhetoric (or at least that of its current president), and its rethinking of some international undertakings that raises the question of the standing of international law in the American legal system.

To the American lawyer, however, it is the status of international law as a source of law in the resolution of legal disputes, the subject of this chapter, and in particular, the interplay between domestic and international law. The interplay between the two has become increasingly critical, because disputes raising international law have, according to Justice Breyer, become a much larger proportion of the Supreme Court's docket. *See* STEPHEN BREYER, THE COURT AND THE WORLD: AMERICAN LAW AND THE NEW GLOBAL REALITIES (2016). Presumably the same can be said of the lower federal courts. The observed trend likely has more to do with private transnational transactions than it does with disputes involving the American government as a legal actor. America's economic interests range globally, and there is an increasingly wide array of other nations that are formidable international business competitors with whom Americans deal. That much over-used term, "globalization," is a reality. Its reach is far more significant than simply a McDonald's restaurant unhappily placed in France. Another overworked term, the "global village," has put strains on an archaic legal order that at times seems more comfortable in the nineteenth, rather than in the twenty-first, century.

Law has not always efficiently dealt with international commercial affairs. History tends to suggest that commercial actors prefer to structure agreements to avoid disputes, and when they arise, their preferred tribunals are those comprised by fellow traders that implemented the le*x mercatoria* (the largely customary law of merchants) rather than by jurists. The modern tendency towards arbitration to resolve commercial disputes, international or domestic, is a contemporary manifestation of this longstanding predisposition.

This chapter sketches the application of both public and private international law in the United States. It begins with the two straightforward questions that each national legal order approaches somewhat differently: first, how (by what process) does the United States enter into international agreements; and second, once created, what is the status of these international obligations in the hierarchy of law in the domestic legal order? It then turns to the export of law: the controversial issue of the extra-territorial application of substantive American law and the reach of its forums. It closes with a discussion of sovereign immunity in American law.

American Process for Entering into International Agreements

Although there is only one type of international agreement expressly mentioned in the United States Constitution, the treaty, American law also recognizes the less-formally created executive agreement. Both are negotiated by the executive branch, the president and the Department of State (or, if the treaty is specialized, the appropriate executive department). The difference between the two lies primarily in congressional oversight. Executive agreements entered into by the president (an inherent constitutional power of the executive) and relating to foreign affairs, as opposed to domestic affairs, need not be formally or expressly ratified by Congress. *See Dames & Moore v. Regan*, 453 U.S. 654 (1981). However, a treaty negotiated by the executive branch must be formally ratified according to a process set out in Article II, Section 2 to have legal effect: it must be presented to the Senate; the Senate must either approve of its terms or suggest modifications; and the Senate must approve the treaty (as amended, if amended) by a two-thirds vote of those senators present. Consent by the Senate may be conditioned on particular interpretations or reservations offered, and the president must then determine whether to proclaim the altered treaty as ratified.

The rather cumbersome nature of the treaty-making process has indeed led to the adoption and judicial acceptance of executive agreements. Congress may empower the president to act in a particular area, or under certain circumstances, essentially giving the concluded executive international agreement its imprimatur prospectively; alternatively, the president may act in the international theatre pursuant to inherent executive powers. Federal courts retain the power to determine whether the subject matter of the executive agreement falls within appropriate bounds.

Status of International Agreements in American Law

The supremacy clause of the United States Constitution (Article VI, Section 2), at first glance, gives international law exalted legal status. Treaties (and, by judicial interpretation, customary international law) are, along with the Constitution and federal law, the "supreme Law of the Land." All three sources of law are co-equal, and they all trump state law. Thus, a state law is invalid if its terms are contrary to provisions of a treaty, and state lawmaking in an area of international affairs may be preempted even in the absence of conflicting federal law.

Moreover, in the much-cited case of migratory bird protection, *Missouri v. Holland*, the Supreme Court may have conceded that the treaty power was not limited by the enumerated powers of the Congress in Article I, Section 8. 252 U.S. 416 (1920). The decision suggests that the federal government might indeed act by treaty in areas in which it could not legislate by statute. Though of interest to constitutional scholars (and examined by law students), the opinion is of little practical consequence because Congress's powers are fairly broadly construed in those areas which are the likely subjects of treaties, most notably, international affairs and commerce.

But equating treaties with the United States Constitution and other federal law does not turn the

United States into a "monist" regime for a number of
reasons. In the first place, the Constitution (*Missouri
v. Holland* aside), and in particular, constitutional
rights, cannot be abrogated by treaty. In some
European nations, international law and treaties
(particularly European Union (EU) law amongst EU
member states) are accorded a higher status than
domestic law. However, in the United States, treaties
are not a superior form of federal law; a subsequently
adopted federal statute that conflicts with provisions
of a ratified treaty repeals the treaty's provisions at
least to the extent of the inconsistency. Finally, many
treaties (or certain provisions therein) are not
regarded as self-executing; they are without
immediate legal effect and require congressional
action before having legal force. Thus, a treaty (or
certain provisions) may be read as one requiring
implementing legislation before being enforceable.

Because they are accorded the status of law,
treaties may be enforced by private parties against
government officials or against another private party
in American courts. One area in which American
courts have recently been involved is in litigation
under the Alien Tort Statute (usually referred to as
the Alien Tort Claims Act). 28 U.S.C. § 1350. Enacted
in 1789 when it was addressing the issue of the
jurisdiction of the federal courts, Congress provided
federal jurisdiction in cases brought by an alien (a
non-American national) for a tort "committed in
violation of the law of nations or a treaty of the
United States." Modern use of the act began in a suit
seeking redress from a Paraguayan governmental
official living in the United States, charging acts of

torture committed in Paraguay. More recently, cases have been brought against the Serbian leader Radovan Karadzic for committing acts of genocide, and against the estate of Ferdinand Marcos for torture. In none of these cases did the acts alleged occur in the United States; likewise the defendants were not present in America.

Extra-Territoriality of American Law: Substantive Law

The extra-territorial reach of domestic American law has long been of interest to foreign lawyers. To what extent can American law prescribe norms that govern conduct abroad; and under what circumstances can claims by foreigners over non-American transactions be entertained in American courts? Before addressing these issues, a brief discourse on the territorial application of American law is in order.

Domestic law, of course, is primarily calculated to apply to legal actors going about their business within national geographic boundaries. Yet it has long been accepted that national law may control the conduct of nationals abroad. An example in American law is the Foreign Corrupt Practices Act of 1977 which bars American corporations from bribing officials of foreign governments in order to receive contracts. 15 U.S.C. §§ 78dd (LEXIS through Pub. L. No. 116–115). In 2008, the German conglomerate Siemens paid over $800,000,000 in fines for its violation even though the actionable conduct occurred outside of the United States. Likewise, in the well-known *Alcoa* case, American antitrust laws were held to cover agreements between American corporations and foreign entities entered into abroad if they have anti-competitive effects within national borders. *U.S. v. Alcoa*, 148 F.2d 416 (2d Cir. 1945). Finally, non-United States flagged cruise ships were subjected to provisions of the Americans with Disabilities Act. *Spector et al. v. Norwegian Cruise Line Ltd.*, 545 U.S. 119 (2005).

Although issues of nationality are relatively straightforward with respect to persons, defining a "national" is not always clear-cut for business entities: for example, is a foreign-based subsidiary of a United States corporation subject to American law? American law has long so maintained. For the purposes of trade embargoes, American law has treated foreign subsidiaries of American corporations as American nationals on the grounds that they are largely controlled by domestic management. American law enforcers have demanded their compliance with American legal restrictions, even when by so doing the subsidiary is required to violate the domestic law of their situs.

American law may also be enforced against non-American nationals for conduct that occurs abroad. A foreign entity that conspires to thwart American antitrust laws abroad is liable to prosecution in American courts, and indeed possibly for treble damages, leading some trading partners to adopt so called "blocking statutes" that attempt to counteract what they regard as draconian monetary penalties for otherwise legitimate business activities. Federal securities law is applied against foreign entities that participate in the American market, even when the fraudulent conduct charged largely occurs outside the United States. In addition, American law, particularly in light of the so-called "war on terror," has attempted to subject foreign nationals abroad to criminal sanctions when they commit acts against American citizens abroad. But it is not just American criminal law to which the United States has sought to subject foreign nationals abroad. Such noncitizens abroad may also benefit from due process protections under the Fifth Amendment, including the privilege to file a writ of *habeas corpus* against unlawful detainment by the United States. *See Boumediene v. Bush,* 583 F. Supp. 2d 133 (D.D.C. 2008) (holding that the writ of *habeas corpus* extends to noncitizens upon a weighing of various factors, including the citizenship status of the detainee and the adequacy of the process in which that status was determined; the nature of the site in which the detainee is apprehended; the practical obstacles inherent in affording the detainee the writ; and any potential threats if the writ is extended).

Extra-Territoriality of American Law: Jurisdiction

American law is thus expansive in its approach whom and for what conduct its substantive laws can control. An issue ancillary to the reach of the law is the range of its courts: the extent to which non-American defendants can be subjected to the jurisdiction of an American forum. This issue is not a novel one for America's federal system. American courts face this problem in purely domestic situations, when a defendant resident in one state is summoned to appear before the courts of a sister state. The governing rule in both contexts is the same: the "minimum contacts" test. Because it is unlikely that a defendant summoned to appear in an American court had no contact with the jurisdiction, the application of the "minimum contacts" rule analyzes the character of the link: was the entity purposely directing business towards or "targeting" clients or customers in the forum state? If so, a sufficient nexus is established to proceed.

Thus, the inquiry into contacts will frequently be fact-specific, and the result may depend upon the particular nature of the business in question. In addition, in domestic personal jurisdiction cases (and probably also when foreign defendants are involved), courts subject their determination of jurisdiction to a "reasonableness" test. Considerations like the burden to the defendant to appear in the forum, the plaintiff's jurisdictional alternatives, the interest of the forum state in resolving the claim, and the "efficient resolution of disputes" are thrown into the mix to determine whether it is reasonable to subject the foreign defendant to the court's jurisdiction. The context in which such cases arise is frequently when non-American nationals seek to bring suits against non-American nationals in American courts, even though the conduct occurred outside the United States, because they believe American courts will award a higher level of damages.

American courts also apply the doctrine of *forum non conveniens* to both domestic interstate and international disputes. The doctrine holds that a pending suit should be dismissed when there is a more appropriate tribunal to adjudicate the dispute than the present court. Foreign plaintiffs may wish to pursue a claim in an American court because they believe that the law and/or pre-trial processes, for example, discovery, will improve their prospects for recovery. Such concerns, however, are not considered. Likewise, the mere fact that the defendant is located in the United States, while relevant in determining a suitable forum, does not necessarily render an American court the best-placed court to adjudicate a dispute where some part of the transaction in controversy occurred elsewhere.

For a court to hear a case, process must be served on the defendant, domestic or foreign. The Hague Service Convention (1965) has provided a framework for signatory states (such as the United States) to create a government office to serve as a clearinghouse for process (complaints) issued against foreign defendants. In addition, in suits against foreign parent corporations, American law permits plaintiffs to serve an American-based subsidiary of the foreign entity. The Hague Service Convention procedure may also be used to serve discovery orders, though in most cases American courts allow the parties to serve notices to foreign defendants directly, in the same manner as they do domestic ones.

Finally, there is the question of judgments rendered abroad: how may they be enforced in

American courts? This question would more easily be resolved if an international convention similar to the Brussels Convention on Jurisdiction and the Enforcement of Judgments in Civil and Commercial Matters was extended beyond European Union members. Most American states will enforce foreign judgments, and even in the absence of reciprocity, where the court that issued the judgment might not enforce an American judgment. More than half of the states have adopted the Uniform Foreign-Money Judgments Recognition Act, which allows the enforcement of foreign judgments if doing so does not violate the state's public policy. The act demands that the forum state jurisdiction have had both subject matter and personal jurisdiction, that its procedures comport with "due process," and that fraud was absent from the proceedings. Arbitration awards are subject to the 1958 Convention on the Recognition and Enforcement of Foreign Arbitral Awards, commonly referred to as the New York Convention, an international treaty adopted by 161 countries (including the United States) which provides that the enforcement of international awards be subject to no greater conditions than those that attach to domestic awards.

American judgments sought to be enforced abroad are more often suspect than the enforcement of foreign judgments in American courts, particularly when punitive damages are at issue. Reciprocity is usually required for American judgments to be enforced abroad, as is some justification for having brought the action in American courts.

A final jurisdictional issue is whether foreign states may be sued in American courts. Prior to 1976, so-called "foreign sovereign immunity" was governed by judge-made common law, which was guided by customary international law as interpreted by the United States Department of State. The Foreign Sovereign Immunities Act (28 U.S.C. § 1604) (hereafter FSIA) sweeps away previous law and provides immunity for a nation state's "sovereign" acts, but not for its "private" acts. Thus, when a sovereign engages in "commercial activity," it may be sued in American courts, on the same terms as if it was a private legal actor, if its conduct has effects in the United States. Whether an act is "commercial" depends upon its nature and not its purpose, so when Argentina floated bonds to stabilize the peso, it was acting "commercially," even though the ultimate goal of its action was governmental. Likewise, sovereign immunity cannot be claimed for personal injuries committed by the sovereign or its agents, unless the conduct on which it is based is discretionary.

To claim sovereign immunity, the state (or its political subdivision or agency) must be recognized by the United States. States may waive their sovereign immunity and choose to be sued in American courts. The act provides for federal jurisdiction in "non-jury civil actions." State courts have concurrent jurisdiction which may allow jury trial, though the sovereign can remove the case to federal court. Questions of sovereign immunity sometimes arise when entities that are owned in part by the state are sued. FSIA simply grants sovereign immunity to entities in which the government owns a majority share.

Related to sovereign immunity is the so-called "act of state" doctrine. Unlike sovereign immunity where the nation state is sued, cases involving the doctrine arise when private parties to a suit raise some act of the sovereign state to support a cause of action. According to the doctrine, American courts will not sit in judgment upon acts of a sovereign undertaken in its own territory; the American court must accept the action of the foreign state as valid, and as legally binding, regardless of whether the act might violate American law or international law. If an individual, for example, sues in an American court, charging that a foreign government's expropriation of her land was illegal, the doctrine precludes the American court from inquiring into that issue. There are exceptions to the doctrine in cases in which the executive branch intervenes in some way to support the claim based upon a government act, or when the act of state is commercial rather than sovereign.

The Interface Between European Union and American Law: An Example of New Frontiers of International Law

The European Economic Community (hereafter EEC) was founded in 1958 when the Treaty of Rome, negotiated in 1956 and ratified in 1957, came into effect. Six nations joined to form this multilateral organization: France, Italy, West Germany, Belgium, the Netherlands and Luxembourg. The EEC was conceived as an area in which national law restricting the free movement of goods (as well as workers, established persons and businesses, services, and capital) yielded to distinct treaty obligations to remove restrictions thereof amongst the signatories, and encourage a so-called "common market" or "internal market."

The succeeding half-century plus has seen vast changes in the original program initially forged. In the first place, there has been a staggering increase in numbers. Membership (even with parting of the ways between the United Kingdom and the bloc) increased by more than four-fold; the institutions (Commission, Court of Justice, Council, and Parliament) created in the Rome Treaty have matured, and others have been added (the European Council and the European Central Bank to name two); additional substantive competencies have been added; a raft of secondary legislation has been promulgated; and nationals of member states are also citizens of the European Union (hereafter EU) as the EEC since the Maastricht Treaty of 1992 is now officially denominated.

All this may be of interest to the historian and political science, but what does this important development have to do with American law? It may be an overstatement to remark that the law follows trade. But assume that they are related, then one of the most important developments in international law for United States legal actors is to navigate a massive body of EU law, because the United States and Europe are amongst one another's largest trading partners (U.S. goods and services trade with the EU totaled nearly $1.3 trillion in 2018; American exports totaled $575 billion, and imports totaled $684 billion).

The law that American businesses must follow to export goods and services to the EU takes on many guises. First, agreements that once were forged with individual member states are now often entered into with the EU. For example, take compacts for American airlines to fly passengers into EU member states (and the reverse); prior to 2008, each European country had negotiated the basis upon which flights from the United States could enter their airspace. These bilateral compacts, so-called "open-skies" agreements, have given way to an "EU-US Open Skies Agreement" that governs access to the EU by American airlines and the reverse. Second, gone is national regulation in many spheres. The "Europeanization" of many areas of what hitherto was domestic law had created what the European Court of Justice has called a "new legal order" in international law. *See Van Gend en Loos v. Nederlandse Administratie der Belastingen* (1963) Case 26/62. A host of national regulatory agencies have been folded into pan-European agencies; domestic law has given way to European law. American corporations doing business in the EU must deal with the Union's lawmakers and regulations, in addition to the domestic law in areas in which the member states still retain lawmaking competence.

Consider the following example. Should an American pharmaceutical company perfect a vaccine or treatment for the novel and widespread coronavirus, regulatory approval of member states' use of the drug will come from the European Medicines Agency, the EU's equivalent to the U.S. Food and Drug Administration (FDA), and not from the governments of the member states. Indeed, most regulatory provisions that deal with food or product safety in the member states are promulgated by the EU.

Product regulation aside, an important area in which European law has become critical to American corporations is antitrust, or competition law as the EU is wont to refer to it. Mergers are regulated by EU law—even those between American companies— if they impact the European "internal market." Likewise, allegedly anti-competitive business practices by American companies operating in the EU have been scrutinized by Directorate-General for Competition (DG COMP), the competition authority of the EU Commission. The operation of large American technology companies like Microsoft, Intel, and Google have been investigated, found to have engaged in conduct in violation of EU competition law, and fined, though the ultimate outcome of some of these cases are still uncertain at this time.

Another flashpoint between the EU and American legal systems is privacy law. The EU has far more stringent data privacy protection than does the United States. Exchanges of personal data between the EU and the U.S., say of employees of European subsidiaries of American corporations, is problematic given America's more lenient privacy regime. The differences have been ironed out through a long and tortuous process of negotiation, or so it was thought by the establishment of so-called "safe harbor" agreements ironed out by the EU Commission and the U.S. government. The most recent iteration, the so-called "shield," however, was recently struck down by the Court of Justice of European Communities, the EU's highest court. The decision upheld other parts of the concord between the United States and the EU so it is unclear what parts of the agreement now remain. *See Facebook Ireland, Ltd. v. Schrems*, C-311/18, Judgment (E.C.J. July 16, 2020).

This brief sketch of the impact on European law illustrates that international law has taken on a new dimension for American companies if they are engaged in business in the EU. Of course, previous international agreements have created law and processes that have been woven into the domestic legal regime. That of the EU is probably the most important because it is the most sophisticated, institutionally and doctrinally, and because of the extent and nature of EU-U.S. trade.

Conclusion

To some, possibly most, American lawyers, international law is irrelevant to their practice. They may regard international law as a dark area of law's kingdom. International law is frequently unfamiliar to domestic American lawyers; its structure differs, as does (frequently) its manner of enforcement. Nevertheless, America's economic interests have led it to take an active role in fostering agreements that facilitate the resolution of international disputes. Moreover, Congress has committed the American legal order to the substantive law of contracts by ratifying the Vienna Convention on the International Sale of Goods (CISG). The current generation of law students realize the central role that transnational transactions may have in their practice. International Business Transactions and European Union Law have become staples of the American law school curriculum. The chapter title posed the question is international law really there. The answer most decidedly is: "Yes, more than ever."

CHAPTER 16

CONCLUSION: THE AMERICAN BAR

Introduction

How does one conclude a book introducing the American legal system to lawyers trained in other legal regimes? Our odyssey can best close with a discussion of the profession which has created much of the law over the course of American history: the lawyers.

Lawyers have long been powerful players in the American experience in government. Thomas Jefferson, the primary author of the Declaration of Independence, was a gentleman of many skills, but he was above all a lawyer. Given the dearth of lawyers in the colonies, it is surprising that nearly half of those participating in the Constitutional Convention were lawyers. Well over half of those who have sat in the House of Representatives and Senate have been lawyers. A co-equal branch of government, the judiciary, is in the custody of the profession; and there have been a fair number of presidents who were members of the bar. Lawyers have been indeed present from the inception of the republic to our own time. Former Vice-President Biden, a lawyer, recently selected Kamala Harris, a lawyer, as his running mate in the 2020 Presidential Election. Vice-President Mike Pence is a lawyer, though the current occupant of the Oval Office is not. That three out of four of the candidates for the highest offices in the land are lawyers is telling.

One should not necessarily conclude that because America's political leaders have frequently been lawyers, that the profession is held is high esteem. There has long been a populist bent in American politics. In our introduction, we noted the national preference for a simple and straightforward law of men and women, and not one comprised of "quiddities, quillets, tenures and tricks" that clever lawyers can devise. In many ways, rhetoric aside, that battle has been lost; American law, as we have discovered, is a body of complex rules largely devised, implemented, and interpreted by astute members of the profession.

What may be staggering to the non-American are the sheer number of lawyers in the United States. Board a jumbo jet, indeed even a smaller 767 airplane, and the statistical probability is that more than one lawyer will be traveling with you. Somewhere in the realm of 1 out of every 250 Americans can claim to be a lawyer, a proportion that has fallen dramatically each year, even though the roughly 200 American law schools churn out (graduate) tens of thousands (33,954 in 2019 to be precise) of law students per year.

This chapter sheds light on a variety of inter-related issues that are raised in this society of lawyers. We begin first with regulation; and then turn attention to the various occupations in which those called to the bar serve. Finally, a law professor reflects on the future of the trade.

Regulation of the Guild

Regulation of the profession is a matter for state government rather than the federal. States either delegate regulatory authority to the state supreme court or establish a board of bar examiners. Regardless of the body empowered, their role is similar: to vet admission to the guild; and to ensure that legal services of reasonable quality is maintained.

The usual path for an aspirant to the bar is as follows: a four-year undergraduate program; three years of law school; a bar review course; and passage of a bar exam. No internship period is required.

Law school is perhaps the key stage in a lawyer's professional development. They have a long and distinguished history in America. Just after independence, the first law school was up and running in Litchfield, Connecticut (1784), and law schools continue to provide entry tickets into the profession. Law school lecture rooms are the primary venue in which the law is learned, though lawyers are said to "practice" law, indicating that the process of assimilating knowledge is ongoing. Indeed, most states now require lawyers to "continue" their legal education by requiring a certain number of classroom hours devoted to "continuing legal education" courses sponsored by the bar or by law schools.

After successfully completing two degrees, the Bachelor of Arts/Sciences and the Juris Doctor, passage of the bar exam is the third rite of passage for the aspiring lawyer. Though many states (like

New York) use the Multi-state test devised nationally, followed by the Uniform Bar Exam, other states (my home state of Louisiana, for example) devise their own questions, on the grounds that their law and procedure is unique. "Our federalism" is at work. It is for that reason most law students spend the month or so after graduation cramming the nuances of state law into their brains, at least for a few weeks, until the two or three-day written ordeal has been completed.

State regulation continues for the remainder of a lawyer's professional career. Although there is a national bar association, the American Bar Association, and state bar groups as well, regulation of lawyers comes from the bench, typically the highest state court. One of the most important issues confronted by bar disciplinary committees is to determine what conduct constitutes the practice of law, and therefore must be undertaken by members of the bar. Each state court also adopts ethical rules that govern professional conduct; these are largely based upon the Model Rules of Professional Conduct, promulgated by the American Bar Association. Specific rules define appropriate conduct in a number of critical areas such as the extent of duties of confidentiality and loyalty and the obligation to avoid conflicts of interest. Disciplinary boards are created to receive complaints of violations of the promulgated rules, and should the board find a violation, it may censure the lawyer. Disbarment, the most serious penalty for violations of professional ethics, is usually meted out by the judiciary.

In addition to disciplinary action by the authorities, clients may undertake their own "enforcement" against their lawyer, if they believe that they have received substandard legal services, by bringing an action for malpractice. These actions can be brought as a tort (the legal service was performed negligently) or in contract (the lawyer agreed to the provision of competent legal service, and then failed to deliver it). Usually, it is the aggrieved client who must sue, though malpractice actions brought by others injured by a lawyer's fraudulent conduct have succeeded. In addition, in certain circumstances, a non-client (like a beneficiary in a poorly-drafted will) may bring an action alleging that she was a third-party beneficiary to a contract for legal services.

The Practice of Law

If diversity can be said to characterize American law, the same can be said of the profession. The profession is unified: there is no distinction between those who advise clients and those who appear in court; those who draft contracts and those that undertake other legal work. American lawyers labor on a variety of tasks and the context in which they do so runs the gamut from sole practitioner to that of associate or partner in multi-office national and/or international law firms employing hundreds (and indeed thousands) of lawyers. Corporations employ lawyers as in-house counsel to serve as the corporation's legal advisors. In addition to the private sphere, many lawyers labor in the public sector. Government, federal, state and local, employ lawyers, both criminal and civil. The poor are likewise served by government-sponsored lawyers. Judges are appointed or elected, usually from senior members of the bar. And there are, of course, law professors, who selflessly dedicate their lives to teaching and scholarship.

Law is no longer a profession dominated exclusively by white males. That said woman have been involved in the law since the nineteenth century. My alma mater, the University of Iowa College of Law, proudly proclaims that it awarded the first law degree to a woman, Mary B. Hickey Wilkinson, in 1873. Law schools seek diverse student bodies, though gender balance has been easier to realize than racial and ethnic diversity. Although economic prosperity can frequently be achieved at the bar, the road to success in the profession is not an inexpensive one to travel, more easily negotiated by children of the wealthy than those of the poor. Yet, the ongoing incorporation of young lawyers into the profession at all levels, and in the variety of practice modes, has changed the overall demographics of the profession, and has arguably infused greater informality into the profession.

Conclusion

Just like the republic itself, the law and the legal profession would probably be unrecognizable to its founders. Lawyering has become a major American service industry. The law is a significant transaction cost included, consciously or otherwise, in the price paid for goods and other services. Theorists can ponder whether American society can or should continue to build-in such charges into its economic order.

Time machines unavailable, one may only speculate on the trajectory of the legal profession. Depending upon personal proclivities, the observer of the past may envision long-term continuity or drastic change for the future. Technology, such as computer-based legal research, has greatly changed the practice of law. The computer is a double-edged sword: it is easier to find the law, but there is so much law that is now readily accessible that researching an issue can take what seems to be a life-time. Competition amongst providers is greater than it has ever been, due in part to more lawyers chasing clients, but the ongoing commercialization of American society certainly has had an effect in stimulating demand for lawyers. Most consumers of legal services would doubt that the plethora of lawyers has driven down their fees.

The American legal world, or what the distinguished scholar Ronald Dworkin called "Law's Empire" in a 1986 book by the same name has a certain timeless quality to it; lawyers draft contracts, write wills, and argue cases in court. They will probably be doing much the same when America begins its third century. It is also likely that they will continue to take a significant role in governing these United States.

INDEX

References are to Pages

ABORTION RIGHTS
Generally, 11–12, 62, 73, 365–366

ACCOUNTS
Receivables, 131–132

ACT OF STATE DOCTRINE
International law, 399

ADMINISTRATIVE AGENCIES
Generally, 371–382
Adjudicatory functions, 377–378
APA, 375–376
Appeals, 379–380
Discretion afforded agencies, 380
Due process requirements, 377–379
Executive control, 380–383
Final rule, publication in CFR, 376
Functions of agencies, 374–379
Guidance, congressional, 374, 376
Hearing rights, 376, 387
Interpretive rules, 376–377, 380
Judicial review, Appeal rights, above
Legislative control, 380–382
Notice and comment period, 377
Policy statements, 372–373, 375, 377, 380
Presidential appointments, 410
Proposed rules, publication in Federal Register, 375
Public inquiries, responses to, 373
Reasoned decision-making, 375
Rulemaking authority, 371, 374–381
Standing to appeal, 379
State agencies, 371–372
Substantial evidence rule, 380

ADMISSIBILITY OF EVIDENCE
Generally, 85–89

ADVERSE POSSESSION
Generally, 180–183

ADVERTISING
Commercial speech, 351

AERIAL SURVEILLANCE
Search and seizure, 330

AFFIRMATIVE ACTION
Generally, 360–362

AFFIRMATIVE DEFENSES
Pleading, 110–111
To Criminal charge, 297–298

AGE DISCRIMINATION
Employment law, 300, 304, 306

AIR POLLUTION
Clean Air Act, 196

ALIENS
Alien Tort Claims Act, 391–392
Discrimination based on alien status, 362

AMERICANS WITH DISABILITIES ACT
Generally, 276–277
Cruise ships, applicability of ADA, 393
Reasonable accommodation, 279

ANSWER
Generally, 104–109
Affirmative defenses, 109
Defenses, alleging, 109

ANTITRUST LAW
Generally, 256–269
Clayton Act, 260, 268
Economic schools of thought, 257–259
Enforcement, political factors, 257–258

Exclusive dealing agreements, 265
Extraterritoriality of antitrust law, 256–257
Federal legislation, 207
Federal Trade Commission Act, 256–259
Horizontal agreements, 261–263, 268, 270
Mergers, 243–248
Monopolies, 260, 265–268
Per se violations, 260–265
Price fixing, 210–211
Rule of reason, 260–265
Sherman Act, 260–268
Territorial exclusivity, 264
Tying, 220, 265
Vertical agreements, 260–265

APPEALS
Generally, 268–270
Administrative appeals, 278–380
Briefs, 69, 102
Courts of Appeal, this index
Criminal defendants, 323
De novo review, 101
Harmless error, 102
Opinion writing, 102
Oral argument, 102
Process, 102
Questions of law, 102
Supreme Court, this index

ARRAIGNMENT
Generally, 316

ARREST
Criminal Procedure, this index

ASBESTOS LITIGATION
Tort reform efforts, 142

ASSAULT
Intentional torts, 150–151

ASSEMBLY, RIGHT TO
Generally, 352–353

ASSOCIATION, FREEDOM OF
Generally, 50, 352–353

ATTORNEYS
  Generally, 405–411
Bar exam, 478
Continuing education requirements, 407
Disciplinary action, 408–409
Ethical rules, 308
Law school, 407
Practice of law, 409–410
Regulation of profession, 407–409
Rules of Professional Conduct, 408
Unified nature of profession, 409

AUTOMOBILES
Search and seizure, 331–332

BAIL
Posting, 310, 314

BATTERY
Generally, 148, 150–151, 155, 158

BENCH TRIAL
Criminal proceedings, 319

BILL OF RIGHTS
First Amendment, this index

BLACKMAIL
Generally, 295

BONDS
Generally, 343, 347, 388

BRIBERY
Generally, 57, 85, 295

BRIEFS
Appeals, 69

BROADCAST MEDIA
Generally, 262, 286, 348, 351

BURDEN OF PROOF
Breach of contract, damage suffered, 162
Civil vs. criminal cases, 145, 297–298

BURGLARY
Generally, 157, 292, 294–295

BUSINESS ENTITIES
Corporations, this index

BUSINESS JUDGMENT RULE
Generally, 338

BUSINESS TRANSACTIONS
Contract and Commercial Law, this index

CAUSATION
But for causation, 290
Proximate cause, 163–164
Torts, 163–165

CHATTEL PAPER
Secured transactions, 131–134

CHECKS AND BALANCES
Generally, 38, 56, 63, 66

CHEMICALS
Regulating manufacture, 198

CHILD PORNOGRAPHY
Phone solicitation, 351

CIVIL RIGHTS MOVEMENT
Federal government, role of, 18

CIVIL TRIAL
Trial, this index

CIVIL WAR
Generally, 16–17
Civil War amendments, 353–354

CLEAN AIR ACT
Discharge standards, 136

CLOSELY-HELD CORPORATIONS
   Generally, 234–235
Personal liability for debts, 241
S corporation status, 236

COLLATERAL
Secured transactions, 106, 133–136

COLLECTIVE BARGAINING
Labor and Employment Law, this index

COLONIAL PERIOD
Historical background, 12–15

COMMERCE CLAUSE
   Generally, 41–48
Dormant commerce clause, 47–48

COMMERCIAL LAW
Contract and Commercial Law, this index

COMMON LAW
   Generally, 8–15, 2–36
Americanization of, 15–26, 76, 142
Writs, 22, 60

COMPARATIVE FAULT
Generally, 166

COMPLAINT
Generally, 50, 76–81

COMPLEXITY
American law, complexity of, 8–9, 40, 76, 90, 264–267

CONFESSIONS
Criminal Procedure, this index

CONGRESSIONAL POWER
Constitutional Law, this index

CONSENT
Congressional, 35, 57, 389
Intentional torts, consent defense, 148, 156, 293–284

CONSIDERATION
Generally, 109–115

CONSTITUTIONAL LAW
Allocation of governmental powers, 30–50
Checks and balances, this index
Civil War Amendments, this index
Commerce clause, this index
Congressional powers
   Generally, 39–50
Commerce clause, this index
Criminal Procedure, this index
Dormant commerce clause, this index
Due Process Clause, this index
Eminent domain, this index
Equal Protection Clause, this index
Federalism
     Generally, 8, 24, 38–41, 337, 341, 408
   Presidential powers, 51–55
   Supremacy clause, 50–51
First Amendment, this index
Impeachment
   Generally, 57–58
Intellectual property, 68, 70, 212
Judicial branch
     Generally, 59–67
   Confirmation of nominees, 55, 65, 71
   Federal bench in constitutional scheme, 58–63
   Federal Courts, this index
   Federal Jurisdiction, this index
  Judicial review, 53, 57–63, 340
  Necessary and Proper Clause, this index
  Ninth Amendment, 62, 342, 364–365
  Police power, 76, 187–194
  Preemption of state regulation, 345–346
Presidential powers,
   Generally, 51–58

Administrative agencies, executive control, 380–381
Foreign Relations, this index
Treaty power, 55–56
Veto power, 56
Privacy, this index
Separation of powers
    Generally, 8, 38, 51, 57, 371, 353
Tenth Amendment, 38–39
Supremacy clause, 50–51
Takings clause, 89, 185–191, 342
Tenth Amendment, 38–39, 364

CONSUMER PROTECTION LAW
Contract and Commercial Law, this index

CONTRACT AND COMMERCIAL LAW
Generally, 105–139
Accounts, 105–106
Agreements to agree, 111–112
Bilateral contracts, 110
Boilerplate, 112
Breach, what constitutes, 124–128
Burden of proof, damage suffered, 123–124
Cash sales, 129–130
Chattel Paper, this index
Check, payment by, 129–130
Collateral, this index
Commercial law
    Generally, 128–139
    Consumer protection law, below
    Credit transactions, below
    Negotiable instruments, below
    Payment, below
    Secured transactions, below
    Wire transfers, 129–130
Conditions
    Offers, conditional, 109–110
    Performance, conditioned, 119–120
Consideration, 112–115
Consumer protection law
    Generally, 136–138

Credit card issuers, 137–138
Credit reporting, 137
Truth-in-lending, 137
Contracts to bargain, 111
Course of performance, 117
Credit cards, consumer protection, see above
Credit reporting, consumer protection, see above
Credit transactions
    Generally, 133–136
Revolving credit arrangements, 135
Damages as remedy for breach, 105, 113–114, 120, 124–128
Default, secured transaction, 134
Delivery, tender of, 119, 129
Duty to perform, conditional, 94–95
Excuses for nonperformance
    Generally, 121–124
Misrepresentation, 122
Unconscionability, 121
Unforeseen circumstances, 122
Firm offers, 110
Floating liens, 135
Foreclosure sale, secured transaction, 184
Foreseeability, 122
Formation of contracts, 109–112
Forms, standardized, 112
Good faith and fair dealing, 117–119, 132, 139
Holders in due course, 132–143
Interpretation of contracts, 115–118
Inventory financing, this index
Jurisprudential aspirations, 107–109
Letters of credit, 129–131
Liquidated damages, 128
Meeting of the minds, 109–110
Merchant agreements, 105, 110–112, 116, 118, 132
Merger, doctrine of, 116–117
Misrepresentation, 122
Money damages as remedy for breach, see above
Negotiable instruments
    Generally, 132–133
Holders in due course, 132–133

Nonperformance
　　Excuses for nonperformance, above
　　Remedies for nonperformance, below
Offer and acceptance, 109–112, 116
Oral contracts, 111, 116
Parole evidence rule, 144–145
Parties' prior dealings, 117
Payment, 129–131
Perfection of security interest, 135–136
Performance of contract, 118–121
Profits, foreseeability, 122–123
Promissory estoppel, 115
Receivables, 131–132
Reliance on promise, 115
Remedies for nonperformance
　　　Generally, 125–128
　　Liquidated damages, 128
　　Money damages, 125–128
　　Specific performance, 127–128
Revolving credit arrangements, 135
Secured transactions
　　　Generally, 133–136
　　Chattel paper, this index
　　Collateral, this index
　　Default, 131–136
　　Floating liens, see above
　　Foreclosure sale, see above
　　Inventory financing, 134–135
　　Perfection of interest, see above
　　Revolving credit arrangements, see above
Services, contracts for, 1–6, 111, 119
Specific performance, 127–129
Statute of Frauds, 116
Time for performance, 82, 118–120, 122
Title to goods, seller's warranty, 168–170
Tort and contract, links between, 92, 122, 141
Trade practices, 117
Unconscionability, 121–122
Unforeseen circumstances, this index
Uniform Commercial Code, 82, 106–108, 138

Unjust enrichment, this index
Wire transfers, 129–130

CONTRADICTIONS
American law, contradictions and paradoxes, 5–7

CONTRIBUTORY NEGLIGENCE
Generally, 165–166

COPYRIGHT
    Generally, 213–216
Commencement and duration of protection, 214
Damages for infringement, 216
Fair use doctrine, 215
First sale doctrine, 215
Infringement, 216
Injunctive relief, 216
Intellectual Property, this index
Rights of copyright holder, 213–214
Sale of copyrighted material, 215
Visual artists, 214–215
Works of authorship, 213

CORPORATIONS
    Generally, 187–199
Acquisitions. Mergers and Acquisitions, below
Advantages to corporate form, 235–237
Annual meeting, 238–239
Articles of incorporation, 236–237
Bonds and bond issues, 243, 247
Business judgment rule, 238, 252
Closely-Held Corporations, this index
Comingling assets, 241
Derivative suits, 239–240
Directors, 235–241
Dissolution, 242–243
Dividends, 236–237, 242–243
Equity and debt
        Generally, 242–243
    Distinction between, 242–243
Fiduciary duties, 231, 237–241

Formation, 231, 237–241
Greenmail, 245–246
Hostile takeovers, 246–248
Limitation on liability, 227
Meetings, 235–241
Mergers and Acquisitions, this index
Organizational structure, 235–237
Parent corporation's responsibility for liabilities of progeny, 214–242
Piercing the corporate veil, 241
Poison pills, 245
Proxy voting, 238–239, 256–257
S corporation status, 236
Securities Regulation, this index
Share price, 242–243
Shareholders rights, 238–242, 248
Shares, common and preferred, 242–244
Spin-offs, 248
Taxation, 232, 234, 236
Tender offers, 244–245
Termination of operations, 247
White knights, 245

COUNSEL
Attorneys, this index

COUNTERCLAIMS
Generally, 82–83

COURTS OF APPEAL
Generally, 67–19
Appeals to, 101

COVENANTS
Race-based, 360

CREDIBILITY
Witness credibility, weighing by jury, 93–94

CREDIT CARDS
Contract and Commercial Law, this index

CREDIT REPORTING
Contract and Commercial Law, this index

CREDIT TRANSACTIONS
Contract and Commercial Law, this index

CRIMINAL LAW
Generally, 285–306
Actus reas, 288
Blackmail, 295
Bribery, 295
Burglary, 187, 292, 294–295
Causation, 290
Death Penalty, this index
Defenses
Generally, 296–297
Burden of proof, 297
Duress, 299
Entrapment, 300–301
Insanity, 298–299
Necessity, 300
Self-defense, 297–298
Duty to act, 288–289
Felonies vs. misdemeanors, 289, 291, 294, 314–315
Felony murder, 320
Forfeiture of property, 296, 323
Homicide
Manslaughter, 293, 299
Murder, 291–293, 298–299, 303, 305, 313, 329, 333, 386
Intervening cause, 290–291
Jury, role of, 287–288
Larceny, 294, 295
Mens rea, 288–292
Model Penal Code, 287, 292
Money laundering, 295
Omissions, 288
Parole, 302–304, 309–310, 324–325
Probation, 309–310, 322, 325
Procedure. Criminal Procedure, this index
Property crimes
Generally, 294–295

Burglary, this index
Larceny, this index
Theft offenses, this index
Punishment
    Generally, 301–307
    Forfeiture of property, above
    Parole, above
    Probation, above
    Sentencing, 309–310, 322
Rape
    Generally, 293
    Shield law, 294
    Statutory rape, 290
RICO, 295–296
Strict liability, 290
Substantive criminal law, basic principles
    Generally, 230–233
    Actus reas, above
    Causation, above
    Duty to act, above
    Mens rea, above
    Omissions, above
    Strict liability, above
    Vicarious liability, 290
Theft offenses, above
Tort and criminal law, links between, above
White collar crime, 287, 296, 307, 317, 322

CRIMINAL PROCEDURE
    Generally, 309–338
Aerial surveillance, 330
Appeal rights, 309, 323–324
Arraignment, 316
Arrest
    Generally, 312–315
    Search incident to, 311–313
    Warrant, 311–314, 328–329, 331–335
Automobile searches, 328–329
Bail, this index
Bench trial, 318–319

Challenges to jurors, 320, 359
Closing argument, 320
Confessions
    Generally, 333–337
  Miranda rights, 334–346
Constitutional protections
    Generally, 248–249, 261–263
  Exclusionary rule, below
  Search and seizure, below
  State action, necessity for, 327–328
Counsel, right to, 312
Cross-examination, 321
Custodial interrogation, 334
Defense motion to dismiss, 320
Delay, defense requests, 318
Electronic listening devices, 329–330
Evidence disclosure, 317
Exclusionary rule, above
Exculpatory evidence, 316–317
Exigent circumstances exception to warrant requirement, 331
Expert witnesses, 321
Forfeiture of property, above
Fruit of the poisonous tree, 335–336
Grand jury, 315–316
Habeas corpus writs, 323–324
Hearsay evidence, 321
Hung juries, 320–321
Indictment, 315–318
Informants, 312
Information, 314, 316, 318
Instructions to jury, 320
Plain view doctrine, 331
Plea
  Bargaining, this index
  Entry of, 316
Post-conviction
    Generally, 321–324
  Forfeiture of property, above
  Probation, above
  Sentencing, above

Preliminary hearing, 315–316
Pre-trial phase, 315–317
Privacy, expectation of, 229
Probable cause,
   Arrest, 311–315
   Search and seizure, 329–332
Probation, above
Prosecutorial discretion, 313
Prosecutor's case-in-chief, 320
Rebuttal case, 320–321
Release on own recognizance, 314
Search and seizure, 311–313, 327–336
Self-incrimination, invocation or waiver of right, 311, 321
Speedy trial, 312, 318
Stop and frisk, 328
Subpoenas, 52
Trial, 175–204
Unanimity requirement, 35, 320
Verdict, 299, 304, 319–324
Voir dire, 92, 319
Warrants
   Arrest, 311, 331
   Searches, warrantless, 331–332
Witnesses, lay and expert, 127, 160, 216, 321

DAMAGES
See Contracts and Commercial law, Torts this index

DE NOVO REVIEW
Questions of law, 101

DEATH PENALTY
   Generally, 305–306, 324
Commutation of sentence, 325
Habeas corpus writs, 324

DECEDENTS' ESTATES
Wills and Trusts, this index

DECLARATORY JUDGMENTS
Patents, 218

DEFAMATION
Generally, 172

DEFENSES
Alleging in answer, 77
Criminal Law, this index

DEPOSITIONS
Generally, 87–88

DISABLED PERSONS
Employment discrimination, 275, 279

DISCOVERY
Generally, 83–90
Confidential information, 84–85
Depositions, 87–88
Interrogatories, 87–88
Production of documents, 84–85
Purpose, 83–84

DISCRIMINATION
Labor and Employment Law, this index

DISMISSAL
Motion to dismiss
At trial, 70, 80, 83, 90
Criminal cases, 320, 327

DIVERSITY OF CITIZENSHIP
Federal jurisdiction, 3

DOCUMENTS
Production of documents, 85–86

DOCUMENTS OF TITLE
Personal property, 178

DUE PROCESS CLAUSE
Generally, 354–357
Administrative agencies, 378–379
Economic regulation, 355
Fourteenth Amendment, 354
Personal rights, 354–356

Privacy, 62, 363
Procedural due process, 354–355
Racial equality, 354
Same-sex consensual relations, 356
State government, extension to, 356
Substantive rights, 354–356

DURESS
Contract, 122
Defense of, 299

DUTY OF CARE
Tort law, 160–162

ECONOMIC REGULATION
Substantive due process, 356–357

ECONOMICS
Law and economics, 30, 108

ELECTORAL COLLEGE
Generally, 52

EMINENT DOMAIN
Generally, 184–187
Fair market value, 186–187
Good will, 186
Public use, what constitutes, 61, 176, 185
Takings clause, 148–149

EMPLOYMENT
Labor and Employment Law, this index

ENFORCEMENT OF JUDGMENTS
Judgments rendered abroad, 396–397

ENVIRONMENTAL REGULATION
Generally, 195–198
Discharge standards, 224
Hazardous substances, 196–197
Impact statements, 196–197
NEPA, 196
Nuisance law and environmental pollution, 158–159

Policy goals, 195–196
Private right of action, 158–159
State law, 197
Sustainable development, 195–196

EQUAL PROTECTION CLAUSE
    Generally, 357–363
Affirmative action, 360–363
Alien status, discrimination based on, 362
Gender discrimination, 362
Historical background, 353–354
School desegregation, 358–359
Separate but equal, 358

ESTATES IN LAND
Property Law, this index

EVIDENCE
Administrative hearings, 378–381
Admissibility, 91, 98, 101
Criminal proceedings
    Generally, 292
  Exclusionary rule, see above
  Pre-trial disclosure, 316
Relevance, 84, 100
Rules of evidence
    Generally, 98–100
  Admissibility, 98–100
  Criminal cases, 92
  Relevance, 100
Witnesses, this index

EXECUTIVE AGREEMENTS
International law, 389–390

EXECUTIVE BRANCH
Constitutional Law, this index

EXECUTORY INTERESTS
Property law, 206

FEDERAL COURTS
Judicial branch. Constitutional Law, this index

FEDERAL JURISDICTION
Generally, 67, 69–72, 302
Challenging, 64
Concurrent jurisdiction with state courts, 71
Diversity jurisdiction, 3, 70
Federal questions, 70
Limited nature, 70

FEDERAL LAW
State vs. National Law, this index

FEDERAL RULES OF CIVIL PROCEDURE
Overview, 75–78

FEDERALISM
Constitutional Law, this index

FIDUCIARY DUTY
Corporations, this index

FIRST AMENDMENT
Generally, 342–352
Assembly, right to, 352–353
Association, freedom of, 50, 352–353, 356
Clear and present danger, 279
Commercial speech, 349–350
Compelling state interests, 343, 349–350
Content-based vs. content-neutral regulations, 347–348
Fighting words, 350
Free expression
Generally, 346–352
Clear and present danger, above
Commercial speech, 350
Compelling state interests, above
Content-based vs. content-neutral regulations, above
Fighting words, above
Flag burning, 349
Historical background, 346
Overbroad regulations, 350
Pornography, 258, 357
Press freedoms, 281
Symbolic speech, 279–280

Overbroad regulations, above
Pornography, above
Press, freedom of, above
Prior restraint, 352
Religious expression and tolerance
    Generally, 342–346
  Accommodation of religion, 344–345
  Excessive entanglement, 346
  Free expression vs. establishment of religion, 275
  Pledge of Allegiance, 277
  Prayer in schools, 9, 344–345
Symbolic speech, 349–351

FIRST IN TIME
Nuisance law, 188–198

FLAG BURNING
First amendment, 349

FORECLOSURE SALE
Secured transactions, 136

FOREIGN JUDGMENTS
Enforcement of judgments rendered abroad, 396–397

FOREIGN RELATIONS
Conduct of, 43–44

FOREIGN STATES
Suing in American courts, 396–397

FORFEITURE OF PROPERTY
Criminal procedure, 296

FORUM NON CONVENIENS
International law, 396

FREEDOM OF SPEECH
First Amendment, this index

GAY RELATIONSHIPS
Due process rights, consensual relations, 367

GENDER DISCRIMINATION
Generally, 93, 272, 276–277, 286
Equal protection clause, above
Title VII, 276–278

HARMLESS ERROR
Generally, 102

HAZARDOUS SUBSTANCES
Regulation, 196–197

HEARSAY EVIDENCE
Civil cases, 99
Criminal cases, 321

HIGHER EDUCATION
Affirmative action, 360–363

HISTORICAL BACKGROUND
Generally, 12–19

HOMICIDE
Manslaughter, above
Murder, above

IMPEACHMENT
Generally, 381

INHERITANCE
Wills and Trusts, this index

INTELLECTUAL PROPERTY
Generally, 212–222
Copyright, this index
Patents, this index
Trademarks, this index

INTENTIONAL TORTS
Tort Law, this index

INTERNATIONAL LAW
Generally, 385–404
Act of state doctrine, 399
Alien Tort Claims Act, 391–392

Antitrust law, extraterritoriality, 284–285
Conflicting federal statute, subsequently adopted, 390–391
Criminal sanctions, acts against American citizens abroad, 394
Enforcement of judgments rendered abroad, 396–397
Executive agreements, 389–390
Extraterritoriality of American law
   Jurisdiction, 392–394
   Substantive law, 394–399
Foreign states, suing in American courts, 392–394
Forum Non Conveniens, this index
Hague Service Convention, 396–397
Judgments rendered abroad, enforcement of, see above
Jurisdiction over non-American defendants
     Generally, 394–396
   Act of State Doctrine, this index
   Foreign sovereign immunity, 398–399
   Forum Non Conveniens, this index
   Judgments rendered abroad, enforcement of, this index
   Minimum contacts, 394–395
Nationality of business entities, 393
Process for entering into international agreements, 388–389
Securities law, application against foreign entities, 393–394
Sovereign immunity, foreign states, 398–399
Status of international agreements, 390–392
Study by American law students, 2
Supremacy clause, 50, 390
Treaties, 29, 50, 56–57, 390–391
Uniform Foreign-Money Judgments Recognition Act, 397

JOINT AND SEVERAL LIABILITY
Partnerships, 184
Torts, 166

JUDICIAL BRANCH
Constitutional Law, this index

JURISDICTION
Extra-territoriality of American law, 392–399
Federal Jurisdiction, this index

JURISPRUDENCE

Contract law, jurisprudential aspirations, 107–109
Export of American jurisprudence, 1

JURORS AND JURY TRIAL

Generally, 91–98
Constitutional guarantee, 71
Credibility of witnesses, weighing, 93
Criminal proceedings, this index
Damages determination, 94
Deliberations, 95–96
Finder of fact, jury as, 68, 77, 93, 149
For cause challenges
    Criminal cases, 320
    Pre-emptory, 71
Impartiality, 92
Instructions to jury, 101
Mock jury trial, 97–98
Potential juror pools, 92
Preemptory challenges, 92
Right to, 91–94
Runaway jury, control by judge, 96
Unanimity requirement
    Civil cases, 35
    Criminal cases, 320
Verdict, 51, 96–97, 101, 145, 299, 304, 319–320, 323, 328
Voir dire
    Civil cases, 92
    Criminal cases, 319

LABOR AND EMPLOYMENT LAW

Generally, 215–226
Affirmative action, 279
Age discrimination, 272, 275–278
At will employment, 271
Back-pay, reinstatement and prospective pay, 275–278
Benefits, 275–276
Collective bargaining. Unions and collective bargaining, below
Disabled persons, 276–279, 283
Discrimination in employment, 276–279
Health and safety standards, 276, 282

Hostile work environment, 278
Laissez faire approach, 271–272
Occupational Health Act, 276
Privacy rights, 218
Public employees, due process rights, 274–275
Retirement packages, 278–279
Sex discrimination, above
Sexual harassment, 278
Tenured positions, 274–275
Title VII, 276–279
Unemployment compensation, 275
Unions and collective bargaining, 279–283
Workers' compensation, 170, 276
Wrongful termination, 274–275

LANDLORD-TENANT LAW
    Generally, 210–212
Business premises, suitability, 211
Covenants, independent, 210–211
Habitability for residential use, 211
Leases, 210–212
Mitigation of damages, landlord's obligation, 168–169
Obligations of landlord, 159, 210–211
Remedies for breach of warranty, 211–212

LAND-USE REGULATION
Generally, 51, 175–176, 184, 187–195

LAW ENFORCEMENT
Federal agencies, 44, 45, 58, 67, 256, 260, 277, 281

LAWYERS
Attorneys, this index

LEGAL MALPRACTICE
Elements of action, 159, 409

LIMITED LIABILITY COMPANIES
Generally, 233–234

LIQUIDATED DAMAGES
Contract, 128

MAGNA CARTA
Generally, 26

MALPRACTICE
Legal Malpractice, this index
Medical Malpractice, this index

MARIJUANA
Medical use, 44–45
Thermal imaging, 330

MEDICAL MALPRACTICE
Generally, 143–144, 159–160

MERGERS AND ACQUISITIONS
Corporations, this index

MINORITY-OPERATED BUSINESSES
Public contracts, 262

MOTIONS
Pre-trial motions, 90–91

MULTIPLE PARTIES
Tort law, 166–167

NATIONAL ORIGIN
Discrimination based on, 278, 362

NECESSARY AND PROPER CLAUSE
Generally, 39, 41, 48–50

NECESSITY
Defense of (Criminal), 156, 300
Intentional torts, necessity defense, 158

NEGLIGENT TORTS
Tort Law, this index

NEGOTIABLE INSTRUMENTS
Contract and Commercial Law, this index

NEW DEAL
Federal government, role of, 17–19

NEW TRIAL
Generally, 96–97

NEWSPAPERS
Press, freedom of, 351–352

NINTH AMENDMENT
Generally, 62, 342, 364–365

NON-ECONOMIC LOSS
Generally, 143–144
Tort reform efforts, 165

NUISANCE
Generally, 153, 176, 198–201
Environmental pollution, 197
First in time doctrine, 156–157, 198–199
Law of, historical development, 16
Majority rule, 199–201
Private nuisance, tort actions, 124
Restatement of Torts, balancing test, 199–201
Unreasonableness, 199–201

OCCUPATIONAL SAFETY AND HEALTH
Generally, 276

OWNERSHIP
Property law, 177–179

PAIN AND SUFFERING
Generally, 143–144
Recovery for, 171
Tort reform efforts, 171

PAROL EVIDENCE RULE
Generally, 116–117

PARTIES
Multiple parties, tort law, 166–167

PARTNERSHIPS
Generally, 227, 229–233
Agreements, 229–230
Creation, 229–230

Death of partner, 231, 233
Fiduciary duty, 231
Joint and several liability, 231
Limited partnerships, 185–186
Losses, allocation of, 230
Management, 230–231
Profit distribution, 230
Revised Uniform Partnership Act, 230–233
Termination, 231, 233
Uniform Limited Partnership Act, 186
Withdrawal of partner, 233

PATENTS
Generally, 216–218
Cross-licensing agreements, 218
Damages, 218
Declaratory judgments, 218
Duration, 218
Infringement, 218
Injunctive relief, 218
Intellectual Property, this index
Inventor, priority given to, 217–218
Novelty requirement, 216
Process for securing, 217–218
Review of rejected application, 173
Utility requirement, 172–173

PAYMENT
Contract and Commercial Law, this index

PERFECTION
Contract and Commercial Law, this index

PERSONAL PROPERTY
Documents of title, 178
Trespass, 123–124

PESTICIDES
Regulating use, 197

PLEA BARGAINING
Generally, 317–319

PLEADING
Generally, 78–83
Affirmative defenses, 81–82
Amendments
Leave to amend, 81
Answer, this index
Code pleading, 76
Complaint, this index
Counterclaims, this index
Defenses, this index
Failure to state claim, 80
Federal Rules of Civil Procedure, this index
Filing fees, 78
Motion to dismiss, 80–81, 90
Service, 79–80
Technical flaws, 81

PLEDGE OF ALLEGIANCE
First Amendment challenge, 345

POLICE POWER
Land-use regulation and zoning, 48, 187–189, 194

POLLUTION
Environmental, 196–197

PORNOGRAPHY
First amendment, 348–349

POSSESSION
Adverse, 180–183
Property law, 177

PREEMPTION
State regulation and federal commerce clause, 45–46

PRELIMINARY HEARING
Generally, 315–316

PRESIDENTIAL POWER
Constitutional Law, this index

PRE-TRIAL CONFERENCE
Generally, 91

PRE-TRIAL MOTIONS
Generally, 90–91

PRIOR RESTRAINT
First Amendment, 352

PRIVACY
Abortion rights, 11, 62, 365–366
Constitutional protections
    Generally, 363–367
  Ninth and Tenth Amendments, this index
  Reproductive privacy, 341, 365
Employee rights, 218
Expectation of privacy, 264
Reproductive privacy, 291, 341, 365

PROBABLE CAUSE
Criminal Procedure, this index

PROBATION
Criminal Procedure, this index

PRODUCTION OF DOCUMENTS
Generally, 85–86

PRODUCTS LIABILITY
Strict liability in tort, 84, 87, 142–144, 168–173

PROMISSORY ESTOPPEL
Generally, 115

PROPERTY LAW
    Generally, 175–224
Adverse possession, 180–183
Contract for sale of real estate, 183–184
Covenants, race-based, 360
Eminent Domain, this index
Environmental Regulation, this index
Estates in land, 201–207
  Future interests, 10, 204, 207

Present possessory interests, 204
Remainder and executory interests, 10, 205–206
Executory Interests, this index
Future interests, above
Historical background, 201–207
Intellectual Property, this index
Land-Use Regulation, this index
Landlord-Tenant Law, this index
Nuisance, this index
Possession and ownership in American law, see Ownership above
Statute of Frauds, 116
Title search, 183–184
Trespass, this index
Wills and Trusts, this index
Zoning, this index

PROSECUTORS
Criminal Procedure, this index

PROXIMATE CAUSE
Generally, 163–165

PUNISHMENT
Criminal Law, this index

PUNITIVE DAMAGES
Generally, 98, 398
Contract cases, 124, 128, 142–143
Deterrence function, 145
Tort cases, 137, 142–143, 146, 171

RACIAL DISCRIMINATION
Generally, 359, 360, 365
Affirmative Action, this index
Equal protection challenges, 287–288
Equality, 340, 353–354
School desegregation, 358–359

RAILROADS
Tort standards, development of, 16

RAPE
Criminal Law, this index

REAL PROPERTY
Property Law, this index

REASONABLENESS
Defenses to intentional torts, 147–149
Nuisance law, 199–201

REASONING
Common law, 21–35

RECEIVABLES
Contract and Commercial Law, this index

RELEVANCE
Rules of evidence, 84, 100

RELIGIOUS EXPRESSION
First Amendment, this index

REMAINDER INTERESTS
Property law, 205–206

REPRODUCTIVE PRIVACY
Generally, 291, 341, 365

RESTATEMENT OF CONTRACTS
Generally, 114–115, 125

RESTATEMENT OF TORTS
Nuisance law, 199–120

REVERSE DISCRIMINATION
Affirmative Action, this index

RIGHT TO COUNSEL
Attorneys, this index

RULES
Federal Rules of Civil Procedure, this index
Rules of evidence. Evidence, this index

SCHOOLS
Desegregation, 263, 358–363
Prayer in schools, 344–345

SECURED TRANSACTIONS
Contract and Commercial Law, this index

SECURITIES REGULATION
Generally, 248–256
Accredited investors, 277
Corporations, this index
Disclosure requirements, 244, 252–253, 368
Federal legislation, 248–250
Financial statements, 249–250, 253–255
Foreign entities, application of American law, 253
Historical background, 248–249
Insider trading, 253–254
Interim reports, 250
Prospectus, 249
Proxy statements, 249–251
Registration statement, 249
Rule 10b–5
        Generally, 251–253
    Elements of violation, 251–252
SEC, role of, 10, 244–245, 249–251
Transparency, 199

SELF-DEFENSE
Criminal law, 279–280
Intentional torts, 156–157

SELF-INCRIMINATION
Invocation or waiver of right, 311, 321

SENTENCING
Generally, 303–305, 309, 321–322

SEPARATION OF POWERS
Constitutional Law, this index

SERVICE OF PROCESS
Complaint, 79–80
International law, 396
Personal service, exceptions to, 108

SERVICES, CONTRACTS FOR
Generally, 110–111, 119, 128

Specific performance, 128

SETTLEMENT
Generally, 83

SEX DISCRIMINATION
Gender Discrimination, this index

SEXUAL HARASSMENT
Employment law, 278

SHAREHOLDERS
Corporations, this index

SHOPLIFTING
False imprisonment, 153, 291

SLAVERY
Debate over, 16–17, 340, 353, 358

SODOMY
Due process rights, same-sex consensual relations, 346

SOLE PROPRIETORSHIPS
Generally, 229–230, 255

SOVEREIGN IMMUNITY
Foreign states, 388, 398–399

SOVEREIGN POWER
Generally, 26, 39

SPECIAL VERDICTS
Generally, 96

SPECIFIC PERFORMANCE
Contract and Commercial Law, this index

SPEEDY TRIAL
Criminal Procedure, this index

STATE ACTION
Generally, 328, 355, 360, 380

STATE OF MIND
Criminal law, 288–292

Intentional torts, 147–149

STATE VS. NATIONAL LAW
Generally, 4–5
Supremacy clause, 50, 60

STATUTE OF FRAUDS
Generally, 109, 116

STRICT LIABILITY
Criminal law, 289
Tort, 167–170

SUBPOENAS
Criminal procedure, 80

SUMMARY JUDGMENT
Generally, 90–91

SUMMATION
Generally, 93–94

SUMMONS
Service with complaint, 79–80

SUPREMACY CLAUSE
Generally, 50–51
International agreements, 390

SUPREME COURT
Generally, 49–63, 67–73

TENTH AMENDMENT
Generally, 38–39
Privacy rights, 364

TITLE TO PROPERTY
Adverse possession, 181–183
Marketable title, 184

TITLE VII
Discrimination in employment, 276–279

TORT LAW
Generally, 141–172

Assault, 150–152

Battery, 150–152, 156

But for test of causation, 152

Causation, 163–165

Comparative fault, 166

Consent defense to intentional tort, 148, 156

Contract and tort, links between, 92, 122, 141, 146–147

Contributory negligence, 156–157

Cost-benefit analyses, 161

Criminal law and tort, links between, 145–146

Damages, 170–172

Defamation, 172

Duty of care, 160–162

False imprisonment, 152–153

Future earnings damages, 171

Intentional torts

    Generally, 147–150

  Assault, above

  Battery, above

  Defenses, above

  False imprisonment, above

  Property, trespass to, 123–125

Joint and several liability, 166

Moral dimensions, 147

Multiple parties, 166

Necessity defense, 56, 158

Negligent torts

    Generally, 158

  Causation, above

  Contributory negligence, above

  Duty of care, above

  Multiple parties, above

Noneconomic losses, 171

Nuisance, this index

Pain and suffering, 116, 137

Proximate cause, 163–165

Prudent persons standard, 161

Reasonableness

  Defenses to intentional torts, 158

Reform efforts, 142–145

Strict liability, 167–170
Wrongful death, 145–146
Wrongful termination, 274

TOXIC WASTE
Cleanup, 196

TRADE PRACTICES
See Contracts

TRADEMARKS
Generally, 215, 219–222
Confusion between competing products, minimizing, 219, 222
Damages for infringement, 222
Distinctiveness requirement, 177, 212, 218–219
Exclusive rights to exploit, 220–221
Injunctive relief, 222
Intellectual Property, this index
Registration, 221–222
Review of rejected applications, 222
Trade dress, 220

TRIAL
Generally, 75–103
Appeals, this index
Criminal Procedure, this index
Damages, this index
Damages determination, above
Discovery, this index
Factual disputes, 79, 90, 101
Federal Rules of Civil Procedure, this index
Instructions to jury, 101
Jurors and Jury Trial, this index
Mock jury trial, 97–98
Motion to dismiss, 81, 83, 90, 96
Opening argument, 85
Pleading, this index
Pre-trial conference, 90
Pre-trial motions, 91
Summary judgment, 90–91
Summation, 94–95

Witness credibility, 93–94

TRUSTS
Wills and Trusts, this index

UNEMPLOYMENT COMPENSATION
Generally, 275

UNIFORM COMMERCIAL CODE
Contract and Commercial Law, this index

UNIFORM FOREIGN-MONEY JUDGMENTS RECOGNITION ACT
Generally, 397

UNIONS
Labor and Employment Law, this index

UNIVERSITIES
Affirmative action, 360–362

VERDICT
Generally, 96, 97, 145, 299, 305, 320, 323, 328

VOIR DIRE
Civil cases, 92
Criminal cases, 319

WARRANTS
Criminal Procedure, this index

WILLS AND TRUSTS
Generally, 207–210
Disinheritance of children, 207–208
Estate plans, 208–209
Trusts, 209

WITNESSES
Competence to testify, 97–99
Credibility, weighing by jury, 73
Criminal trials, 312, 316, 318, 321
Expert, 160
Legal conclusions, 78–79
Questioning, 93, 95, 117

WORKERS' COMPENSATION
Generally, 170

WORKPLACE
Health and safety standards, 170, 276–277

WRITS
Abolition, pleading rules, 75–76
Certiorari, writ of, 69, 101, 323
Common law, 32
Habeas Corpus, 326, 394
Mandamus, 59–60

WRONGFUL TERMINATION
Generally, 275

ZONING
Generally, 193–195
Comprehensive plans, 194–195
Exclusionary policies, 153–154
Non-conforming uses, 193
Police Power, this index
Variances, 195